English Gentlemen and World Soccer

The significance of the Corinthians Football Club, founded in 1882, has been widely acknowledged by historians of football and by sports historians generally. As a 'super club' comprising the best amateur talent available, they were an important formative influence on football in England from the 1880s to 1930s. As a touring club – they first travelled to South Africa in 1897 and made regular forays into Europe and also to Canada, the United States and Brazil – they were the self-proclaimed standard bearers for gentlemanly values in sport.

Indeed, for many years, they were the most famous football club in the world, drawing huge crowds and helping to ensure that the version of football emanating from the English public schools and universities in the mid-nineteenth century became a global game. Though their playing strength and influence waned after the First World War, they remained a significant force through to 1939, upholding 'true-blue' amateurism at a time when football was increasingly associated with professionalism and seen as a branch of commercial entertainment.

While much has been written about the Corinthians, mainly by club insiders, this is the first complete scholarly history to cover their activities both in England and in other parts of the world. It critically reassesses the club's role in the development of football and fills a gap in existing literature on the relationship between the progress of the game in England and globally. Most crucially, the book re-examines the sporting ideology of gentlemanly amateurism within the context of late nineteenth- and early twentieth-century society.

Chris Bolsmann is a Professor in the Department of Kinesiology at California State University Northridge, USA and Visiting Professor, Faculty of Health Sciences, University of Johannesburg, South Africa.

Dilwyn Porter is an Honorary Professor of Sports History and Culture at De Montfort University and Visiting Professor of Modern History at Newman University, Birmingham.

Routledge Studies in Modern British History

15 **Charles Pelham Villiers: Aristocratic Victorian Radical**
   The Member for Wolverhampton, 1835–1898, and Father of
   the House of Commons
   Roger Swift

16 **Women, Mission and Church in Uganda**
   Ethnographic encounters in an age of imperialism, 1895–1960s
   Elizabeth Dimock

17 **British Politics, Society and Empire, 1852–1945**
   Essays in Honour of Trevor O. Lloyd
   David W. Gutzke

18 **Deprivation, State Interventions and Urban Communities in Britain, 1968–79**
   Peter Shapely

19 **Private Secretaries to the Prime Minister**
   Foreign Affairs from Churchill to Thatcher
   Edited by Andrew Holt and Warren Dockter

20 **Liberal Reform and Industrial Relations**
   J.H. Whitley (1866–1935), Halifax Radical and Speaker
   of the House of Commons
   Edited by John A. Hargreaves, Keith Laybourn and Richard Toye

21 **Neoliberal Thought and Thatcherism**
   'A Transition From Here to There?'
   Robert Ledger

22 **English Gentlemen and World Soccer**
   Corinthians, Amateurism and the Global Game
   Chris Bolsmann and Dilwyn Porter

For a full list of titles in this series, please visit www.routledge.com/history/series/RSMBH

English Gentlemen and World Soccer

Corinthians, Amateurism and the Global Game

**Chris Bolsmann and
Dilwyn Porter**

LONDON AND NEW YORK

First published 2018
by Routledge
2 Park Square, Milton Park, Abingdon, Oxon OX14 4RN

and by Routledge
711 Third Avenue, New York, NY 10017

Routledge is an imprint of the Taylor & Francis Group, an informa business

© 2018 Chris Bolsmann and Dilwyn Porter

The right of Chris Bolsmann and Dilwyn Porter to be identified as authors of this work has been asserted by them in accordance with sections 77 and 78 of the Copyright, Designs and Patents Act 1988.

All rights reserved. No part of this book may be reprinted or reproduced or utilised in any form or by any electronic, mechanical, or other means, now known or hereafter invented, including photocopying and recording, or in any information storage or retrieval system, without permission in writing from the publishers.

Trademark notice: Product or corporate names may be trademarks or registered trademarks, and are used only for identification and explanation without intent to infringe.

British Library Cataloguing-in-Publication Data
A catalogue record for this book is available from the British Library

Library of Congress Cataloging-in-Publication Data
Names: Bolsmann, Chris, author. | Porter, Dilwyn, 1947– author.
Title: English gentlemen and world soccer: Corinthians, amateurism and the global game / Chris Bolsmann, Dilwyn Porter.
Description: Abingdon, Oxon; New York, NY: Routledge, 2018. | Series: Routledge studies in modern British history | Includes bibliographical references and index.
Identifiers: LCCN 2017058012
Subjects: LCSH: Corinthian Football Club—History.
Classification: LCC GV943.6.C59 B65 2018 | DDC 796.334/640941—dc23
LC record available at https://lccn.loc.gov/2017058012

ISBN: 978-1-4724-6613-6 (hbk)
ISBN: 978-1-315-57975-7 (ebk)

Typeset in Times New Roman
by codeMantra

Contents

	List of Figures	vii
	Acknowledgements	ix
	Introduction	1
1	'A scratch team with gentlemanly instincts': The Corinthians and English soccer in the late nineteenth century	20
2	Decline and fall: The Corinthians in the twentieth century	41
3	'Missionaries of Empire': The Corinthians on tour in South Africa	62
4	Communing with continental amateurism: Corinthians in Europe, *c.* 1904–39	80
5	'Joy the Corinthians are coming!' The Corinthian Football Club on tour in Canada and the United States	101
6	*Noblesse Oblige* and the Corinthian sojourns in Rio de Janeiro and São Paulo	117
	Conclusion	130
	Bibliography	139
	Index	151

List of Figures

I.1	Corinthian FC, 1885–86	1
1.1	Crystal Palace, Sheriff of London Shield, Corinthians v Sheffield United, 19 March 1898	20
2.1	Corinthian FC, Sheriff of London Shield v Sheffield United, Crystal Palace, 19 March 1898	41
3.1	Corinthians v Orange River Colony, Bloemfontein, 24 July 1907	62
4.1	Corinthians v Hannover 96, Hannover, 12 April 1936	80
5.1	Corinthians v Fore River, Boston, 14 September 1906	101
6.1	Corinthians v Brasileiros, Rio de Janeiro, 24 August 1913	117
C.1	Banquet in honour of the Corinthians, Paris, 1904	130

Acknowledgements

Thanks are due to our editors at Routledge, Rob Langham and Michael Bourne, who took on this book in difficult circumstances and have kept faith with the authors over a lengthier period than they could possibly have anticipated. Stuart Allison, James Hall, Gary James, Nick Piercey, Evie Stevenson and Christoph Wagner were each very generous in setting time aside to help with translations and access to sources. The content of this book is much richer for their efforts. Peter Holme and Alex Jackson at the National Football Museum Archive at Preston came up with leads I would never have found myself. Thanks are also due to Neil Carter, Richard Holt, Kristian Naglo, Harvey Osborne, Kevin Tallec Marston and Matt Taylor for various services rendered.

Sandra Porter was an endless source of encouragement and support throughout. Without her love and kindness, my half of the project would never have been completed.

Working with my co-author Chris Bolsmann has been a real pleasure. I have been involved in a number of co-authored and co-edited projects over the course of my career and know that they often test the strength of a friendship. We know each other much better now than when we started and yet somehow remain the best of friends. See you on Route 66, buddy.

Finally, thanks are due to our friend and colleague Tony Mason who began this journey with us and to whom all historians of association football are indebted.

Dil Porter

Several colleagues and friends have helped me immeasurably with this project. Thank you all. In England, Tony Mason read some of my earlier work and provided critical insights. Aidan Hamilton assisted with contacts in South America and shared sources. Rob Cavallini spent several hours answering my questions watching the Corinthian-Casuals. Alex Jackson at the National Football Museum in Manchester helped me access excellent source materials. Ana Maria Madrigal, Juan Carlos Guataqui, Olga Castro and Ovande Furtado assisted with Spanish and Portuguese translations.

Acknowledgements

In Brazil, Maria Quinteiro tracked down Brazilian newspaper sources. Dante Grecco, Celso Unzelte and Matthew Shirts were generous with their time in São Paulo and introduced me to their club Corinthians. Chris Gaffney assisted me in Rio de Janeiro. In Argentina, Sergio Lodise helped me find excellent sources and showed me around Boca's La Bombonera Stadium. In South Africa, Mafadi Bapela at the State Library in Pretoria greatly assisted in finding materials. Tony Wilcocks provided access to his archive. Diana Bolsmann, my mother in Cape Town, regularly visited the National Library on my behalf.

In the United States, several colleagues shared sources, read drafts, discussed ideas and helped sharpen arguments. They are Steven Apostolov, Brian Bunk, Ed Farnsworth, Colin Jose, Stephen Kerber, George Kioussis, David Kilpatrick, Gabe Logan, Tom McCabe and Cesar Torres. In addition, Kathleen Burns, Marcia Henry, Lynn Lampert, Dave Litterer, Osvaldo José Gorgazzi, Miki Goral, Nick Guoth, Gary James, Martin Johnes, Les Jones, Plínio Labriola, Jan Luitzen, John Mills, John Nauright, Leonardo Pereira and Wray Vamplew kindly shared sources with me. Finally, Dil Porter became my mentor during this project. I am now happy to call him my friend, thanks mate.

Chris Bolsmann

Introduction

Figure I.1 Corinthian FC, 1885–86.
From N. Lane ('Pa') Jackson, *Sporting Days and Sporting Ways* (Hurst & Blackett, Ltd., London 1932).

Association football is a global phenomenon. *Fédération Internationale de Football Association* (FIFA), its governing body, currently has 211 countries in membership. In 2014, the sixty-four matches played by the thirty-two national teams competing in the final stages of the World Cup tournament in Brazil attracted a total attendance of almost 3.5 million spectators while reaching an estimated 2.1 billion television viewers worldwide. 'Soccer', as we shall mostly call it so as to distinguish it from other forms of football, has come a long way from Kennington Oval, London, where the first international match was contested between England and Scotland in 1872 in front of 2,500 enthusiasts.[1] It was once commonplace to argue that it spread from Britain to the rest of the world by a relatively uncomplicated process of one-way diffusion. Historians and sociologists – increasingly aware of the complexities of globalization – are now less inclined to favour this view, preferring instead to emphasize the emergence of multi-directional cultural connections, some of which bypassed Britain altogether. This does not mean that Britain's role in the development of the globalized game was unimportant, merely that its contribution has to be located in a wider context and subjected to more nuanced interpretation.

Revisiting the history of the Corinthian Football Club provides an opportunity to address some of the issues arising from this turn in modern scholarship. The club's role in the development of the association game in England has long been acknowledged. As standard bearers for amateurism, the Corinthians found themselves at the centre of inter- and intra-class tensions centred on the moral ownership and institutional control of a middle-class recreational activity that was fast being transformed into a form of commercial entertainment with mass appeal. Their cultural legacy in terms of a value system that could be applied primarily in sport but which also had wider applications has probably been underestimated. 'Corinthianism' or 'the Corinthian spirit', essentially the amateur code of the public-school educated Victorian gentleman, still has its adherents. Arguably, it remains 'a vital part of the behavioural cocktail that makes us who we are and what we are to become'.[2] It was these values as well as soccer itself that the Corinthians carried with them on their tours to the Midlands, the North of England and Scotland and when they travelled overseas to Europe, South Africa, the United States, Canada and Brazil. We now understand that these events triggered complex responses, not least because they involved engagement with football cultures that were alive and kicking before 'Corinth', as insiders referred to the club, ventured beyond the familiar territory of London and its surrounding 'Home Counties'.

Who were the Corinthians?

'We may suppose that in the beginning was a ball, and [that] men kicked it about', one of rugby union's early chroniclers has explained.[3] In respect of soccer, however, the English claim to original ownership is solidly based, not least on account of the existence of a foundation text, the rules published by the newly formed Football Association (FA) in 1863 after a series of meetings between representatives of various clubs. The intention had been to arrive at a compromise that would facilitate matches between those who had attended various English 'public' (i.e. private) schools where they had learned different versions of football. This act of codification, fixing the game form in print, was an important step and marks the beginning of football as most people have come to know it. *The Rule Book of Association Football* (1863) has been nominated as one of the twelve books that 'changed the world', alongside the King James Bible (1611), Adam Smith's *Wealth of*

Nations (1776) and Charles Darwin's *On the Origins of Species* (1859).[4] It was this version of the game – give or take a few modifications – with which the Corinthian Football Club, founded in 1882, was primarily associated and which it carried on its travels.

Social exclusivity was a defining characteristic of the club from the start. It had taken its name from the ancient Greek city of Corinth whose delights were accessible only to a privileged minority. 'Not everyone is able to go to Corinth', the saying went.[5] Though N.L. ('Pa') Jackson, the journalist and sports promoter who founded the Corinthians, claimed in his autobiography that he had been motivated principally by the patriotic intention of finding eleven Englishmen capable of beating Scotland, there were self-imposed limits when it came to team selection. 'At that period', he recalled, 'the public school and university men provided most of the players for the English side, so I thought that by giving these plenty of practice together they would acquire a certain measure of combination'.[6] This was important because, though football was widely played in the public schools and universities, it also had a long history as a game of the masses or, at least, as an activity that permitted young men to prove their masculinity in contests, often involving hundreds of participants, in which a ball was carried, hurled, kicked or otherwise propelled towards the opposition line or goal. As England industrialized, folk football of this kind had given way to more 'rational' forms of physical recreation, effectively those favoured by employers, magistrates, schoolmasters and clergy. In this climate, codified versions of football that effectively curtailed the potential for mayhem – soccer from 1863, rugby from 1871 – could be regarded as respectable pursuits.[7]

Some historians and sociologists have framed these developments within the idea of sport as part of a 'civilizing process', assigning a key role to the public schools. Thus, for Eric Dunning and Kenneth Sheard, 'new forms of football' flourished in the late nineteenth century partly because 'they had become acceptable as media for expressing "gentlemanly" values'.[8] At the same time, the expansion of these and other recognizably modern sports owed much to the impetus from below. 'There had always been a considerable popular appetite for sport in England', as Peter Bailey has observed, 'and it had been far from extinguished'.[9] Working-class enthusiasm for and participation in soccer was a factor that could not be ignored and the focus of academic inquiry shifted from the classes to the masses. 'An increasingly influential body of work', Dave Russell noted in 2013, 'now challenges established narratives placing public school football and ex-public schoolboys at the heart of the game's codification and dissemination'.[10] Yet, while recognizing the importance of explaining how and why soccer became embedded in popular culture, it would be perverse to deny the public schools and their old boys a place in the story.

Given the rise of professional football from the 1880s onwards – with working-class players employed by clubs owned by syndicates of small businessmen who Jackson believed were 'in the game for what they could get out of it' – the symbolic significance of the Corinthians was enormous.[11] Jackson's gentlemen crossed geographical, social and cultural boundaries when playing away from home. In industrial Lancashire in the mid-1880s, they encountered both 'class resentment' and 'provincial hostility to the Metropolis'.[12] C.B. Fry, for many the epitome of the gentleman amateur, believed that the 'foul play' he found so irritating when playing for the Corinthians on tour could be accounted for by 'the way everybody all round up there looked at things'. The essential difference, he explained, 'was that football in the Midlands and the North was played by wage-earners whereas in the South most of the strong clubs were composed of relatively leisured men'.[13] In these circumstances, it was important to ensure that Aston Villa, Blackburn Rovers and Preston North End, however technically proficient they might be, should not have the field to themselves when it came to setting standards. It had been gratifying, one of the club's historians recorded, having been incorrectly labelled as the 'Old Corinthians' before a match at Blackpool in 1885, to be approached by a spectator anxious to know the whereabouts of Corinth School, 'as if they turned out such fine players he would like to send his son there'.[14]

Style – playing in a way that would make a favourable impression wherever they went – was also important. Having settled by the end of the 1880s on an attacking formation with five forwards and using sweeping passes to advance swiftly on the opposition goal, the Corinthians liked to believe that they were superior in terms of football aesthetics. 'There can indeed be no more pleasant sight in the eyes of the appreciative onlooker than a line of forwards going straight down the field without swerving aside or turning back, but making direct for goal', claimed G.O. Smith, centre-forward for the Corinthians and England. Professionals, playing a cagier game with the emphasis on ball retention, did things differently, 'but it compares very unfavourably with what we have called the amateur system'.[15] It was important to make such distinctions, especially for those comprising what the *Morning Post* in 1898 called 'the large community who look to the Corinthians for a maintenance of the true traditions of football in these days, when the sport is overrun by a great wave of professionalism'.[16] In the late nineteenth century, as Britain's political establishment grappled with the problem of how best to accommodate the perceived threat posed by organized labour, the idea that gentlemen amateurs could match and sometimes beat teams of working-class professionals was immensely reassuring, not least when such victories could be depicted as demonstrations of effortless superiority. 'It is singular, but nevertheless true', noted a Sheffield sports weekly after an interview with Smith, 'that the famous Corinthian never trains'. Yet, not only was he England's centre-forward, but also 'a cricketer of no mean ability', having scored 132 for Oxford against Cambridge in 1896, 'pulling the match out of the fire'.[17] With such natural talent on your side, the disconcerting thought that the world might be turned upside down, even for ninety minutes, could be kept at bay.

As a cultural phenomenon, the Corinthians were significant on account of what they represented. When they wore the club's white shirt with its distinctive 'CFC' monogram, its players embodied the amateur ideal. 'The true amateur', as Richard Holt has argued, 'was an ideal type and the banal realities of play can rarely have taken on such a high moral tone'.[18] Newspapers – especially when the opposition were professionals – left readers in no doubt as to what was at stake when the Corinthians took the field. 'In Saturday's match at the Crystal Palace', ran one match report, 'there was renewed that well-known rivalry between those two branches of sport – the one body who devote their leisure to a game and the other who make it their means of livelihood'. The Corinthians were said to 'represent all that is best in amateurism'.[19] This meant rather more than simply not being paid for their efforts. Amateurism constituted a sporting ideology rooted in the chivalric traditions of the English aristocracy and the cult of athleticism, which flourished at the schools to which Victorian middle-class parents sent their sons. It involved an idealized code of behaviour in which how a sportsman conducted himself was more important than winning. As Holt has observed, it was 'more a matter of being a gentleman than of strict compliance with the principles of amateurism'.[20] This was just as well, as these principles were not always strictly adhered to even by those who advocated them most vehemently.

If Corinth School had existed, it would have been located in the South of England, which the Corinthians were often said to represent. 'Southerners', the *Morning Post* noted after Preston North End had been defeated in 1892, 'will hail with no small degree of satisfaction the brilliant victory of the Corinthians in the match at the Queen's Club, West Kensington, yesterday'.[21] Socially exclusive definitions of amateurism had more purchase in the South, where sport was dominated by ex-public schoolboys, than in the Midlands or the North. In the late nineteenth century, there was a sufficient supply of young men meeting these qualifications to be found in and around London so that fielding teams of the desired quality was rarely a problem. Sometimes the Corinthians claimed to represent 'England', when boasting, for example, that they had supplied the national team with all eleven players for the international matches against Wales in 1894 and 1895. It is clear, however, that the Corinthians aligned themselves with a variant of Englishness more closely identified with what has been called 'the Southern Metaphor' (romantic, aristocratic, traditional, frivolous) than with its Northern counterpart (pragmatic, bourgeois, enterprising, serious).[22] 'The great event, or series of events, of a Corinthian season', Fry recalled, 'was the Christmas tour in the north of England and the south of Scotland'.[23] How could it have been otherwise when it invoked symbolic rivalry between the classes and the masses, amateurs and professionals, the South and the North, not to mention England and Scotland?

By the time that Fry was playing for the Corinthians in the early 1890s, they were being referred to in the press as 'the leading peripatetic team'.[24] Touring was of critical importance for the club, though it followed paths already trodden by others rather than breaking new ground. The London-based Wanderers, according to some accounts, were the first to tour, visiting Oxford and Cambridge to play various college teams in 1867. A brief history of soccer tourism in the *Pall Mall Gazette* pointed to the Royal Engineers, based at Chatham, Kent, as significant pioneers, having visited Nottingham, Sheffield and Derby in 1875 'to try their strength with the leading club of each town'.[25] Neither were the Corinthians the first to travel abroad. They played in Vienna on their first European tour at Easter 1904 but had been preceded by Oxford University whose goalkeeper had distinguished himself during a 15-0 victory in 1899 'by signing autographs for admirers, eating sweets and, seated on a chair, keeping a safe goal'.[26] When the Corinthians arrived in 1904, the Austrians were improving and had already been exposed to professional opposition, notably Southampton and Glasgow Rangers 'on whose style [they] were to mould their game'.[27] By the time they visited Copenhagen later the same year, their Scottish counterparts, Queen's Park, had already made three trips to Denmark in 1898, 1900 and 1903.[28]

That other English and Scottish clubs had preceded them did not detract from the fame of the Corinthians or the enthusiasm with which they were received. As early as 1895, when soccer tours to 'the continent', as the English liked to call Europe, were still regarded as adventurous, concerns were expressed regarding the possibility that 'a class of players may take part in them who will not enhance the reputation of Englishmen for courtesy off the field or fair play on it'.[29] The elite social provenance of the Corinthians, underpinned by the club's adherence to the sporting code of the gentleman amateur – modest in victory, gracious in defeat – ensured that they were ideally suited to an ambassadorial role. When they toured abroad, the Corinthians were regarded as representatives not just of English soccer but of English *amateur* soccer. They were invariably described as 'the best amateur team in England', or 'the famous English amateur football team', or even 'the best amateur footballers in the world'.[30] Their hosts, especially in the years before the First World War, expected the Corinthians to delight them with an exhibition of soccer as it could only be played by the English masters. Yet, the Corinthians were also concerned to teach foreigners how to play the game in the right spirit. Continental tours, as the club's first chronicler B.O. Corbett noted in 1906, 'have done much to popularise the British idea of true sportsmanship'.[31] They set standards to which other English tourists could aspire, even if they did not wear the club's colours.

The missionary dimension of soccer tourism was especially evident when the Corinthians sent teams to far-flung parts of Britain's informal and formal overseas empire, and to the United States. Soccer tended to follow the flag in the late nineteenth century; it certainly followed trade. Charles Miller, son of a railway engineer working in São Paulo, is often credited with bringing the game to Brazil when he returned from school in England, though this is an over-simplification. As a schoolboy, Miller had made a guest appearance for the Corinthians when they were one man short against Hampshire in 1892.[32] Two years later, he organized the first match played under association rules in Brazil, the teams comprising expatriates working for British companies in São Paulo, though other influences, especially German and Swiss, were soon apparent. Oscar Cox, who in 1897 founded the Fluminense club in Rio de Janeiro, had learned his football in Lausanne. In São Paulo, the founding members of Sport Club Internacional in 1899 were Brazilian, French, German, Portuguese and English.[33] Moreover, Brazil entertained touring teams from South Africa in 1906 and Argentina in 1907, well in advance of the Corinthians, who in 1910 became the first team from Britain to visit. Thus, when they arrived, they encountered a soccer culture that had already gained a foothold and which had been shaped to some extent by external connections, not all of them English. It was, however, a culture which the Corinthians had already influenced to some extent. When the referee mistakenly awarded a penalty against the tourists, Charles Miller, playing his last match, 'was so sporting as to kick the ball gently to our goalkeeper Rogers who cleared'.[34] In as far as they were missionaries for soccer in Brazil, the Corinthians were to a large extent preaching to the converted, while the exhibition matches played and the various dinners and receptions at which they were entertained provided opportunities for the expatriate British business community to wave the flag.[35]

Much the same could be said of their visits to South Africa, though these had a more obvious political significance given the crisis in British-Afrikaner relations at the turn of the century. The South African Football Association had been established in 1892, five years before the first Corinthians tour, and it was not unusual to encounter opponents who had played as professionals in England and Scotland. This does not mean, however, that the Corinthians did not think of themselves as missionaries. According to Tony Mason, for the English gentlemen who wore the club's shirt, touring – whether at home or abroad – was probably regarded 'as part holiday and part football missionary work'.[36] Corbett's in-house history of the club, published in 1906, added a political dimension, claiming that they had visited South Africa as 'Missionaries of Empire', helping to bring the 'Mother Country' and the colonies closer together.[37] 'Missionaries of Empire', Joseph Chamberlain had urged in 1903, 'must spread the faith by personal intercession'.[38] Football may not have been exactly what the Colonial Secretary had in mind, but sport was one of the cultural ties that bound the Empire together, and Corbett's appropriation of the then fashionable phrase is significant.

It clearly did not apply in quite the same way to the United States, first visited in 1906, where soccer was struggling to establish itself in a crowded and highly competitive sports marketplace, suffering in particular from 'the perception of the game as separate from American sports culture by both its practitioners and enthusiasts ... and the vast majority of the American public'.[39] Local enthusiasts, in the words of the *American Cricketer*, anticipated '[that] the visit of so renowned a team will give a tremendous fillip to the game', demonstrating how it should be played to both the initiated and uninitiated.[40] Nevertheless, as John Benson has argued in connection with the Oxford-Cambridge athletics team that visited Canada and the United States in 1901, we should not underestimate the impact of such tours in terms of cementing international relationships between English-speaking social elites.[41] This may not have been the primary purpose of visiting the United States, but it may have been one of the most important outcomes.

What this suggests is that the Corinthians had a significance that extended beyond sport into other spheres. It was not simply that the club fulfilled an important role in helping to popularize soccer both at home and abroad. The excitement generated by the FA Cup after 1871 indicates that the game was well on its way to achieving widespread popularity at home some years before it was formed. Moreover, though the Corinthians and other tourists played a part in ensuring that soccer acquired an international dimension, powerful agencies were already at work, not least the economic factors that persuaded European migrants – and not only those from England – that it was in their best interests to seek work overseas, taking their native sports with them or taking up those that others had brought from elsewhere. That said, the Corinthian Football Club was important because it represented a particular kind of football, played by a particular kind of footballer and because it effectively embodied a particular set of values, specifically those associated with gentlemanly amateurism and British imperialism. They carried an impressive amount of cultural baggage with them wherever they went, whether at home or abroad.

Surveying the field

One reason why a reassessment of the Corinthians is overdue is that they have had such a very good press to date. In part, this was because they were able to write their own story. Jackson, the club's founding father and guiding light, was a journalist and magazine proprietor who exploited opportunities presented by the growing public interest in sport. By 1882, the year in which it was founded, Jackson had a London office from which he and FA Secretary Charles Alcock issued *Football*, a weekly paper. 'As Football is becoming more popular every year', the first issue explained, 'the necessity for such a periodical becomes apparent'.[42] A year later, *Football* was superseded by *Pastime*, a sports weekly launched independently by Jackson. He claimed that it was 'the leading weekly paper for all the principal amateur sports throughout the next thirteen or fourteen years'.[43] 'Pa' also supplied 'three or four weekly articles on sport for daily, or weekly journals and a few for monthly magazines'.[44] The Corinthians would not suffer for want of representation in the sporting press.

Jackson's connections remained useful in securing favourable publicity. It was gratifying, no doubt, to read in Alcock's *Handbook of Athletic*

Sports for 1892, during a period in which Jackson was increasingly at odds with his critics on the FA Council, that improvements in the style of play in recent years were due largely to 'the work of the Corinthian Football Club'.[45] Other Corinthians were very active in the burgeoning sports press, notably C.B. Fry who wrote regularly for the *Athletic News* and recalled that the editor 'always put my articles in without diminution or correction'.[46] Fry, never too shy to cash in on his name, also edited his own weekly, *C. B. Fry's Magazine*, from 1904 until it folded in 1914. In addition, until its demise in 1924, the *Sportsman* could be relied on for sympathetic coverage, not least because its chief football writer, H.V. ('Pa') Stanton, was firmly embedded in London amateur football circles and had a particular feeling for the public-school old-boys clubs from which the Corinthians recruited many of their players.[47] As we shall see, bulletins appearing in the *Sportsman* when the Corinthians travelled abroad were often supplied by the tourists themselves. Suffice to say that those who write on the history of sport rely more heavily than most on evidence in newspapers as sources and that, in the English press of the late nineteenth and early twentieth centuries, the Corinthian element was well placed to shape opinion.

This impression is reinforced by the extent to which the Corinthians contributed to contemporary histories of soccer written around the turn of the century, when the club's best days had just passed. What we are seeing here is an example of a process that Anthony Bateman has identified as 'literaturisation' – usually applied to cricket – whereby a particular version of sports history achieves a kind of literary hegemony.[48] Unsurprisingly, Jackson was well to the fore, arguing in *Association Football* (1899) that the Corinthians' policy of eschewing league and cup competitions 'permitted its members to enjoy the best sort of football, *viz.* that played for sport alone'.[49] The authors of the section on 'Association Football' in the Badminton Library volume on *Football* (1904) were W.J. Oakley and G.O. Smith, both Corinthians. In a key chapter assessing the impact of professionalism, Smith underlined the idea that original ownership lay with the public schools and the universities, supporting their claim 'both to have started the game and to have given it to the world'. He was also anxious to seize the moral high ground, noting that gamesmanship and trickery were on the increase, before adding by way of explanation that professionals, though 'excellent men', were 'paid to do the best for their side, not the best for sport'.[50] Chapters on different aspects of play allowed the authors to define what constituted good football and often looked no further than the Corinthians for role models. This process of idealization was repeated in Corbett's history of the club, which contained 'Hints on the Game' by well-known Corinthians and a series of 'Character Sketches' by Fry. 'I think we may decide on the game as played by Cobbold and his contemporaries as the ideal style', he observed magisterially, referring to what has often been described as the club's 'golden age'.[51]

It is important to remember that the printed word played an important part in creating the Victorian and Edwardian sporting world. The press, Mike Huggins has argued, actively constructed 'the very meaning of sports, since what people understood of them was largely shaped by the way they were represented'.[52] Match reports made it possible for readers to grasp what was at stake when the teams in opposition were referred to as 'The Southerners' (Corinthians) and 'The Northerners' (Preston North End), or when a victory over Aston Villa was described as 'a triumph for amateurism'.[53] Even if they never saw them play, it seems likely that readers would have become aware of the particular qualities said to characterize the Corinthian style, so frequently were they mentioned. 'The dashing runs and long passing of the Corinthians were very attractive to watch, and the 4,000 people grew very enthusiastic', was not untypical.[54] Reporting of this kind prepared the ground in which myths regarding the superiority of the Corinthians and the values they represented could take root and grow. Few who wrote at any length about the club and its history were able to resist the temptation to repeat tales of Corinthian glory, especially as they kept returning to the same sources. Moreover, it was a myth that lived on, resurfacing from time to time long after the original club had ceased to exist after merging with the Casuals on the eve of the Second World War. It helped to sustain the diminishing constituency, which continued to insist, even in the 1940s, that 'Association Football at its best is played by the public schools, the universities, and by various amateur clubs'.[55]

Writing in 1954 of the Corinthians of the late nineteenth century, Ivan Sharpe of the *Sunday Chronicle* admitted that 'These men performed before I could study them'. He then went on to nominate the Corinthians as one of the four 'greatest club teams' in English football history.[56] Geoffrey Green, chief association football correspondent of *The Times*, was more judicious. 'I never saw him', he wrote of Smith, 'but those who did swore that he was England's greatest centre-forward ever'. What was certain, he added, was that 'to these worshippers G.O. Smith was a god, equivalent in his way to the legendary "W.G." at cricket'.[57] Edward Grayson's sycophantic *Corinthians & Cricketers*, with a foreword by Fry, published in 1957, effectively repeated the by now familiar tale of 'The Glory that was Corinth'.[58] Significantly, this adulatory tendency appears to have peaked around 1960, just as the amateur hegemony in British sport was beginning to crumble. As English cricket prepared to ditch the distinction between 'Gentlemen' and 'Players', the appearance of a four-volume history of English soccer, edited by Green and A.H. Fabian, both of whom had played for the club between the wars, testified to the enduring myth of Corinthian supremacy. 'The name still means more to the discerning follower of association football', observed Norman Ackland in a chapter dedicated to the Corinthians, 'than all the professional titles strung together in the history of the game'. As if to illustrate the point, Ackland, who had been covering amateur soccer for various London newspapers since 1923, reminded his readers that the Corinthians had behaved and dressed like gentlemen. 'With an intelligent nonchalance', he recalled, 'and in their tailored shirts and well-cut shorts, they brought a quality and culture to the game'.[59]

James Walvin's *The People's Game* (1975) and Tony Mason's groundbreaking *Association Football and English Society* (1980) began the important process of supplying a context in which the role played by the Corinthians in the development of English and world soccer could be better understood. Significantly, Mason was the first historian to critique early twentieth-century accounts on which others had relied as sources, dismissing Gibson and Pickford's assessment of Smith in their monumental *Association Football & the Men Who Made It* (1906) as an example of the 'hyperbole' that characterized much of the writing about Jackson's Corinthians by contemporaries and near contemporaries.[60] This was a striking development, especially as Gibson and Pickford's assessment, for the period in which they were writing, was probably more considered than most. While acknowledging brilliant performances in the past, they were aware that 'the palmy days of the Corinthians have gone'.[61] Much of the emphasis in the historical writing on English football that ensued, however, was on the Corinthians as the last representatives of an old order that had been swept away at the end of the nineteenth century. Walvin had argued that the history of the club was indicative of what was happening to English soccer in the late Victorian and Edwardian era as commerce and professionalism gained the ascendancy. 'In the 1880s', he argued, 'the Corinthians were typical of the game's founding fathers; by 1914 they were utterly exceptional – toffs in a world taken over by the plebs', a judgement that was not revised when *The People's Game* was republished in 1994.[62]

The danger now was that the Corinthians and other gentlemen amateurs might be pushed to the margins of soccer historiography simply because the working class seemed more important to cultural and social historians at the time. 'Scholarly overkill of one group', warned Mike Huggins, 'has been coupled with neglect of another. The middle-classes have been made second-class citizens'.[63] Arguably, Dave Russell had already begun to address this concern in relation to English football by recasting the amateur-professional divide as an 'intra-middle-class conflict, with the provincial, non-public-school educated business and commercial classes uniting in support of professionalism, against the public school elite'.[64] Even this, however, as Russell acknowledged, was an oversimplification. As in the political crisis of 1910–11 over the powers of the House of Lords, some toffs were inclined to compromise, while others wanted to fight to 'the last ditch'.

By this time, however, it was also possible to locate the history of the Corinthians in the context of a growing body of work on amateurism, notably Richard Holt's seminal chapter on 'Amateurism and the Victorians' in *Sport and the British* (1989). It became clear that the club had been formed during a period between the mid-nineteenth and mid-twentieth centuries when the ideology of amateurism exerted a hegemonic grip over British sport. 'At its peak', Lincoln Allison elaborated a few years later, 'sport was run as if amateurism were the ideal condition; it was run by amateurs and large areas within its space ... were cleared for the use of amateurs only'. This did not mean that professionalism and commerce were eradicated, but they were contained, 'bounded and subordinated for the most part'.[65] The amateur ethos supplied a framework within which governing bodies in Britain and elsewhere drafted and applied rules designed to keep commerce at a safe distance. Sometimes these rules were bent, sometimes expediency prevailed and they were applied selectively or ignored altogether, but generally the idea that sport was 'a moral end in itself' rather than 'a source of enrichment' was powerfully influential.[66]

Reawakened to the importance of amateurism as an ideal, historians began to locate it more precisely via explorations of the relationship between the middle class and sport, with John Lowerson's *Sport and the English Middle Classes* (1993) to the fore. In many sports played by middle-class men, he noted, 'the spread was lateral rather than downwards ... it was the peer groups who mattered'.[67] More recent work on the history of English football has benefited from these insights. 'For an important group of individuals and clubs based mainly around the English Home Counties', Matthew Taylor has observed, 'amateur football existed not as a resource for the professional arm of the sport but as an antithesis to it'. It was played, as the Corinthians always insisted, in a different spirit, and was, in many ways, 'a different game entirely'.[68] This line of argument has recently been reinforced by Terry Morris in his excellent survey of the history of amateur soccer in England where he sets the history of the socially exclusive Corinthians in the context of a battle to 'save the gentleman amateur'.[69] This involved 'confronting the Northern professionals', though, as we shall see, it did not preclude working with them when it was perceived to be mutually beneficial.

Thus, the Corinthians took their own game with them on their travels. In so far as they were ambassadors, it was largely for their own gentlemanly version of association football. Their refusal to take advantage of penalty kicks when touring South Africa in 1907 was a significant indicator in this respect. Though eventually abandoning this ruse when persuaded that it was disrespectful to local referees, the point had been made.[70] Norman Creek's history of the club, published in 1933 and containing brief accounts of tours abroad up to 1931, makes it clear that the Corinthians found satisfaction in being regarded as representatives of the amateur tradition in football, especially in the 1920s and 1930s when it was becoming increasingly difficult for them to mount a sustained challenge to professionals at home. He recycled an article from 'the foremost Austrian daily paper' describing the Corinthians as the 'most prominent representatives of the amateur idea in sport' and 'true champions of fair play'. He also seized on a Swiss newspaper report after a match against Zurich Grasshoppers in 1931, which urged the Corinthians to 'return to our country every year'. They were preferred to visiting teams of English professionals who were said 'never take their

Continental matches seriously'.[71] In this way, Creek, who had played in the match that had prompted these observations, re-emphasized the club's commitment to amateurism in soccer. Moreover, the underlying assumption that only the English knew how to play the game properly remained intact, even though the focus in Creek's accounts of the later tours was increasingly on playing it in the right spirit. The implication was that diffusion remained very much a one-way process despite the rapid development of the game in Europe, South America and elsewhere since the Corinthians had first ventured abroad thirty years previously.

This view has persisted despite its critics. 'The standard theory', it was noted as recently as 2010, 'is that Britain is the birthplace of modern sports and that sports diffused from the homeland to the rest of the world'.[72] More specifically, recent work in Latin America continues to identify tours undertaken by the Corinthians and other visitors from England as one of the three 'vectors' – along with education and trade – through which football culture made its way across the South Atlantic.[73] However, what we are more aware of now, given our understanding of the historical relationship between sport and globalization, is the global historical context in which the Corinthians operated. Between the mid-nineteenth and early twentieth centuries, revolutions in communications and transport made the world a smaller place. Technology-driven change facilitated international travel along with the rapid transmission of ideas and information, while simultaneously enhancing personal and social interconnections between people living in different countries and even on different continents. These developments, as Taylor has observed, 'were crucial prerequisites for the emergence of the modern sporting world'.[74] One factor that helps to explain the adoption of English sports across Europe in this period was that 'there was a greater interdependency between these nations than ever before'.[75] The Corinthians demand our attention because no other soccer club engaged so actively in the new global public sphere and sustained that engagement over so many years. Ironically for a club that was in the process of being swept aside by the commercial juggernaut of professional football at home, these gentlemanly amateurs, the game they played and the values they represented were welcomed by modernizers and progressives elsewhere who tended to look to Britain as an example. Thus, at a critical juncture in what is now regarded as the initial phase of globalization, the Corinthians were especially well placed to assist as association football became 'the game of the *fin de siècle* urban elites of Europe and Latin America'.[76]

Summary

Writing in the 1950s, Geoffrey Green assigned a major role in the development of world soccer to the Corinthians, for whom he had made a few appearances in the 1930s. The club and the values that it represented, he claimed, had been 'a shining light, diffused, not only throughout Britain but overseas, too, in their tours to the Continent, South Africa, America and other distant climes'.[77] This view, heavily underpinned by the assumption that Britain, or at least that part of England with which the Corinthians were primarily associated, was the world's true centre and also a source of football enlightenment, now seems dated and simplistic. It is important to remember, however, that explanations of this kind, which envisaged soccer as a product of the English public schools, disseminated throughout the United Kingdom and then exported to the rest of the world, carried considerable weight at the time. Perhaps it was inevitable that the Corinthians, simply because they travelled more than most and so widely, should have been regarded as such important agents in this process of cultural diffusion, though, to some extent, this may have resulted from the favourable treatment they had been able to secure in the sporting press and in early twentieth-century accounts of the history of the game. The myth thus had an enduring appeal. It seems likely that many of those who turned to Green's match reports and features in *The Times* found comfort in the idea that the people's game owed its success to former public schoolboys playing soccer of 'the best sort' at home and abroad.

Recent work in sports history suggests that a reassessment of the Corinthians is overdue, not least because so little – Chris Bolsmann's work on South Africa and Piercey and Porter's work on the Netherlands aside – has been written about their overseas tours.[78] Sports historians are learning to read their primary sources critically, interrogating the language of match reports, for example, to reveal embedded assumptions about gender, class, nation and ethnicity. Club histories based on compilations of match reports, such as Rob Cavallini's *Play Up Corinth* (2007), serve a useful purpose but raise as many questions as answers. However, we now have greater awareness of the embattled social context in which the Corinthians operated at home and of the complex web of cultural connections in which they were enmeshed every time they set out on tour, especially if it involved a trip to the 'distant climes' to which Green alluded. It would be easy to write the Corinthians and the gentlemanly amateurism that they represented out of the story of world football altogether or to consign them to the margins, not least because they had such an inflated view of their own importance. Instead, we should seize the opportunity to view them in a new perspective informed by an enriched understanding of the contexts in which they played both at home and overseas.

The discussion that follows falls into two parts. Chapters 1 and 2 trace the rise and fall of the Corinthians as a force in English soccer. Initially, the focus is on Jackson, the amateur 'super club' that he created and the strategies deployed to sustain gentlemanly amateurism as a force within the domestic game in an era characterized by the onwards march of professionalism. For Morris, 'the mission of the Corinthians was to maintain as much as possible of a doomed status quo'.[79] Yet, the tenacity with which they pursued this ambition across half a century suggests that they did not necessarily see themselves as doomed nor their cause as irredeemably lost and that they were engaged in a protracted negotiation to secure for themselves a place in the modern game which acknowledged the historic significance of the social elite from which they drew their players and supporters. This was the logic underpinning the club's decision to join the breakaway Amateur Football Association (AFA) in 1907, surely the most significant reverse ever suffered by the Corinthians and entirely self-inflicted. Chapter 2 explores the reduced circumstances in which the Corinthians found themselves as a result of English soccer's 'great split' and the increasing difficulties encountered in promoting the cause of gentlemanly soccer in the 1920s and 1930s, when the 'rush to rugby' in the public schools cut the ground from under their feet.

The second part of the discussion seeks to assess the impact made by the Corinthians as overseas tourists and the ways in which they interacted with pre-existing football cultures in the countries that they visited. The focus here reflects our view of the importance of a more complex and less Anglo-centric view of soccer diffusion than would have once been conventional with an emphasis on the bilateral cultural exchanges that soccer tourism facilitated. Connectivity is a key theme here, not least because it opens up opportunities to explore the development of amateurism as a global phenomenon. South Africa was an important part of the British Empire, and between 1897 and 1907, the Corinthians visited on three occasions. Chapter 3 considers the club's role as 'Missionaries of Empire' in South Africa where, following in the footsteps of English cricket and rugby tourists, the Corinthians undertook three long and arduous tours in 1897, 1903 and 1907. South Africa was an important part of the British Empire, and the Corinthians arrived, especially in 1897 and 1903 – the tours neatly bracketing the South African War of 1899–1902 – as high-profile representatives of the mother country at a critical juncture in imperial history. All major centres were visited, and the Corinthians were welcomed and feted by the football authorities and local elites alike. While they were superior to local opposition, particularly in 1897 and 1903, South African football had made steady progress by the time of their third visit in 1907. Not only were some local teams now able to defeat the Corinthians, but the tourists also encountered a reluctance to take their side in the ensuing conflict between the AFA and the FA in England despite their determined efforts to make the case for amateurism.

Chapter 4, which follows the Corinthians on their travels to Europe between 1904 and 1938, builds on some of the arguments developed in Piercey and Porter's account of the club's impact on Dutch soccer. Short continental tours, as McDowell has concluded in his recent work on Queen's Park, meant making bilateral connections with sportsmen drawn from a similar background to themselves and 'communing with the broad church of European amateur sport'.[80] Those who hosted such tours often had good reasons to embrace Corinthianism, which was then appropriated and adapted to meet their particular requirements. This was especially evident in countries like France and the Netherlands where middle-class footballers were becoming an embattled minority by the 1920s and 1930s. Amateurism is very much a key theme here. The Corinthians' decision to join the breakaway AFA made it very difficult to consolidate the relationships established in Europe before 1907, and this difficulty was accentuated by the impact of the First World War. By the time continental tours were resumed in the 1920s, the Corinthians were in decline at home, and the club's capacity to influence the development of the game in Europe was thereby significantly reduced.

The following chapter explores the club's three visits to North America in some detail. George Parker, integrally involved in the South African tours, arranged their early tours to Canada and the United States. On their first trip in 1906, the Corinthians sought to demonstrate the benefits of association football in the context of a 'crisis' in the American version of the game. Though some small inroads were made, their second visit in 1911 was more successful in that the Corinthians unintentionally contributed to the reconfiguration of soccer in the United States. On their final trans-Atlantic trip in 1924, a visit that took in both Canada and the United States, it was clear that North American soccer had made significant strides since 1911, while the Corinthians were markedly poor and no longer the attraction they once had been. Finally, in Chapter 6, the tours to Brazil are considered. In their two short visits to Rio de Janeiro and São Paulo in 1910 and 1913, the Corinthians played against sides representing the Anglo-Brazilian social elite. The game in Brazil was not as developed as in neighbouring Argentina during this period, and the English tourists were able to defeat the local opposition convincingly. They were, however, invited to visit Argentina in 1914, an important year as the gentlemen amateurs renegotiated their way back into the FA fold. En route to South America, the Corinthians were drawn into the conflict between rival football associations in Argentina, potentially compromising their status at home. No soccer, however, was played on the ill-fated 1914 tour. Instead, a much larger conflict saw the Corinthians return home to take up arms.

Notes

1 *2014 FIFA World Cup Brazil TM: Television Audience Report* (London: Kantar Media, 2014), p. 7; total in-home audience reach calculated on the basis of individual viewers watching matches for 20+ minutes; also Andy Mitchell, *First Elevens: The Birth of International Football and the Men Who Made It Happen* (Glasgow: Andy Mitchell Media, 2012), p. 50.
2 D.J. Taylor, *On the Corinthian Spirit: The Decline of Amateurism in Sport* (London: Yellow Jersey Press, 2006), p. 118.
3 Jerome J. Rahilly, *Rugby Football* (London: C. Arthur Pearson Ltd., 1904), p. 15; for ancient versions of the game worldwide, see David Goldblatt, *The Ball Is Round: A Global History of Football* (London: Penguin, 2006), pp. 4–18.
4 Melvyn Bragg, *12 Books That Changed the World* (London: Hodder & Stoughton, 2006), pp. 93–118.

5 See Rob Cavallini, *Play Up Corinth: A History of the Corinthian Football Club* (Stroud: Stadia, 2007), p. 9.
6 N. Lane ('Pa') Jackson, *Sporting Days and Sporting Ways* (London: Hurst & Blackett, 1932), p. 66.
7 See Peter Bailey, *Leisure and Class in Victorian England: Rational Recreation and the Contest for Control, 1830–1885* (London: Routledge and Kegan Paul, 1978), p. 144.
8 Eric Dunning and Kenneth Sheard, *Barbarians, Gentlemen and Players: A Sociological Study of the Development of Rugby Football* (Oxford: Martin Robertson, 1979), p. 107.
9 Bailey, *Leisure and Class*, p. 139.
10 Dave Russell, 'Kicking Off: The Origins of Association Football', in Rob Steen, Jed Novick and Huw Richards (eds), *The Cambridge Companion to Football* (Cambridge: Cambridge University Press, 2013), p. 14.
11 William Pickford, *A Glance Back at the Football Association Council 1888–1938* (Bournemouth: Bournemouth Guardian, 1938), p. 16.
12 Bailey, *Leisure and Class*, p. 142.
13 C.B. Fry, *Life Worth Living* (London: Pavilion Books, 1986; first published, 1939), pp. 264–65; see also Iain Wilton, *C.B. Fry: King of Sport* (London: Metro Publishing, 2002), pp. 141–42.
14 F.N.S. Creek, *A History of the Corinthian Football Club* (London: Longmans, Green and Co., 1933), p. 12.
15 G.O. Smith, 'The Attack', in Montague Shearman (ed), *Football* (London: Longmans, Green and Co., 1904), pp. 104–5.
16 *Morning Post* (London), 11 November 1898.
17 *Sports (Illustrated)* (Sheffield), 6 April 1898, p. 29; see also Edward Grayson, *Corinthians & Cricketers* (London: Sportsmans Book Club, 1957), p. 31.
18 Richard Holt, *Sport and the British: A Modern History* (Oxford: Oxford University Press, 1989), p. 100.
19 *Morning Post*, 21 March 1898.
20 Richard Holt, 'Amateurism and its Interpretation: The Social Origins of British Sport', *Innovation*, vol. 5, no. 1, 1992, p. 21.
21 *Morning Post*, 22 March 1892.
22 See Martin J. Wiener, *English Culture and the Decline of the Industrial Spirit, 1850–1980* (Cambridge: Cambridge University Press, 1981), pp. 41–42.
23 Fry, *Life Worth Living*, p. 270.
24 *The Sportsman* (London), 22 February 1892.
25 See Rob Cavallini, *The Wanderers F.C.: Five Times F.A. Cup Winners* (Worcester Park: Dog N Duck Publications, 2005), pp. 58–59; *Pall Mall Gazette* (London), 4 January 1895.
26 Colin Weir, *The History of Oxford University Association Football Club 1872–1998* (Harefield: Yore Publications, 1998), p. 26.
27 Willy Meisl, *Soccer Revolution* (London: Phoenix Sports Books, 1955), pp. 56–57.
28 See Matthew McDowell, 'Queen's Park FC in Copenhagen, 1898–1903: Paradoxes in Early Transnational Amateurism', *Idrottsforum*, 2014, 1–18, available at www.idrottsforum.org.mcdowell140514, accessed 19 April 2016 and McDowell, M.L., '"To Cross the Skager Rack", Discourses, Images, and Tourism in Early "European" Football: Scotland, the United Kingdom, Denmark and Scandinavia', *Soccer & Society*, vol. 18, nos. 2–3, pp. 245–69.
29 *Pall Mall Gazette*, 4 January 1895.
30 See, for example, *Le Matin* (Paris), 15 April 1904, 26 December 1907; *Berliner Tageblatt*, 2 February, 13 April 1906; *Pester Lloyd* (Budapest), 30 March 1904.
31 B.O. Corbett, (ed), *Annals of the Corinthian Football Club* (London: Longmans, Green and Co., 1906), pp. vi–vii.

Introduction

32 Aidan Hamilton, *An Entirely Different Game: The British Influence on Brazilian Football* (Edinburgh: Mainstream, 1998), pp. 20–21; Rob Cavallini, *Play Up Corinth*, p. 33.
33 Goldblatt, *The Ball Is Round*, p. 131; Tony Mason, *Passion of the People? Football in South America* (London: Verso, 1995), pp. 10–11.
34 'How English-schooled Charles Miller set the tone for football in Brazil', www.theguardian.com/football/blog/2014/jul/05, accessed 20 July 2014.
35 Hamilton, *An Entirely Different Game*, pp. 67–78.
36 Mason, *Passion of the People?* p. 22.
37 Corbett, *Annals of the Corinthians*, p. vi.
38 Chamberlain's speech at the Guildhall, London, 20 March 1903, cited in Julian Amery, *The Life of Joseph Chamberlain*, vol. V, *Joseph Chamberlain and the Tariff Reform Campaign* (London: Macmillan, 1969), p. 148.
39 Andrei Markovits and Steven Hellerman, *Offside: Soccer and American Exceptionalism* (Princeton: Princeton University Press, 2001), p. 109.
40 *American Cricketer* (Philadelphia), vol. 28, no. 609, 1905, p. 20.
41 John Benson, 'Athletics, Class and Nation: The Oxford-Cambridge University Tour of Canada and the United States of America, 1901', *Sport in History*, vol. 3, no. 1, 2013, pp. 13–14.
42 *Football*, 4 October 1882, cited in Keith Booth, *The Father of Modern Sport: The Life and Times of Charles W. Alcock* (Manchester: The Parrs Wood Press, 2002), p. 85.
43 Jackson, *Sporting Days*, p. 73.
44 N.L. (Pa) Jackson, *Always Fit and Well* (London: George Newnes Ltd., 1931), p. vii.
45 Jackson, *Sporting Days*, pp. 140–41.
46 Fry, *Life Worth Living*, p. 153; for *Fry's Magazine*, see Wilton, *C.B. Fry*, pp. 193–216.
47 W.E. Greenland, *The History of the Amateur Football Alliance* (Harwich: Amateur Football Alliance/Standard Publishing Company, 1965), p. 49.
48 For literaturisation, see Anthony Bateman, *Cricket, Literature and Culture: Symbolising the Nation, Destabilising Empire* (Farnham: Ashgate, 2009), pp. 3–5.
49 N.L. Jackson, *Association Football* (London: George Newnes Ltd., 1900), p. 332.
50 Smith, 'The Attack', pp. 173, 184.
51 C.B. Fry, 'Character Sketches', in B.O. Corbett (ed), *Annals of the Corinthian Football Club* (London: Longmans, Green and Co., 1906), p. 212.
52 Mike Huggins, *The Victorians and Sport* (London: Hambledon and London, 2004), p. 142.
53 *Morning Post*, 19 November 1889; 9 November 1899.
54 *Morning Post*, 22 October 1894.
55 Eric Parker, *British Sport* (London: William Collins, 1941), p. 38.
56 Ivan Sharpe, *40 Years in Football* (London: Sportsmans Book Club, 1954), p. 101.
57 Geoffrey Green, *Soccer: The World Game: A Popular History* (London: Pan Books, 1956), pp. 72–73, 76.
58 Grayson, *Corinthians & Cricketers*, pp. 150–72.
59 Norman Ackland, 'The Corinthians', in A.H. Fabian and Geoffrey Green (eds), *Association Football* (London: Caxton Publishing Co., 1960), vol. 1, pp. 386–87.
60 Tony Mason, *Association Football and English Society, 1863–1915* (Brighton: Harvester Press, 1980), p. 217.
61 Alfred Gibson and William Pickford, *Association Football & the Men Who Made It* (London: Caxton Publishing Company, 1906), vol. 3, p. 66.
62 James Walvin, *The People's Game: The History of Football Revisited* (Edinburgh: Mainstream, 2nd ed., 1994), p. 92.

63 Mike Huggins, 'Second-Class Citizens? English Middle-Class Culture and Sport, 1850–1910: A Reconsideration', *International Journal of the History of Sport*, vol. 17, no. 1, 2000, p. 1.
64 Dave Russell, *Football and the English: A Social History of Association Football in England, 1863–1995* (Preston: Carnegie Publishing, 1997), p. 27.
65 Lincoln Allison, *Amateurism in Sport: An Analysis and a Defence* (London: Frank Cass, 2001), pp. 18–19; 49; see also Holt, 'Amateurism and Its Interpretation', p. 19.
66 Holt, *Sport and the British*, p. 103.
67 John Lowerson, *Sport and the English Middle Classes 1870–1914* (Manchester: Manchester University Press, 1993), p. 25.
68 Matthew Taylor, *The Association Game: A History of British Football* (Harlow: Pearson Longman, 2008), p. 83.
69 Terry Morris, *In a Class of Their Own: A History of English Amateur Football* (Sheffield: Chequered Flag Publishing, 2015), pp. 164–73.
70 Chris Bolsmann, 'South African Football Tours at the Turn of the Twentieth Century: Amateurs, Pioneers and Profits', *African Historical Review*, vol. 42, no. 1, 2010, p. 106.
71 Creek, *A History of Corinthians*, pp. 105, 118.
72 Marteen van Bottenburg, 'Beyond Diffusion: Sport and Its Remaking in Cross-Cultural Contexts', *Journal of Sport History*, vol. 37, no. 1, 2010, p. 43.
73 Matthew Brown, *From Frontiers to Football: An Alternative History of Latin America since 1800* (London: Reaktion Books, 2014), p. 68.
74 Matthew Taylor, 'Editorial – Sport, Transnationalism, and Global History', *Journal of Global History*, vol. 8, no. 2, 2013, p. 204.
75 Marteen van Bottenburg, 'Why Are the European and American Sports Worlds So Different? Path Dependence in European and American Sports History', in Alan Tomlinson, Christopher Young and Richard Holt (eds), *Sport and the Transformation of Modern Europe: States, Media and Markets 1950–2010* (London: Routledge, 2011), p. 215.
76 Goldblatt, *The Ball Is Round*, p. 114.
77 Green, *Soccer: World Game*, p. 75.
78 Bolsmann, 'South African Football Tours', pp. 95–99; 103–7; Nicholas Piercey and Dilwyn Porter, 'Transnational Connectivity, Cultural Interaction and Selective Adaptation: English Corinthians and Amateur Football in the Netherlands, c.1906–39', *Sport in History*, vol. 37, no. 2, 2017, pp. 124–45.
79 Morris, *In a Class of Their Own*, p. 168.
80 McDowell, 'Queen's Park in Copenhagen', p. 3; see also Piercey and Porter, 'Transnational Connectivity', pp. 140–41.

1 'A scratch team with gentlemanly instincts'

The Corinthians and English soccer in the late nineteenth century

Figure 1.1 Crystal Palace, Sheriff of London Shield, Corinthians v Sheffield United, 19 March 1898.
From *Sports* (Illustrated), pub. Sheffield, 6 April 1898.

In the *Oxford Dictionary of National Biography*, where the lives of the great and the good are recorded, the headline descriptor for Nicholas Lane Jackson is simply 'sports administrator'. As assiduous in promoting himself as the business ventures and sports activities in which he was involved, Jackson would not have been so modest. The autobiographical note with which he prefaced *Always Fit and Well* (1931), a volume offering advice on living to a ripe old age, left readers in no doubt as to his achievements over the course of a busy and successful career. He had 'played nearly every English game with a certain amount of success' and edited numerous magazines as well as handbooks on various sports, thus acquiring 'an all-round knowledge possessed by few'. All this had been achieved without neglecting his many business interests.[1] It helped, of course, that so much of Jackson's business was sports-related, such as the affairs of the Corinthian Football Club, with which he was closely associated from 1882 to 1898, the first sixteen years of its history. What follows is an account of the club's origins and progress set in the context of the *modus vivendi* between amateurism and professionalism that emerged in England after the mid-1880s. The spotlight is then turned on to 'Jackson's Corinthians', as they were sometimes known, and the practicalities of running a successful amateur club from the early 1880s through to the turn of the century.

During his career, Jackson exhibited many of the qualities often attributed to entrepreneurs. He was an outsider, the son of a cheesemonger, who affected the gentility required to do business with the rich and famous; he was an opportunist who made connections between sports and sports-related activities to create new products; he was a publicist who recognized instinctively the value of a distinctive brand. Much of this was evident from the notice published in *Football* in October 1882, announcing the arrival of 'A NEW ASSOCIATION CLUB', open to 'international and well-known players', which would play on Wednesdays. Should anyone doubt the club's credentials, there was 'some probability that it would amalgamate with the old Wanderers' – they had won the English Cup five times in the 1870s – 'and if so a club historical in football annals will be revived'. Jackson, honorary secretary of the London Football Association (LFA), would arrange fixtures, 'some of which will be with strong provincial clubs'.[2] It is possible to discern here the essence of the project that was eventually to unfold. What was being proposed was an elite club for soccer players of social standing and exceptional ability. Playing on Wednesdays indicated that it would be open only to those untroubled by the constraints that kept most young men at work mid-week. Finally, the prospect of matches with clubs from outside London was intriguing, especially when it was announced later that tours would be arranged two or three times a season.[3]

At the time, Jackson was also the assistant secretary of the Football Association (FA), the English game's governing body. Later, when explaining his motives for establishing the club, he was inclined to take a patriotic line. In the early 1880s, aside from the FA Cup Final, the most prestigious fixture as far as the small world of English soccer was concerned was the annual match against Scotland. Jackson believed that Scotland's superior record in this series was due to most of its team being drawn from the Queen's Park club. Having played together regularly there, they were likely to combine more effectively than any England team that the FA could select and, as readers of *Football* – one of the magazines that Jackson was editing in October 1882 – were reminded, 'the success of a football team depends on its combination'.[4] The Corinthian Football Club, its name suggestive of both soccer excellence and social exclusivity, was Jackson's solution to this problem. Potential England players would have the opportunity of playing together regularly on Wednesdays and on tour, thereby enhancing the possibility of beating Scotland. It was this account of the club's origins that Jackson recalled whenever he recounted the circumstances of its foundation.[5] The story has been recycled many times by those who have chronicled the history of the Corinthians over the years and has only recently been subjected to critical scrutiny.

Terry Morris has questioned Jackson's claim that Scotland had a settled side based around players from Queen's Park.[6] However, given the situation as Jackson may have seen it in 1882, his often-repeated explanation for starting the club remains plausible. For those who followed English soccer at the time, there was genuine cause for concern. 'In the ten matches now played', observed *The Times* in 1881, 'the Scotch have kicked 34 goals and the English 20', winning six matches to England's two. A further 5-1 defeat for England followed in March 1882.[7] Jackson recalled that it was this particular disaster that prompted him to invite 'a few of the more prominent Association footballers in the South of England to meet in his office', though it seems likely that the meeting at which the Corinthian Football Club was founded actually took place just after the start of the following season in October.[8] England's inferiority in terms of combination was taken up subsequently by *Football* when criticizing the team selected to play against Scotland in 1883 and referred to again when England was defeated a few weeks later: 'Another contest past! Another fought and won! And won by the side that has so often proved victorious on former occasions. Why is it?'[9] England was on a bad run, losing again in 1883 and 1884.

Morris, however, rejects Jackson's 'patriotic' explanation for the establishment of the Corinthian club, implying that its main purpose from the start was to confront the growth of professionalism in English soccer, 'a far greater threat to all that Jackson and his associates stood for'.[10] Professionalism in Lancashire was certainly a concern in October 1882 when *Football* referred darkly to 'insidious whispers' that would soon demand the attention of the London-based FA. Some wild rumours were circulating: 'All expenses paid. All *wages* paid ... Hearty suppers every evening when "the team" is in training, Disgraceful orgies. Public houses and beer-shops purchased'.[11] Given these circumstances, it seems odd that Jackson, having taken the initiative, should then have allowed the club to drift for two seasons. If anxieties regarding either England's form or professionalism were pressing, they were insufficient to prompt decisive action in this respect. The 1882–83 campaign was problematic, and on occasions, it was a struggle for Archer Secretan, on whom secretarial duties had been devolved, to raise a team. Jackson himself – hardly an England prospect – turned out in the club's third fixture when the Corinthians lost 3-1 at Brighton College.[12] A comprehensive 6-0 defeat at Cambridge University was followed by a match with the Royal Engineers at Chatham for which the Corinthians arrived with only six players. Somehow, with the assistance of 'a trio of musicians' and two 'subs' supplied by their hosts, they achieved an unlikely victory, but this was most definitely not the stellar combination that had originally been envisaged.[13] After this embarrassment, the Corinthians rallied sufficiently to make their first tour at Easter 1883, travelling to Lancashire to play Accrington, Church and Bootle before returning via Stoke where they lost 5-4, 'having played one short throughout'.[14]

At this point and for more than a year thereafter, the prospect of the Corinthians making a significant mark on English football was highly unlikely. Only three matches were played in the season that followed, the departure of Secretan, 'called abroad' in October 1883, leaving both the accounts and the membership list in disarray.[15] By autumn of 1884, however, when Jackson began to devote more of his time and energy to the Corinthians, it was clear that the FA could no longer ignore 'the subtle and subversive growth of professionalism'.[16] Blackburn Olympic had won the FA Cup in 1883, beating Old Etonians in the final. Their victory – the first time the trophy had been won by a team from the North – assumed huge symbolic significance, not least because it could be represented as a triumph for the plebs over the patricians.[17] Extra time was required, but only 120 minutes had been enough to turn the world upside down, albeit temporarily. This match proved to be a significant watershed in English football history, but at the time, it simply increased antipathy between the 'gentlemen' from the South and the 'players' from the North. One of the Old Etonians recalled that he and his colleagues had been exhausted after ninety minutes, 'while the Blackburn men were in strict training and they just managed to get a winning goal'.[18] Critics, including *Football*, pointed out that the Cup-winners had trained at the seaside for a week before the final at their club's expense, signifying 'that the amateur clause of the competition rules is set at naught'. Concern was expressed that other clubs, including Olympic's ambitious neighbours Blackburn Rovers, would follow this example, gaining an advantage so significant that it would 'entirely spoil the Cup competition'.[19]

By mid-November 1884, when the Corinthians once again took to the field, the controversy surrounding professionalism was at its height. The focus was very much on Lancashire, especially the cotton-manufacturing towns of Accrington, Bolton, Blackburn, Burnley, Darwen and Preston, where 'because of an intense network of local rivalries, clubs began paying or offering other inducements to good players in order to better their rivals'.[20] Up-and-coming Preston North End were a particular cause for concern. 'The Prestonian players posed as amateurs', one newspaperman recalled, 'but everyone knew they were not'.[21] Their manager, William Sudell, after a complaint by Upton Park following an FA Cup-tie in January, had openly admitted finding employment in order to attract professionals from Scotland, justifying the club's policy as normal custom and practice for Lancashire. Blackburn Rovers, also suspected of bending the rules, had won the FA Cup a few months earlier. Jackson at first aligned himself with those who opposed 'veiled professionalism', backing the rigorous imposition of the FA's Rule 16, passed in 1882 to discourage excessive payments to cover expenses or to compensate for 'broken time' at work. In October 1884, this went a stage further with the introduction of three new rules designed to curb importation by prohibiting FA Cup entry to clubs that could not prove the legitimacy of players signed after 1 September 1882 or had arranged matches with opponents who had failed to meet this requirement. Their fixture lists and future gate money in jeopardy, many Lancashire clubs signalled their willingness to break away from FA jurisdiction, over thirty of them attending a meeting of the newly formed British Football Association at Manchester on 30 October.[22] As yet, there was nothing to suggest that the Corinthians were seen as part of the solution to the problem of professionalism by Jackson or anyone else. Their first two matches in 1884–85 against Notts (lost 1-7) and Cambridge University (lost 0-5) supplied no indication of the role that they would play over the next few months.

The particular circumstances pertaining in late October and early November were critical. Alcock, the FA's secretary, recalling these events a few years later, was in no doubt that the crisis had been serious. Professionalism 'boded real danger to, if not the actual destruction of the Association'.[23] Confronted with the threat of secession, as Dave Russell observes, the FA 'beat a remarkably swift retreat'. This was signalled on 3 November when Jackson supported a sub-committee resolution recognizing that 'it was now expedient to legalise professionalism under stringent conditions'. For the next six months or so, whatever his reservations, he aligned himself with Alcock who had long favoured a compromise by which the Association would effectively licence professionalism, leaving the gentlemen still in control of the game, an outcome finally achieved in July 1885.[24] The tours undertaken by the Corinthians in December 1884 and April 1885 have to be seen in this context. Jackson, who had taken over as secretary on Secretan's departure, now breathed new life into the club, not primarily to confront the professionals but to build bridges while helping to assemble the two-thirds majority required to bring the necessary rule change into effect. There was some antipathy between North and South, between the provinces and the metropolis; some class feeling. One Lancashire newspaper complained towards the end of November that the people's game was being manipulated by 'a few mashers who wish to have the English Cup back in London'.[25] There was all the more reason, therefore, for a charm offensive, especially as class relations had not actually broken down. The aim was to demonstrate that amateurs and professionals, just like gentlemen and players in cricket, could achieve peaceful co-existence.

It seems likely that the December tour was hastily improvised. The *Athletic News* was inclined to be disparaging, describing the Corinthians as 'a scratch team with gentlemanly instincts'.[26] The tour was announced by the *Sportsman* only on the day of departure, and the published list of fixtures included two in Scotland, against Queen's Park and St Bernard's, which were never played.[27] Jackson assembled a party of sixteen, comprising five internationals and eleven 'cracks', all university or public-school old boys. The inclusion of Dr John Smith, a Scottish international, suggests that the England team was no longer a priority. They were to take on five of the strongest clubs in Lancashire, along with Sheffield and Notts, playing seven games in eight days. The results were rather mixed. A spectacular and, as we shall see, historic victory over Blackburn Rovers was followed by a defeat at Darwen; a draw at Blackburn Olympic; a win at Sheffield; and defeats at Bolton, Preston and Nottingham. In terms of what it was meant to achieve, however, the tour was a success. As the soccer correspondent of the *Sunday Times* concluded in January 1885, 'The question of professionalism has, of course, proved a great bugbear, but after the recent happy experience of the Corinthians in the North, I anticipate that its legalisation will be secured on the 19th inst'.[28] It took a little longer than he anticipated to achieve the desired outcome – professionalism was not sanctioned until July – but pragmatism had triumphed and the FA had been saved.

Building the Corinthian brand

The first match of the 1884 tour against FA Cup-holders Blackburn Rovers proved to be the most momentous played by the Corinthian club in its entire history. The result was an enormous surprise. 'Certainly the visitors were a fine lot of fellows', observed one of Blackburn's historians, 'but 8-1 against the acknowledged champions of the world was unexplainable'.[29] For whatever reason, the Rovers were outplayed by the visitors who thus made an immediate impact. 'It may be said with safety', purred the *Athletic News*, 'that such magnificent football as that shown by Mr N. L. Jackson's Corinthian team at Blackburn on Monday was never seen in Lancashire'. It had been 'simply marvellous all round – the dribbling, passing, tackling, and kicking of all the various players being as near perfect as possible'.[30] Jackson, who travelled with the team and wrote a detailed account of the tour for *Pastime*, noted that 'the forwards were a fine lot, the speed and passing exhibited by them evoking tremendous cheers from the spectators'. The Corinthians had won on merit and with style and, though unable to repeat this spectacular success in their other fixtures, made friends and influenced people wherever they went, playing 'in the best of spirits' and 'setting a really good example to all'. Significantly, 'good fellowship prevailed throughout'. It seemed that the North was not such a bad place after all and the professionals had been most hospitable, not least at Preston where Sudell, 'that most genial of sportsmen and a right good fellow', had provided 'a sumptuous repast' after the match. Sudell was praised for his honesty in admitting that his players were paid, Jackson concluding that 'if all professionals would play as well and as fairly as the North Enders did on Saturday, their advent should be hailed with pleasure'.[31] The tour allowed the Corinthians to make their mark; the club, as Jackson later claimed justifiably, 'jumped in to prominent position at one bound'.[32] It also facilitated *rapprochement* by providing opportunities for contending factions within the FA to demonstrate goodwill.

A template had been established for subsequent tours to districts where professional football flourished. These continued throughout Jackson's tenure as honorary secretary and for some years afterwards. Blackburn Rovers quickly gave way to Preston North End as the showpiece match on the northern tour, attracting the most interest and the largest attendances.

Extensive coverage in *Pastime* continued throughout the 1880s, effectively promoting the idea that the Corinthians were 'the *crème de la crème* of Association footballers'. It was no surprise that a fixture with Preston should have attracted such a large crowd as it represented the meeting of 'the best amateur and professional clubs in the kingdom'.[33] From 1886, matches in Scotland were added to the schedule with those against fellow amateurs Queen's Park – 'the best that can be played' – described in *Pastime*'s most purple prose. 'The relations of the two clubs are most friendly', it was reported, 'the play is gentlemanly, and the skill and science of the highest order'. No wonder then that the meeting of England's and Scotland's finest should generate 'a large amount of excitement among the football loving populace of Glasgow', an estimated 15,000 of whom flocked to Hampden Park to see the game at New Year 1887.[34] It was as if football traditions were being invented and reinforced every time the Corinthians went on tour, serving a useful purpose for the upper middle-class community that looked to the men in white shirts to demonstrate their superiority. At the same time, the Corinthians underpinned social cohesion, not least because soccer provided 'a common ground for conversation between virtually any two male workers in England and Scotland'.[35] For a while this strategy could operate at both levels. 'Not only did everyone love a lord', as Tony Mason has observed perceptively, 'but they loved an amateur too, especially when he was a gentleman who was quite capable of giving the professionals a good run for their money'.[36] The popularity of the tours was thus assured.

Congeniality remained a dominant theme despite occasional lapses. Even before they began touring in earnest, there were links between the Corinthians and their rivals in the North. The club's first committee had included W.F. Beardshaw (Sheffield), H.A. Cursham (Notts) and D.H. Greenwood (Blackburn Rovers) along with players from southern clubs.[37] Jackson and Sudell found that they had much in common and were happy to co-operate, even when, as in December 1886, there was much comment in the Lancashire press 'about the rough play of the Corinthians at Preston'.[38] Far from confronting North End, however, the Corinthians were happy to help them out. Mills-Roberts, a Welsh international goalkeeper, having played for the Corinthians against Preston, appeared for Preston in the FA Cup Finals of 1888 and 1889; at least five others signed for Sudell's 'Invincibles' in December 1889, though only Fred Dewhurst went on to make League appearances.[39] Cordiality also marked the relationship with Scottish clubs once the Corinthians began to visit regularly. This was hardly surprising given that the principal objective, when north of the border, was to support Queen's Park, 'kindred spirits' recruiting from a similar pool of upper middle-class talent and steadfastly attached to amateur principles even after the Scottish Football Association (SFA) had sanctioned professionalism in 1893.[40] Personal connections also helped shape the Corinthian touring experience. Matches at Kirkcaldy in the early 1890s sustained a link with Dr John Smith, who had 'a deep interest in the welfare of the Kirkcaldy club'.[41]

By this time, the pattern of the Corinthians' season was well established. It centred largely on two tours, one over the Christmas/New Year period, with around eight matches scheduled in the North and Scotland, the other at Easter, when three or four games were played. The team travelled in a style befitting middle-class gentlemen, assembling in London before heading north by rail, sometimes in the comfort of a private saloon, and then staying at hotels with which they became familiar over the years. In Manchester, for example, the Corinthians put up at the Grand, 'so comfortable that we can recommend it to any club touring in that district'; in Edinburgh, they favoured 'our old resting place, the Waterloo Hotel, where they were greeted by Fritz, that most obliging and most genial of head waiters'.[42] Like many middle-class men of the late Victorian era, they seized the opportunity to enjoy each other's company away from the domestic sphere. 'Naturally enough', Jackson recalled, 'there was a good deal of horseplay and practical joking', but there were also club rules, one of which 'prohibited anyone from being absent from our party at dinner or afterwards without permission'.[43] It was, of course, an expensive business to keep the team on the road for as long as ten days – no less than twenty-six players were listed for the Christmas/New Year tour in 1890–91 – even if they did pay for their own drinks. Above all, it was important to make a good impression, leaving the Corinthian brand intact and unsullied, even when defeated. It would have been gratifying to read, after an away game at Preston, that it had been in every way worthy of the reputation of the two teams, 'undoubtedly the best amateur and professional clubs in the country'. Both had 'played the passing game to perfection'.[44] Gentleman amateurs could look the best of professionals in the face.

Winning was important, even though it was not always possible. 'Despite the club's amateur ethos', as Neil Carter has argued, 'it could not hide the competitive sentiment behind its creation'.[45] When on tour, the available playing strength was managed with a view to fielding the strongest team in the most prestigious matches. This sometimes caused difficulties, as in December 1887 when calls on players to represent their regular London clubs in FA Cup-ties prompted Jackson to reschedule a fixture at Preston because he could not raise a team of sufficient quality. When the match was played a few days later, the Corinthians 'included no fewer than eight internationals, while North End had their best eleven'.[46] Unfortunately for Jackson, the Corinthians were beaten, but there was credit to be gained simply by taking part. 'A capital game being worthily won and honourably lost' was the *Sportsman*'s verdict on a defeat at Queen's Park.[47] It was critical, however, to offer something distinctive in the way of entertainment that would remind spectators of their place in the immutable social order. The Corinthian club, observed the *Pall Mall Gazette*, helping to define the Corinthian brand, was composed of 'gentlemen' whose game was 'much faster and altogether different to that played by the Northerners'.[48] It was also important to look the part.

Writing of R.C. Gosling, his team-mate of the early 1890s, C.B. Fry recalled that he 'played in perfectly valeted brown boots which must have cost him a fiver'. Not surprisingly, those who played with Gosling 'were suspected of being Guards officers and young squires'.[49] Form was temporary, but class, in every sense, was permanent. It was an important part of what the Corinthians had to offer.

Money, money, money

Keeping the Corinthians in the manner to which they were accustomed meant maximizing the income to be derived from their share of the gate money, a significant proportion of which came in the form of guarantees negotiated with host clubs. By the end of the 1880s, some serious questions were being raised, especially in the Lancashire sporting press where the Bolton-based *Football Field* supplied *Tit-Bits*-style 'Nuggets' for its patrons to chew over. 'People want to know why it costs more to run the "amateur" Corinthians than the best professional clubs', it observed mischievously in 1887, thereby alerting readers, not for the first time, to an issue that was later to cause Jackson some difficulty.[50] There is no doubt, however, that the touring Corinthians were an attraction. 'Fancy the Corinthians meeting Everton', noted the Manchester-based *Umpire* newspaper in November 1886. 'What a gate there will be!'[51]

Estimates appearing in the press should not be relied on too heavily, but if 11,000 spectators did turn up to see them at Preston in April 1888, it compared favourably with the average of 6,275 that watched North End win the Football League a year later.[52] Everton's committee was happy to guarantee £30 for a match to be played on the northern tour in January 1888; two years later a deal was struck on the basis of £40 guaranteed or half the net gate for a fixture to be played at Easter 1891. Everton were by then the best supported club in the Football League with estimated home crowds averaging over 11,275. If the *Sportsman* was correct, their committee would not have been disappointed with an attendance of more than 10,000, especially as the kick-off was considerably delayed by the late arrival of Tinsley Lindley, the famous Corinthians and England forward.[53] Ten years later they remained a significant attraction. 'Fix with Corinthians home April 16th and return if possible', ran the relevant board minute, 'failing them Rangers'.[54] Jackson's team, it seems, were just ahead of the Scottish Cup-holders when an attractive friendly was required to fill a gap in the fixtures. Indeed, at times, he appeared to enjoy and exploit a very strong bargaining position. Queen's Park believed that they had agreed to each club keeping the entire proceeds from its home games. Jackson, 'too good a financier to give way', knowing that attendances in Glasgow tended to be higher than those in London, held out for half the net gate plus a £50 guarantee. Even though this was later amended, the new arrangements still represented 'a good bargain for the amateur Corinthians'.[55]

Some years ago, Stephen Hardy pointed out that sports organizations, as they developed, were inevitably drawn into the marketplace through 'the staging of events, the minimization of costs, the garnering of publicity; in short the concerns of a business'. Erik Nielsen has recently revisited this idea, arguing that these concerns were important in the late nineteenth- and early twentieth-century sporting world, even for institutions 'that purported to be antagonistic to the profit motive'.[56] For the Corinthians, the sports business involved a good deal of complicated juggling. On the one hand, it was a soccer club established on true-blue amateur lines and determined to keep its own reputation, in the words of a rival, 'as pure and clean as the driven snow'.[57] On the other, it needed sufficient funds to finance its activities, maintain its social standing and sustain its performances at an elite level. In practical terms, this sometimes involved making arrangements in order to maximize revenue and brand exposure simultaneously, not always with entirely satisfactory results. The challenge of playing matches on consecutive days sometimes proved too much. 'Oh, ye much vaunted Corinthians', crowed the *Football Field* at Christmas 1887. 'Beaten, Beaten. Beaten. Preston. Burnley. Leek'.[58] Sometimes two teams were sent out on the same day. This had especially disastrous consequences on New Year's Eve 1892, when one team of Corinthians lost narrowly at Bolton, while another was humiliated 8-1 at Newcastle, hardly the most glorious day in the club's history.

If Preston North End, Burnley and Leek, not to mention Newcastle, exposed the Corinthians' inconsistency against northern professionals, then A.N. ('Monkey') Hornby achieved the same result in respect of the club's financial affairs. Principally renowned as a cricketer – he played for Lancashire and England – Hornby had also captained his county at rugby. Educated at Harrow, his family owned cotton mills in Blackburn, and he was very well connected. In September 1893, at a meeting of the Lancashire Rugby Union, he made some characteristically blunt remarks about 'broken-time' payments, at that time a highly contentious issue in English rugby. The *Umpire* newspaper reported that he had expressed his 'great dislike for a system which admits of well-to-do players getting as much of the money as the working man without sharing the odium, and he wants to stamp this out'.[59] The Corinthians objected to Hornby's suggestion that, when on tour, they 'received big gates, which covered more than their expenses, and nobody ever heard of the rest', along with the implication that its gentlemen amateurs were no better than working-class rugby players paid 'boot money' by their clubs. When Hornby failed to respond, Jackson went to extraordinary lengths to prove that his players received only the expenses allowed to amateurs under FA and club rules. A four-man 'Committee of Investigation' was set up at the Sports Club, an upmarket establishment in London's West End, which Jackson had founded a few months earlier, comprising an ex-president of the FA, an ex-president of the Rugby Football Union, a Marylebone Cricket Club committee member and a chartered accountant. It duly expressed itself satisfied that the books were in order and that no irregular or excessive payments had been made. Hornby was unmoved, convinced that touring generated a surplus that the committee had failed to investigate.[60]

This 'blazing war of words', as Cavallini describes it, rumbled on inconclusively for a few months. Like the poor, observed a weary sports columnist, it was 'always with us'.[61] The *Umpire*, taking Hornby's side, believed that Jackson's Sports Club committee was simply 'an attempt to throw dust in the eyes of the public'. It sensed that double standards were being applied. Noting the reluctance of 'this swell team of hippodroming footballers' to publish its balance sheets it contended that 'between the working man and the amateur who receives travelling and out-of-pocket expenses, there really is no difference'.[62] Finally, Jackson turned to the weekly *Truth*, publishing some relevant financial details and arguing that the club's share of the gate at Queen's Park, which Hornby had used to illustrate his point, was untypical. Where profits were made, it was claimed, they simply subsidized losses incurred elsewhere. The *Sportsman* then reprinted the *Truth* article claiming that it was 'evidently from someone in the know' and 'took away much of the ground' on which Hornby had made his stand.[63] Yet, though Jackson and his maligned band of brothers may have hoped that this would bring controversy to an end, rumours continued to circulate. A year later, with the rift in English rugby which had prompted Hornby to speak out still an open wound, an article in the *Pall Mall Gazette*, suggested that the case against Jackson and his team was still open. It was fashionable it claimed, 'even among the best of our amateur clubs, to go touring round the country, relying on halved gate money to pay the expenses' while enjoying 'luxurious living at first-class hotels for services rendered on the field'. This prompted a rapid response – it might be described as Jacksonian – suggesting that this criticism was unjustified. The Corinthians travelled third class, wines and spirits were not paid for by the club and the hotel fare was 'always of the simplest, being usually of the ordinary *table d'hôte* type'.[64] The Midland Railway Company, which had placed a 'cosy saloon' at the party's disposal would have been disappointed. So, too, would have been the genial Fritz at the Waterloo Hotel, not forgetting Mrs Brown at the Three Tuns, Durham, who treated her customers 'as private guests', provided dinners 'liberal enough for the old coaching days' and greeted new arrivals with 'a glass of cherry brandy'.[65]

By focusing on touring, however, the club's critics were missing the point for Jackson's Corinthians had developed other ways of generating revenue. Fry, writing in 1906, claimed that they were not at all like professional soccer clubs in that they had no business history. Unlike, for example, Chelsea Football Club, owned by the Mears family, who had bought and developed the Stamford Bridge grounds before acquiring what was in effect London's first Football League franchise, 'Corinth' had no proprietors, had 'never possessed a ground of its own' and 'never had to consider finance'.[66] This was somewhat disingenuous. The Corinthians may not have had a permanent home base until 1922, when they moved to Crystal Palace as co-tenants with the Casuals, but they played fairly regularly at Kennington Oval, at the County Ground, Leyton, and at Queen's Club, West Kensington. Attendances at Cup Finals and international matches suggests that there was an audience for elite soccer in the metropolis in the late nineteenth century and that it was growing. The FA Cup had proved very important in this respect, ensuring that 'crack' teams from the North, the Midlands and Scotland were known in the South. By the mid-1880s, even readers of *The Times* were expected to take an interest in *the* Cup Final. When Blackburn Rovers met Queen's Park in 1885, 'an immense number of spectators, numbering about 15,000, visited Kennington Oval to watch the contest'. The match was reported at some length, the results of all the season's Cup-ties were provided and space was found for a brief notice of an important match played between Bolton Wanderers and Renton, 'holders of the Scotch Association Challenge Cup'. By the end of the decade, the final of the premier national competition could attract 27,000, not all of them visitors in town for a big day out, to see Preston play Wolverhampton Wanderers in 'one of the finest games ever witnessed'.[67] Soccer in the South had yet to develop the characteristics of the professional game that flourished in the North, but there were opportunities to promote prestigious matches if a team of local heroes could be found and, through connections made on their tours, the Corinthians were particularly well placed to arrange return fixtures with elite opponents likely to generate public interest and a good gate.

The first requirement was to find suitable venues. This was achieved mainly by utilizing the spare capacity available at cricket grounds during the winter months. The Oval, where they first played in 1885, had obvious potential in this respect, not least that the indefatigable Alcock, in addition to being honorary secretary at the FA, was similarly engaged at the Surrey County Cricket Club and was aware that soccer generated a significant proportion of its income.[68] In 1884–85, Surrey's total receipts for the year were £15,667, of which £1,011 were derived from football. The corresponding figures for 1891–92 were £20,979 and £3,158.[69] Moreover, when the Corinthians played at the Oval, they tended to generate more revenue than other London clubs that used the venue. An FA Cup-tie in December 1892 featuring two of the capital's better sides, Casuals and Polytechnic, generated receipts of £41, whereas at the Corinthians versus West Bromwich Albion match two months later £222 was taken at the gate.[70] Factors such as the weather, the days on which matches were played and other matches being played in London at the same time make comparison difficult, but the overall trend was upward. 'On an average', Creek noted of the 1880s, 'some 2,000 people would watch an ordinary Corinthian game at the Oval; 5,000 was a good crowd, and on occasions this might be considerably increased'.[71] It was important, therefore, to provide as many 'occasions' as possible.

Jackson's dealings with the Surrey club were indicative of a businessman who was confident of his position. In March 1889, its committee agreed to his request that the Corinthians 'should be allowed three-quarters of all money taken for ground and enclosures in their matches'. But there were limits. The agreement, slightly modified, was extended in 1894, though the hosts were clearly unimpressed by Jackson's suggestion that they should pay all matchday expenses, this being the arrangement that he had negotiated elsewhere. Surrey played a straight bat, convinced 'that the expenses ought to be paid by the Corinthians'.[72] Evidence relating to the arrangement with Queen's Club is unavailable but is clear that Jackson was in a strong position in relation to the impoverished Essex County Cricket Club for whom additional revenue was especially important. So anxious were the Essex committee to do business that they had thanked both clubs profusely and offered Sudell honorary life membership after hosting the Corinthians-Preston match in 1889. A net profit of around £200 from soccer was anticipated when preparing accounts for an emergency meeting later in the year, and this was clearly very welcome given a projected net loss of £230 on county cricket.[73] The arrangements at Leyton were certainly more advantageous to the Corinthians than those at the Oval, principally because Essex paid 'all ground expenses', as correspondence copied into the minutes confirms. When a dispute arose relating to the number of complimentary tickets available to the Corinthians, Jackson was prepared to flex his muscles, threatening to take his business elsewhere. 'Unless I receive tickets by two o'clock or hear from you that they shall be sent', he informed the Essex secretary by telegram, 'I shall on my own responsibility arrange to play Army at Queen's Club'.[74] Suffice to say that the match took place a few days later at Leyton as scheduled.

Being able to stage matches in London became increasingly important to the Corinthians. In the mid-1880s, they were primarily a touring team convening twice a year to fly the flag for gentlemanly amateurism in the North and Midlands. By the mid-1890s, their fixture list was longer and might include as many as twelve matches 'at home', that is at the Oval, Leyton or the Queen's Club. In January 1889, the Corinthians fielded two teams in London on the same day, at the Oval against Nottingham Forest and at Leyton against Preston North End, more than 10,000 spectators turning up to see the League champions, 'an enormous number for a place like Leyton'.[75] At the turn of the century, in season 1900–01, when twenty matches were played, ten were effectively home fixtures, staged either at the Queen's Club or, occasionally, at the Crystal Palace. That admission prices were higher in London than elsewhere, a shilling rather than sixpence, may have influenced this changing pattern of fixtures.[76] Sometimes difficulties arose. Surrey were not prepared to put the playing surface at the Oval at risk unless they could be guaranteed a good return, refusing a request from the Corinthians who were hoping to play Middlesbrough there just before the start of the cricket season in 1893. Essex wanted a slight improvement on their usual terms to stage the match at Leyton, and the match was eventually played at Richmond, an occasional venue for the Corinthians in London. The Oval became unavailable in 1895 just as access to Leyton became more difficult, Essex having come to an arrangement with the Casuals and Old Carthusians giving them priority in the football season.[77] Thereafter, most London matches were played at Queen's Club.

The 1890s: a change of emphasis

By the 1890s, the Corinthian Football Club was able to sustain itself by fulfilling three functions. First, it was a touring side, as it had been from the start; second, it established a brand, becoming synonymous with gentlemanly amateurism at its very best; and third – this has previously been neglected in accounts of the club's activities – it staged high-profile matches in London against professional opposition from the North, the Midlands and Scotland at a time when football in the South of England remained almost exclusively amateur. These were important contributions to the development of English soccer, not least because the balance of power appears to shift so decisively between the early 1880s and the early 1890s from London and the South-East, the first heartland of the association game, to the towns and cities of industrial England. Historians to date have been somewhat bedazzled by this transformation, focusing their attention on Lancashire, where the future seemed to lie, rather than on London, where the game seemed to fall behind, though it was actually progressing quite rapidly in terms of increasing participation and enthusiastic support.[78] Close examination of the history of the Corinthian club helps to redress this historiographic imbalance. At the very least, as Gibson and Pickford observed in their influential survey published in 1906, Jackson's team of toffs sustained soccer in the South during 'those dull and dead seasons', which followed the decline of the first wave of clubs such as the Wanderers, but which preceded the establishment of professionalism in and around the capital at the turn of the century. 'Cockneys', they noted perceptively, 'were proud of the men who could thrash League teams before their eyes, and they would patronise a Corinthian match where they would not cast a glance at another'.[79] At the same time, the game was changing, and this had an impact on the way in which the club conducted its affairs.

This is evident, first, in the changing pattern of Corinthian tours from 1893 onwards. In the 1880s, their Easter tours, though shorter than the nine- or ten-match roadshows at Christmas and the New Year, involved hard games against testing opposition. However, the establishment of the Football League in 1888 and its expansion during the 1890s from one division of twelve clubs to two divisions of eighteen was a striking development, reducing the number of free dates on which teams would be free to play the Corinthians, either at home or away. Moreover, by the end of the 1890s, professional clubs tended to prioritize cup-ties and league matches where points were at stake. From about 1893, the quality of opposition encountered on tour, especially at Easter, was often diluted. This was apparent in the fixtures that were arranged, with an away match at a League club now followed by easy matches against relatively poor sides. Thus, a match against the professionals at Derby County in 1893, 'splendidly contested' but with the home team not at full strength, was followed by an easy win against Hampshire at Southampton. 'Early on', the *Sportsman* reported, 'it was apparent that the county stood no chance against their formidable opponents'. Moving on to Bournemouth, they trounced a local representative eleven 10-0.[80] Though Christmas-New Year tours remained quite challenging, over the following seasons, through to 1900, five Easter tours were arranged in the South and West where, as Creek admitted, 'the opposition was generally less formidable than the teams met on the tours in the North, and the social element was more pronounced'.[81] There was some rather pointed press criticism. Touring the southern counties was, no doubt, 'very pleasant and a cheap way of getting a holiday but scarcely what one likes to see in amateur football'.[82] There were, perhaps, lessons to be learned about the attractiveness of such fixtures when the Bucks and Berks FA turned down an offer from the Corinthians to play them in 1895 for a £20 guarantee, claiming that it was too great a financial risk.[83] It was a while before the implications became fully apparent, but a significant corner had been turned.

Second, it is important to consider the Corinthian brand. Jackson's Corinthians occupied a particular niche in the market for sporting entertainment. This meant that their status as gentlemen amateurs had to be constantly re-affirmed, the matches played twice annually against Queen's Park continuing to serve this function. By the 1890s, these had taken on the characteristics of invented tradition. They had become, according to the *Morning Post* in 1895, 'an institution in the football world'.[84] There were occasional lapses – even gentlemen could get over-excited – but generally the fixture supplied a pretext for some very favourable copy in the posher London prints. According to the *Pall Mall Gazette*, for example, the 1891 match at the Oval 'afforded an exhibition of scientific and gentlemanly football such as is now rarely seen'; it was, the *Sunday Times* observed a few years later, 'a fixture calculated to serve the best interests of the game'. Even when it did get a little overheated, such incidents were merely 'a subject for good humoured chaff at the dinner which usually follows in the evening'. In the closed world of gentlemanly sport, these encounters were quasi-internationals; 'they practically decide the supremacy of amateur football in England and Scotland', it was noted in 1898.[85] Moreover, the continuing presence of Corinthians in the national team helped to sustain the link between gentlemanly amateurism and elite performance, even though it was increasingly dependent on the influence Jackson could exert at the FA. When Fry indicated his unavailability for a Corinthians' fixture, Jackson advised him to play, adding that he would almost certainly be picked to play for England if he turned out. 'Pa was on the Selection Committee', Fry explained, 'so he was not telegraphing through his hat'.[86]

That all eleven players who represented England against Wales in 1894 and 1895 were Corinthians offered reassurance to those becoming increasingly anxious about maintaining the pre-existing social order in sport at a time when rugby was contemplating its 'Great Split'.

Third, the role of the Corinthians in promoting football at London venues, particularly in the 1890s, has to be considered. 'A football game', as it has been observed in another context, 'may be an ephemeral, inconsistent, and intangible experience ... but it is still a product to be bought and sold'.[87] For a few years, there was a window of opportunity, in the absence of professional soccer in the South, to promote events that would bring the best teams from the North, the Midlands and Scotland to play challenge matches against Jackson's men in London. Symbolic rivalries – England versus Scotland, the capital versus the provinces, amateurs versus professionals, especially when underpinned by class differences – meant that these events provided an opportunity to create and capture a market. A fixture card issued by the Queen's Club in 1896–97 made a point of informing potential customers that the visiting teams included Sheffield Wednesday, 'Holders of the English Cup', and offered admission at a discount if tickets for five home games were purchased. The press played its part, and readers were left in no doubt as to what was at stake. Previews were especially important in this respect, simultaneously framing the expectations of London readers while enhancing their knowledge of the game. When the Corinthians entertained Scotland's Third Lanark in 1889, both clubs had already defeated Preston North End, the reigning Football League champions; readers of the *Pall Mall Gazette* were advised that 'the result of this match may be considered as deciding ... the best club in the United Kingdom at the present time'.[88] The *Morning Post* observed in 1894 that Londoners were indebted to the Corinthians 'who of late have provided them with a pretty regular diet of first-class Association football', before going on to preview a match with Bolton Wanderers at Leyton. 'The public', it noted, 'may rest assured of a good game at a ground which the special facilities afforded by the Railway Company have done much to make popular'.[89] Sometimes, the previews read like routine puffery: 'By far the most attractive match under Association rules in London this afternoon is that between the Corinthians and Notts County at Queen's Club'.[90] Jackson's concern for publicity is evident from his earlier correspondence with the Essex County Cricket Club.[91] It seems likely that he would have approved.

Jackson withdrew from soccer in 1898 to concentrate on his other sporting enterprises. By then his influence at the FA and the LFA was waning, and this became evident when the practice of assembling so-called 'scratch teams' came under scrutiny. 'All the desire to make money out of football was not on the side of the professionals', recalled William Pickford, a member of the FA's Council, rather pointedly. Jackson had often sent out teams playing as 'Mr. N.L. Jackson's XI' for one-off games at public schools and the universities in aid of various charities. The players, he protested, had met their own expenses. Possibly Pickford was more concerned about 'Crystal Palace', a scratch team including several Corinthians, which had played against Aston Villa in December 1895 and Sheffield Wednesday in March 1897.[92] Perhaps recalling the Hornby affair, Jackson resented the implication of impropriety and took no interest in soccer thereafter.[93] Significantly, his final intervention on behalf of the Corinthians was to create a new way of maintaining their profile now that the kind of tours that had been undertaken since the 1880s were becoming less viable. That it also provided Jackson and his club with a way of confounding any critics who remained suspicious was an additional advantage. The Hornby episode had inflicted some reputational damage. The attacks may or may not have been justified, it had been observed at the time, 'but the public feels that those who are the object of criticism deserve it in some way or another'.[94]

Noblesse oblige was entirely compatible with the Corinthian brand; they had sometimes played charity matches and had staged an inter-club athletics festival with the Barbarians, their rugby-playing counterparts, to raise money for good causes in 1892.[95] The club had hitherto made a virtue of its reluctance to go 'pot-hunting' and had previously spurned competitive matches, but broke with this tradition in 1898 when they made an exception for the Sheriff of London's Charity Shield [hereafter the Charity Shield] to be contested annually between the best amateur and professional clubs. Staged, at least for the first few seasons, at the Crystal Palace, where FA Cup Finals were played, the match could be promoted unambiguously as one of the events of the season and soon began to exhibit the characteristics of an invented tradition. The Corinthians, it was noted before the first Shield 'final' in 1898, were 'undoubtedly the strongest amateur team in existence'; their opponents, Sheffield United, were 'the best professional club of the year', eventually going on to win the Football League championship.[96] Jackson was largely responsible for this initiative. He had 'happened to suggest' the idea to Lord Dewar, who was looking for a way to mark his year as Sheriff and went on to serve as the competition's first honorary secretary, responsible for distributing the money raised.[97] In so doing, he breathed new life into the Corinthian project just as it was beginning to flag.

By this time, touring at home had ceased to be of prime importance for the Corinthians. The sense of mission that had accompanied the club on its travels in the 1880s had largely disappeared. Tours were now undertaken, it was observed at the start of the 1896–97 season, 'as they invariably prove very enjoyable, and are highly popular with the members'.[98] That appeared to be sufficient. After 1898, the Charity Shield supplied a new way of maintaining their high profile as gentlemen amateurs, but it was becoming difficult to provide matches against professional opposition that would satisfy an increasingly discerning public who, even in the South, were becoming accustomed to League competitions. Woolwich Arsenal had become the first London club to join the Football League in 1893, and a Southern League, including a number of clubs that were at least semi-professional, had started in 1894. The Corinthians were themselves beginning to look for pastures new where their reputation for effortless superiority on and social exclusivity off the pitch might yet be appreciated. After an uncertain beginning, Jackson had shaped Corinthianism to meet the challenges of the mid-1880s. While this meant confrontation on the field of play, it also involved a large degree of co-operation from which both amateurs and professionals could benefit. The temptation to over-emphasize differences should be resisted. Jackson and Sudell were entrepreneurs and not so very far apart in temperament and ambition. Both appreciated that recognizable brands were important, whether 'Corinth' or 'Proud Preston', and that a soccer match was an entertainment product that the public could be persuaded to buy. This is not to say that the Corinthians were insincere in their protestations of true-blue amateurism, but simply to argue that the sporting creed they professed was also a commodity that could command a price.

Notes

1. N.L. (Pa) Jackson, *Always Fit and Well* (London: George Newnes Ltd., 1931), pp. v–vii; A.M. Bryant, 'Jackson, Nicholas Lane [Pa] Jackson, (1849–1937)', *Oxford Dictionary of National Biography* (Oxford: Oxford University Press, 2004) doi:10.1013/ref.odnb/50296.
2. *Football: A Weekly Record of the Game*, 4 October 1882, p. 13. For links between the Wanderers and the Corinthians, see Rob Cavallini, *The Wanderers F.C.: "Five Times F.A. Cup winners"* (Worcester Park: Dog N Duck Publications, 2005), pp. 58–59.
3. *Football*, 18 October 1882, p. 41.
4. *Football*, 14 February 1883, p. 304.
5. N.L. Jackson, *Association Football* (London: George Newnes, 2nd ed., 1900), pp. 329–30; see also N. Lane Jackson, 'The Corinthians', *The Times*, 26 October 1932; N.L. ('Pa') Jackson, *Sporting Days and Sporting Ways* (London: Hurst & Blackett, 1932), p. 66.
6. See Terry Morris, *In a Class of Their Own: A History of English Amateur Football* (Sheffield: Chequered Flag Publishing, 2015), pp. 164–66.
7. *The Times*, 14 March 1881; 13 March 1882.
8. Jackson, *Association Football*, pp. 329–33. See Creek's letter to the *Sunday Times*, 1 May 1932.
9. *Football*, 14 February 1883, p. 304; 14 March 1883, p. 368.
10. Morris, *Class of Their Own*, p. 166.
11. *Football*, 25 October 1882, pp. 56–57.
12. Rob Cavallini, *Play Up Corinth: A History of the Corinthian Football Club* (Stroud: Stadia, 2007), p. 230.
13. *Football*, 13 December 1882, p. 163; *Athletic News* (Manchester), 13 December 1882.
14. *Sportsman*, 29 March 1883.
15. Douglas Chapman, *Dubbined Boots and Shinpads: A History of Leyton F.C.* (London: Leyton and Leytonstone Historical Society, 2012), pp. 22–23, speculates that Secretan had a more important role than has been recognized. Jackson may have simply let him get on with it until circumstances prompted him to intervene.
16. Geoffrey Green, 'The Football Association', in A.H. Fabian and Geoffrey Green, (eds), *Association Football* (London: Caxton Publishing Company, 1960), vol. 1, pp. 58–59.

17 See especially Matthew Taylor, *The Association Game: A History of British Football* (Harlow: Pearson Longman, 2008), pp. 43–44.
18 W.H. Macauley quoted in Shane Leslie, *Men Were Different: Five Studies in Late Victorian Biography* (London: Michael Joseph, 1937), p. 159.
19 *Football*, 21 March 1883, p. 390; 4 April 1883, p. 402.
20 Robert W. Lewis, 'The Genesis of Professional Football: Bolton-Blackburn-Darwen, the Centre of Innovation 1878–85', *International Journal of the History of Sport*, vol. 14, no. 1, 1997, p. 45.
21 J.A.H. (Tityrus) Catton, *The Story of Association Football* (Cleethorpes: Soccer Books Ltd., 2006; first published 1926). p. 9.
22 For the crisis over professionalism, see Dave Russell, 'From Evil to Expedient: The Legalization of Professionalism in English Football, 1884–85', in Stephen Wagg, (ed), *Myths and Milestones in the History of Sport* (Basingstoke: Palgrave Macmillan, 2011), pp. 32–56; see also Taylor, *The Association Game*, pp. 44–52; Tony Mason, *Association Football and English Society 1863–1915* (Brighton: Harvester, 1981), pp. 69–81.
23 Charles W. Alcock, *The Association Game* (London: Routledge and Sons, 1891), p. 71.
24 See Russell, 'From Evil to Expedient', pp. 37–39.
25 *Bolton Chronicle*, 22 November 1884, cited in Peter Bailey, *Leisure and Class in Victorian England: Rational Recreation and the Contest for Control, 1830–1885* (London: Routledge and Kegan Paul, 1978), p. 142.
26 *Athletic News* (Manchester), 10 December 1884.
27 *Sportsman*, 15 December 1884.
28 *Sunday Times*, 4 January 1885.
29 Joseph Baron's history of Blackburn Rovers, cited in *Blackburn Weekly Standard and Express*, 3 March 1894.
30 *Athletic News*, 17 December 1884.
31 *Pastime*, 24 December 1884, pp. 449–51.
32 Jackson, *Association Football*, p. 332.
33 *Pastime*, 6 January 1886, pp. 4–5; 22 December 1886, pp. 410–12.
34 *Pastime*, 5 January 1887, pp. 4–5.
35 Eric Hobsbawm, 'Mass-Producing Traditions: Europe 1870–1914', in Eric Hobsbawm and Terence Ranger, (eds), *The Invention of Tradition* (Cambridge: Cambridge University Press, 1993), pp. 288–89, 298–303.
36 Mason, *Association Football and English Society*, p. 216.
37 *Football*, 18 October 1882.
38 *Pastime*, 22 December 1886.
39 National Football Museum [NFM], Preston North End Football League Player Registrations, 1889–90. For Dewhurst and Mills-Roberts, see Michael Joyce, *Football League Players' Records 1888–1939* (Nottingham: SoccerData, 2002), p. 68, 173; see also Neil Carter, 'Football's First Northern Hero? The Rise and Fall of William Sudell', in Stephen Wagg and Dave Russell, (eds), *Sporting Heroes of the North: Sport, Religion and Culture* (Newcastle upon Tyne: Northumbria Press, 2010), p. 136.
40 Matthew L. McDowell, *A Cultural History of Association Football in Scotland, 1865–1902: Understanding Sports as a Way of Understanding Society* (Lampeter: Edwin Mellen Press, 2013), pp. 40–41.
41 *Sportsman*, 3 January 1891.
42 *Pastime*, 24 December 1884, pp. 449–51; 9 January 1889, pp. 23–24.
43 N. Lane ('Pa') Jackson, *Sporting Days and Sporting Ways* (London: Hurst & Blackett, 1932), pp. 141, 146–48.
44 *Sportsman*, 8 January 1889.
45 Neil Carter, *The Football Manager: A History* (Abingdon: Routledge, 2006), p. 37.

46 *Sportsman*, 20 December 1887.
47 *Sportsman*, 2 January 1891.
48 *Pall Mall Gazette*, 28 December 1891.
49 C.B. Fry, *Life Worth Living: Some Phases of An Englishman,* (London: Pavilion Library, 1986; first published 1939), p. 269.
50 *Football Field and Sports Telegram* (Bolton), 17 December 1887; for *Football Field*, see Tony Mason, 'Sporting News, 1860–1914', in Michael Harris and Alan Lee, *The Press in English Society from the Seventeenth to the Nineteenth Centuries*, (London: Associated University Presses, 1986), p. 178.
51 *Umpire* (Manchester), 21 November 1886.
52 *Sportsman*, 3 April 1888; Brian Tabner, *Football through the Turnstiles ... Again* (Harefield: Yore Publications, 2002, p. 92).
53 Everton Collection at evertoncollection.org.uk, Committee Minutes, 31 October 1887, 14 July 1890; Tabner, *Football through the Turnstiles*, p. 92; *Sportsman*, 1 April 1891.
54 Everton collection, Board of Directors Minutes, 14 March 1898.
55 Richard Robinson, *A History of the Queen's Park Football Club 1867–1917* (Glasgow: Hay, Nisbet & Co., 1920), pp. 238–39.
56 Stephen Hardy, 'Entrepreneurs, Organizations, and the Sports Marketplace: Subjects in Search of Historians', *Journal of Sport History*, vol. 13, no. 1, 1986, p. 16; Erik Nielsen, *Sport and the British World, 1900–1930: Amateurism and National Identity in Australasia and Beyond* (Basingstoke: Palgrave Macmillan, 2014), pp. 26–27.
57 Robinson, *History of Queen's Park*, p. 233.
58 *Football Field*, 24 December 1887.
59 *Umpire*, 17 September 1893.
60 See Cavallini, *Play Up Corinth*, pp. 36–37, the only club history to give this incident the attention it merits, albeit from a sympathetic perspective. For the Sports Club, see Jackson, *Sporting Days and Sporting Ways*, pp. 152–54.
61 *Western Mail* (Cardiff), 5 January 1894.
62 *Umpire*, 17 December 1893.
63 *Sportsman*, 4 January 1894.
64 *Pall Mall Gazette*, 19, 23 January 1895.
65 *Pastime*, 6 January 1887, pp. 4–5; 12 January 1887, pp. 17–18.
66 C.B. Fry, 'Character Sketches', in B.O. Corbett, (ed), *Annals of the Corinthian Football Club* (London: Longmans, Green & Co., 1906), p. 33; for the Mears family and Chelsea FC, see Mason, *Association Football and English Society*, pp. 45–46.
67 *The Times,* 31 March 1885; 1 April 1889.
68 For Jackson's working relationship with Alcock, see Keith Booth, *The Father of Modern Sport: The Life and Times of Charles W. Alcock* (Manchester: The Parrs Wood Press, 2002), pp. 183–84.
69 Surrey History Centre [SHC], 2042/1/4, Surrey CCC, General Minute Book 1879–88, p. 235, Statement of Accounts 1 April 1884 to 31 March 1885; 2042/1/5, Surrey CCC, General Minute Book 1888–98, pp. 183–85, Statement of Accounts, 1 April 1891 to 31 March 1892.
70 SHC, 3035/8/3, Surrey CCC Match Receipt Books, 26 October 1890 to 17 August 1893.
71 F.N.S. Creek, *A History of the Corinthian Football Club* (London: Longmans, Green & Co,. 1933), p. 17.
72 SHC, 2042/1/5, Surrey CCC, General Minute Book 1888–98, p. 35, meeting 21 March 1880; SHC, 2042/6/2, Surrey CCC, Football Sub-Committee Minutes, meeting 10 December 1894.
73 Essex Record Office [ERO], D/Z 82/1/1, Essex CCC Minute Book 1886–93, meeting held 28 February 1889. For the county club's dire financial condition, see David

Lemmon and Mike Marshall, *Essex County Cricket Club: The Official History* (London: Kingswood, 1987), pp. 68, 75.
74 ERO, D/Z 82/1/2, Essex CCC Minute Book 1893–1900, meeting 31 October 1893.
75 *Sunday Times*, 27 January 1889.
76 See *Sunday Times*, 7 February 1886; also Tinsley Lindley interview, *Pall Mall Gazette*, 24 March 1888. At the Oval, there were additional charges for entrance to the stand and the enclosure, SHC 3035/8/2, Surrey CCC, Match Receipt Books, 26 August 1888 to 18 June 1889.
77 SHC, 2042/1/5, Surrey CCC, General Minute Book 1888–98, meeting 16 March 1893; ERO, D/Z 82/1/1, Essex CCC Minute Book 1886–93, meeting 21 March 1893; Minute Book 1893–1900, meeting held 8 January 1895.
78 See Dilwyn Porter, '"Coming on with Leaps and Bounds in the Metropolis": London Football in the Era of the 1908 Olympics', *London Journal*, vol. 34, no. 2, 2009, p. 103.
79 Alfred Gibson and William Pickford, *Association Football & the Men Who Made It* (London: Caxton Press, 1906), vol. 3, pp. 69–70.
80 *Sportsman*, 5, 6, 10 April 1893.
81 Creek, *History of the Corinthian Football Club*, p. 33.
82 *Sunday Times*, 1 April 1894.
83 *Sportsman*, 19, 23 December 1895. It may or may not be significant, but a fixture arranged later with the South Wales Football League for a £35 guarantee was not fulfilled, possibly for the same reason, *Western Mail*, 14 October 1898, 13 January 1899.
84 *Morning Post*, 11 March 1895.
85 *Pall Mall Gazette*, 16 February 1891; *Sunday Times,* 29 February 1896; *Morning Post*, 1 January 1898.
86 Fry, *Life Worth Living*, pp. 266–67; see also Sir Frederick Wall, *50 Years of Football 1884–1934* (Cleethorpes: Soccer Books Ltd., 2006; first published, 1935), p. 59.
87 Stephen Hardy, Brian Norman and Sarah Sceery, 'Toward a History of Branding in Sport', *Journal of Historical Research in Marketing*, vol. 4, no. 4, 2012, pp. 484–85.
88 *Pall Mall Gazette*, 18 March 1889.
89 *Morning Post*, 10 November 1894.
90 *Morning Post*, 8 December 1900.
91 ER0, D/Z 82/1/2, Essex CCC Minute Book 1893–1900, meeting 31 October 1893, letter from Jackson to Borradaile, 16 October 1893 (copy): 'What of the bills and posters [?]', he had asked.
92 *Sunday Times*, 1 December 1895; 28 March 1897. Jackson is specifically mentioned in connection with the first match but not the second. He is, however, likely to have been involved in both as nine Corinthians played against Aston Villa and seven against Sheffield Wednesday.
93 William Pickford, *A Glance Back at the Football Association Council 1888–1938* (Bournemouth: Bournemouth Guardian, 1938), pp. 33–34; see also Jackson, *Sporting Days and Sporting Ways*, pp. 174–75.
94 *Sunday Times*, 21 January 1894.
95 *The Times,* 11 April 1892.
96 *Morning Post*, 17 March 1898.
97 Jackson, *Sporting Days and Sporting Ways*, pp. 142–43.
98 *Sunday Times*, 1 September 1896.

2 Decline and fall

The Corinthians in the twentieth century

Figure 2.1 Corinthian FC, Sheriff of London Shield v Sheffield United, Crystal Palace, 19 March 1898.
From *Sports* (Illustrated), pub. Sheffield, 6 April 1898.

During the First World War, there was consolation to be found in recalling the joys of pre-war sport. Writing to the *Sunday Times* from The Curragh, headquarters of the British military in Ireland, a Mr Madden-Strangeways reflected on the nature of the Corinthians club and what it represented. 'To be a Corinthian', he declared, 'is a distinction of the highest kind known to the athlete'. Indeed, if an international cap was 'the footballer's Victoria Cross', then to play for this highly exclusive club was 'surely the Order of the Garter'. The columnist to whom this was addressed agreed and went on to assign much of the credit for the development of soccer to those who had worn 'the coveted white shirt with the monogram "C.F.C." on the left breast'. They represented 'the cream of amateur talent' and were especially praised for their 'ever-increasing missionary work', taking the game 'into places where first-class contests were otherwise impossible'.[1] Such comments testified to the efforts of Jackson, assisted by a generally sympathetic sporting press, to create and market the Corinthian brand in the late nineteenth century. Moreover, when he withdrew from active involvement in the club's affairs in 1898, the founder could be confident that his legacy was in safe hands. The secretary's role passed first to G.O. Smith and W.J. Oakley until 1902, then to B.O. Corbett until 1904 and then to S.H. Day until 1906. Thereafter, it was taken on by W.U. Timmis, who saw the club through English soccer's 'Great Split' and the disruption caused by the war. Each of these sporting gentlemen had played for the club in the Jackson era; each could regard themselves as members of soccer's most exclusive order.

It was clear in the early years of the twentieth century that the Corinthians had left their mark. The 1890s had been a critical decade in the expansion of sports coverage in the press. 'Sport sold newspapers, or was thought by their owners to do so', Tony Mason has observed perceptively, 'and they were prepared to see that it had all the space it needed'.[2] At the most fundamental level, according to Kennedy Jones of Harmsworth's *Daily Mail*, there was 'always a special demand for news which contains a result'.[3] In addition to the specialist reporting supplied by the *Athletic News*, the *Sportsman* and the proliferating football 'pinks', it featured increasingly in daily and evening papers and in the weekly local press. 'Football Notes by Free Kick', appearing every Monday in the *Lincolnshire Echo*, was not alone in providing details of important matches, including those played by the Corinthians.[4] Thus, the Corinthians club was known throughout the United Kingdom wherever soccer was reported, which was more or less everywhere. Accounts of the first Sheriff of London's Shield [Charity Shield] match with Sheffield United, albeit brief, were to be found as far afield as the *East and South Devon Chronicle*, the *Ludlow Advertiser* and the *Aberdeen Press and Journal*, to name but three. The Victorian press determined to a large extent the way in which its readers understood or imagined sport, not least by promoting personalities. C.B. Fry, for example, became legendary for his versatility because it was so often referred to by journalists. In 1894, after playing rugby for the Barbarians on their tour in South Wales, 'he proceeded to join the Corinthians, the leading Association club, who are on tour in the North'.[5] This was, of course, excellent publicity, not only for Fry, but also for the Corinthians.

Familiarity with the club and what it represented encouraged various forms of imitation. The link between gentility and amateur status was well publicized and widely accepted. Soccer clubs, adopting the name 'Corinthian' or 'Corinthians', were not uncommon by the turn of the century, often indicating a middle-class membership. They could be found from Colchester to Kettering and from Hull to Hartlepool, in England,

Wales, Scotland and Ireland. There was, of course, a world of difference between *the* Corinthians and the Fareham Corinthians, fined five shillings by their local association in Portsmouth when they failed to turn up for a fixture with Gosport Progressive Reserves, but the choice of name almost certainly signified something, if only an intention to play in the sporting spirit with which the famous Corinthians were associated.[6] Loughborough Corinthians in Leicestershire, formed in 1897, were quickly into their stride, entering the Loughborough and District League and manifesting many of the characteristics of a middle-class club with an annual dinner featuring a 'pianoforte selection' and various songs, mainly 'humorous'. A speaker at this event in 1900 was warmly applauded when he announced that 'he was heart and soul in favour of amateur football'.[7] The status and orientation of a club may well have varied over time – Loughborough Corinthians later played in the semi-professional Midland Counties League – but the choice of name remains relevant.

Cardiff Corinthians, also formed in 1897, who included local rivals Barry Corinthians and Penarth Corinthians among their opponents, are a better documented example. Their title, it would seem, was very carefully chosen. 'Cardiff Alpha', the name of the cricket club to which most of its members belonged, was under consideration, but 'a large majority' favoured 'Corinthians'.[8] Possibly, they were influenced by concerns that surfaced a little later when the president of their local association complained that 'amateurism such as some clubs in South Wales professed was nothing but cloaked professionalism'.[9] Initially, the Cardiff Corinthians followed their illustrious English counterparts by refusing to enter their first team in league and cup competitions, though there appears to have been no objection in principle. The reserves joined a league in 1900, and a few years later, the club entered the Rhymney Valley League, the South Wales Senior Cup and the Llanbradach Charity Cup.[10] A note on its history, however, indicates a commitment to Corinthianism that was more than nominal, claiming that it was 'one of the few truly amateur clubs at this highest level of Welsh football', thus confirming Martin Johnes's view that 'it tried to carry on the traditional amateur values of Victorian sport that its name evoked'.[11] The establishment of a Corinthians club in Cardiff, as with the Loughborough example, testifies to the extent to which the project was known and understood at the turn of the century and to the desire of many amateur soccer enthusiasts to follow the example set by Jackson's men while making the adjustments required by the particular circumstances of their locality.

What this suggests is that the Corinthians remained capable of flying the flag for gentlemanly amateurism. At the turn of the century, the club was sometimes referred to as if it were an institution. 'The Corinthians, of course, will always be with us', one Scottish newspaper noted, 'they will no doubt maintain a high standard'.[12] Credibility in terms of playing performance, however, was critical if the club was to enjoy a high profile, and there were indications that this was becoming more difficult to achieve. They were by now 'a very different lot from the eleven which defeated Preston North End when it was at the height of its power'.[13] Those who sympathized with the club and what it represented were increasingly inclined to look backwards rather than forwards. 'They may well sigh for their old days', observed the *Sportsman* in April 1903 at the end of disappointing season, 'for someone to act as their "director-general" with the same persuasive powers and managing ability as "Pa" Jackson'.[14] Such opinions were often repeated in the Edwardian era, with the most authoritative contemporary history of the English game observing in 1906 that the club was past its prime.[15] A tipping point had been reached, and the principal concern of this chapter is to chart and explain the club's decline and fall over the thirty years or so that followed. The Corinthians remained an institution in English sport – it was not just soccer clubs that appropriated its title – and the gentlemanly values it represented still counted for something, even in the 1930s, but the scope of its activities was progressively reduced.

Playing themselves into a corner: the Corinthians and English soccer before 1914

As the Corinthians and their supporters looked back, they were more likely to recall spectacular victories achieved in the 1880s and 1890s than the mundane reality of a playing performance that by the early 1900s was remarkable mainly for its inconsistency. Norman Creek, the most reliably reflective of the club's historians, concluded that the five seasons prior to the 'great Split' in 1907 were characterized by 'a mediocre standard of play ... occasionally relieved by sudden and fleeting exhibitions of greatness'.[16] Some of the difficulties that had first appeared in the 1890s became more pressing. Prestige fixtures became more difficult to arrange, Corbett observing in 1906 that, on account of the extension of the Football League, it was becoming 'harder, season by season, to arrange friendly matches with big professional teams'.[17] Moreover, when such fixtures were arranged, there was no guarantee that their opponents would field their strongest side or that they would approach the game seriously. At around the turn of the century, home matches were sometimes played at the Crystal Palace where cockney pleasure-seekers could be induced to take in the match as part of the afternoon's entertainment. 'An enormous Bank Holiday crowd', estimated at 25,000, turned up to watch the Corinthians take on championship contenders Sheffield United at Easter 1900. It seems likely that many of them would have been disappointed for while the Corinthians 'had not a bad side ... the Sheffielders had only four of their best eleven engaged'.[18]

This became a familiar theme whether the playing at home or away. The first three matches of the Christmas tour in 1904 pitched 'the leading amateur combination' against Aston Villa, Stoke City and Sheffield United on consecutive days, but the credibility of the Corinthians' achievement in emerging from these matches undefeated was diminished by the quality of the opposition. Villa's team was very different from that which had played in its previous match against Arsenal; at Stoke, 'neither side was at full strength and less than a couple of thousand spectators were present'; and Sheffield United 'made several changes from their full side', resting five regular first-team players.[19] It is clear from the teams selected by Everton's directors over the Christmas period in 1906 that they had effectively downgraded their 'friendly' with the Corinthians to a reserve team fixture.[20] It was hardly surprising in these circumstances that matches with professional opposition sometimes lacked a competitive edge. Though they managed to win, Notts County, visiting in 1903, 'gave anything but one of their best displays, and did not appear to enter very seriously into their task'; Southampton were 'inclined to take matters rather too easily' and were beaten.[21] Spectators in the South, had become accustomed to the cut and thrust of competitive soccer since the foundation of the Southern League in 1894. They were sometimes offered rather tame fare. Though the Corinthians enjoyed a run of successes against Queen's Park – 'undoubtedly the greatest club fixture in the amateur calendar' – their old enemies may well have had other priorities as they struggled to achieve a respectable position in the Scottish League, which they had joined in 1900.[22]

In these circumstances, the Charity Shield match assumed great importance, despite the club's previous aversion to 'pot-hunting'. The first match in 1898 featured the Corinthians and Sheffield United, representing the best in the amateur and professional games, respectively. A Sheffield sports weekly predicted that both teams would play 'for all they are worth', noting that this would be very welcome as previous matches between the Corinthians and United had been 'invertebrate exhibitions, pertaining of all the evils of the despised "friendly"'.[23] As it transpired a spirited contest ensued over two matches, both drawn, which generated sufficient controversy to satisfy those critics who were alert to its potential for symbolizing class conflict. The replay featured a heated argument following a disputed free kick, which led to a goal for the Corinthians after which 'a lot of feeling was imported into [the game] by both teams'. It ended abruptly when United refused to play extra time, the club's president explaining that the League championship, which they were contesting with Sunderland, was of 'the utmost importance', far more than the Charity Shield, which the Corinthians prized so much.[24] Yet, even before this controversy was resolved – the trophy was awarded to both clubs jointly – another story had surfaced, which suggested that relations between amateurs and professionals were less problematic than readers might have imagined. Sunderland had refused to release two players wanted by Scotland for the forthcoming international with England so that they could play in a vital league match against United, adamantly rejecting suggestions that the fixture should be re-arranged. United, meanwhile, had released Ernest Needham to play for England. It was revealed that G.O. Smith and Wreford-Brown, both Corinthians and Needham's England team-mates, had been persuaded to sign for United, thus making themselves available for their remaining fixtures if required. This gesture of solidarity, though some thought it misplaced, suggests that the gap between amateur and professional, middle class and working class, North and South remained bridgeable, just as it had been in 1885. For Needham, a quintessential northern 'pro', it is likely to have confirmed his view of Smith as 'one of the most brilliant and gentlemanly players who ever stepped on to a football field'.[25] This episode was especially significant as class differences were hardening in the 1890s, as evidenced by the schism in English rugby.

In the following season, the form of the Corinthians was so inconsistent that Queen's Park were invited to take their place in the Shield match. Thereafter, through to 1907, the Corinthians competed annually against various club sides representing the professionals. Observers tended to note contrasting styles. Against Aston Villa in 1899, in the third match of the series, 'the individual play of some of the Corinthians was both brilliant and fast but the combination of the Midland men enabled them to make their way up the field repeatedly in a fashion which their rivals seldom equalled'.[26] A similar contrast was apparent in the fourth match, also against Villa, played in 1901, though some reports pointed out that an important element was missing. 'Perhaps to some of the Villa enthusiasts', a Birmingham daily suggested, 'the game seemed somewhat tame after the fierce delights of the Cup fight at Nottingham', an opinion endorsed by the influential *Athletic News*.[27] With interest starting to fade, the match was moved from the Crystal Palace and played at Tottenham, where the Corinthians lost to Spurs in 1902 and Sunderland in 1903, this match attracting only 3,000 spectators. The Corinthians were well beaten on both occasions, and criticism after the match with Sunderland was especially severe. Sunderland won easily without having to play at all well; 'the contest was too one-sided to be exciting'.[28] The *Athletic News* was especially scathing, arguing that all future matches should be played on the home ground of one of the competing clubs in order to ensure a respectable gate. 'The Corinthians', it added, '... are not quite the attraction they were: indeed, I think we could now find one or two purely club teams in the Metropolis who could give them a good game'.[29] It could no longer be taken for granted that they were the best amateur side in the country and serious consideration was given to the idea that Cambridge University, who were having an excellent season, would replace them in the 1904 match.[30] The mystique that had attached itself to Jackson's team appeared to be evaporating.

'Then, as if by some magician's touch, the Corinthians somehow clicked'. For once, the words of the club's most adulatory chronicler are appropriate.[31] They were eventually invited to play in the 1904 match, this time staged at Queen's Club, where they inflicted a 10-3 defeat on FA Cup-holders Bury. At the time, their opponents were in the First Division of the Football League and their team included nine of the eleven who had beaten Derby County by the record score of 6-0 in the 1903 Cup Final. As if this was not enough for the myth-makers, the match was won in recognizably Corinthian style.

Praising the forwards, *The Times* declared that such 'dashing work ... has not been seen since amateurs could always be regarded as sure to hold their own with the best professional teams'.[32] Even the *Bury Guardian* was impressed. The local favourites had been outclassed, the Corinthian forwards 'giving a display that has probably never been excelled'.[33] It was a performance in which Corinthian propagandists and sympathizers, both at the time and for years afterwards, could rejoice. In the words of Geoffrey Green in the 1950s, it was for the Corinthians 'the most famous victory of all – certainly the one most quoted'.[34] It was as unexpectedly sensational as the 8-1 win at Blackburn with which they had announced their arrival as a power in the English game twenty years previously.

On this occasion, however, the context was very different. 'Grasshopper', the jobbing journalist who wrote 'Southern Notes' each week for the *Athletic News*, had to take note – 'BRILLIANT PERFORMANCE BY AMATEURS' – and was duly complimentary, but devoted as much space in his article to the bread and butter of the Southern League as to the caviar on offer at 'the swagger West End enclosure', the label he attached to Queen's Club.[35] Thus, when measured in terms of coverage in the most important sports weekly, Plymouth Argyle versus Millwall or Reading versus Fulham was of equal or greater importance than Bury versus Corinth for those who cared about the game. The sensational victory passed into Corinthian folklore but was quickly put into perspective by their manifest failure to follow through as inconsistency continued to prevail. There were some more notable triumphs to come – a Manchester United team were beaten 11-3 at Leyton a few months later – but not in a match that mattered. Interest in the Charity Shield revived, and attendances rose for a while, but whether the Corinthians played well and lost, as they did against Sheffield Wednesday in 1905, or badly and lost, as they did against Liverpool in 1906 had given way but at a cost. Hunting for this particular trophy had little impact on their profile. In 1907, making what was to be their last Charity Shield appearance until 1931, the amateurs lost again, 5-2 to Newcastle United, while treating the spectators to 'a delightful exhibition of [the] clever, quick passing, for which they are so famous'.[36] But something more was now required if the interest of the public in London or elsewhere was to be engaged. Friendlies and charity games were all very well, but by the early twentieth century, spectators wanted 'to see a match in which something is at stake'.[37] They wanted some excitement rather than an exhibition of Corinthian soccer skills.

There was no domestic tour in 1907, the club's attention being focused on its third and most controversial trip to South Africa and on the crisis then enveloping English football at home.[38] This storm had been brewing for some time as the compromise that Jackson and his touring Corinthians had facilitated in 1884–85 became unsustainable. The FA's insistence that its county associations should admit professional clubs into membership prompted a rebellion. It was not difficult for most counties – most of them already operated on this basis – but it was a problem for the London, Middlesex and Surrey associations where gentlemanly amateurism was numerically strong and deeply entrenched. London, after much bitterness and recrimination, had given way in 1906. That Lord Kinnaird, an Old Etonian, used his influence to persuade the London association to accede to the FA's request was regarded by many 'Old Boys' as an act of class treachery.[39] When the accommodation between amateurism and professionalism had been reached in the 1880s, the contending forces had been more evenly matched. Over the years that followed, professional soccer had grown enormously and so had the influence exerted by middle-class men of business who saw football as a way of enhancing their social status, sometimes making money too, though the FA imposed constraints to preclude mere speculation. In pursuing their interests and those of their clubs, they undermined the *modus vivendi*, which had been reached. The gentlemen amateurs suffered frequent reminders that their influence was waning. Professionalism had at first been subject to stringent conditions, but these were progressively relaxed. County Cup competitions were now dominated by professional clubs, and the FA Cup was out of reach. Amateurs appeared less frequently at international level. Penalty kicks, introduced in 1891 to deter the 'professional foul' that denied a goal-scoring opportunity, were much resented. Those who considered themselves gentlemen were offended by the implication that they might behave in an ungentlemanly fashion. The Amateur Football Association (AFA), explained Henry Hughes-Onslow, its first secretary, had no objection to professionalism as such, 'but they did object to the passing of power into the hands of the representatives of professional clubs'. Soccer, he declared, 'must be governed as a sport and not as a commercial undertaking'.[40]

The pretext for the movement that led to English soccer's 'Great Split' was the FA's decision to force the Middlesex and Surrey associations into line in 1906–07. This resulted in a number of clubs, including the Corinthians setting up an Amateur Football Defence Federation in April 1907, an organization that morphed into the breakaway AFA a few months later. The split in some ways reflected inter-class and inter-regional tensions but was principally a trial of strength between two fractions of the middle class clustered around commerce and the professions respectively, around new money and old. Most secessionists wanted to run their clubs and county associations with as little interference from above as possible. They also claimed that the FA had neglected the amateur game, a charge that secretary Frederick Wall denied by reminding them of such initiatives as the Amateur Cup competition introduced in 1893 and the more recent innovation of amateur international matches. The Old Boys, he recalled, were beyond a point where they could be persuaded, having mostly convinced themselves that their grievances were genuine. In reality, they had simply been outflanked and outmanoeuvred; 'he [the gentleman amateur] relaxed his grip, the reins fell from his hands, the professional clubs got the upper hand'.[41] A letter to the *Sportsman* from one amateur soccer enthusiast in June 1907 set out the position of many who favoured a fresh start. Why should they remain with the FA 'which for years has legislated purely and simply in the interest of the money side of the game?'[42] In the end, the AFA overestimated their support and overplayed their hand. 'What was actually "split" between 1907 and 1914', as Morris has perceptively observed, '... was the amateur game itself'.[43] Most amateur clubs – by now predominantly working or lower middle class – remained loyal to the FA. For some reason, probably a misplaced sense of loyalty underpinned by personal connection, the Corinthians decided to take a leading part in this movement.

Geoffrey Green went as far as to claim that the split had been 'instituted by a clique within the Corinthians, largely for personal motives'.[44] It was rather more complicated, but members of the club featured prominently. Among the vice-presidents elected by the AFA at its first meeting were numerous Corinthians, many of them stars of the 1880s and 1890s, and a few current players – N.C. Bailey, W.N. Cobbold, S.S. Harris, M.M. Morgan-Owen, W.J. Oakley, P.M. Walters, C. Wreford-Brown and, inevitably, G.O. Smith, were among this elite. Other celebrated Corinthians were quick to identify themselves with the AFA including C.B. Fry, R.E. Foster and Tinsley Lindley.[45] That they should align themselves with the rebels was regarded as highly significant, adding lustre to a cause that, so far as many gentlemen amateurs were concerned, was far from lost. 'The mere fact of the Corinthians taking the lead', in the view of a not especially sympathetic *Athletic News*, 'is another potent factor towards its ultimate success'.[46] Rugby union, after all, had emerged from the split of the mid-1890s as a viable organization running an amateur game in the interests of amateurs. 'Despite the devastation it had brought to rugby, [the] RFU had got what it wanted', as Tony Collins has argued.[47] This time it was the amateurs that were in revolt, but there was some reason to feel confident, at least at the start, that the eventual outcome would compensate for whatever problems the split might bring. When the club announced its decision to back the secessionists in June 1907, one critic, writing under the pseudonym 'Ardent Amateur', inferred that it had been made 'by men whose honours at the game are already won and their playing days practically over'. He went on to ask if younger Corinthians approved 'of the club practically committing suicide as far as first-class football is concerned'. Timmis responded rapidly, reporting that he had 'not received any intimation from a single member expressing dissent from the recent decision of my committee'.[48] Significantly, however, he agreed with 'Ardent Amateur' that 'sacrifices' would be required.

What this would entail soon became clear. The Christmas-New Year tour undertaken by the Corinthians in 1906 may not have been quite up to the standard of the Jackson era, but it involved matches against major professional clubs such as Everton (effectively the reserves), Hearts, albeit 'wanting four of the usual forwards and a back and a half-back', then 'practically the full strength' of Newcastle United, who were beaten. It also included the New Year match with Queen's Park in Glasgow, which was 'still looked upon as an annual function of no little importance'.[49] A year later, the tour was less ambitious and the opposition more modest. It began at Reigate and moved on to Ramsgate, the Corinthians taking on teams representing the Surrey and Kent branches of the AFA. Considerable local interest was reported at Ramsgate but principally because 'the county eleven included four members of the of St George's (Ramsgate) club'. The Corinthians then returned to London to play New Crusaders, one of the AFA's top clubs, who were beaten easily. Matches were then played at Ipswich and Eastbourne. At Ipswich, both sides were at 'full strength', the Corinthians winning 7-1, though generally they 'had been handicapped by the number of players *hors de combat* or otherwise engaged'.[50] Ipswich Town, somewhat isolated on account of being simultaneously the most eastern and most northern outpost of the AFA's Southern Amateur League, probably came to regard the annual visitation as a mixed blessing. The 15-1 defeat inflicted on them in 1910 remains the worst result in the club's long history and was said to have been 'one of the most one-sided games ever-witnessed in Ipswich'. To lose only by 4-0 a year later, note the club's historians, 'was considered quite a feat'.[51] In short, the quality of the Corinthians' fixture list declined now that they could no longer arrange matches with professional clubs or even the many senior amateur clubs that refused to follow them into the backwater of AFA soccer.

The reason why the Corinthians had to be content with such modest opposition was that the FA was determined to crush the threat to its authority that the rival association represented. It had taken pre-emptive action in July 1907, just before the AFA was formed, in order to minimize any possible exodus. The position to which it was to adhere throughout the split was ratified a few months later when its council resolved that 'All Clubs and Players under the jurisdiction of The FA who shall play with or against Clubs or Players who are not under the jurisdiction of a recognized Association will be forthwith suspended *sine die*'.[52] Judicious exceptions were allowed later for school, college and university players. Clubs that had joined the AFA were cornered; they were at liberty to play anyone, but those clubs who remained loyal to the FA were not free to play them, thus precluding the home and away fixtures with against professional opposition, which had been staples of the Corinthians fixture list since the 1880s. It helped the FA that other national associations fell into line. The Football Association of Wales was thanked in November 1907 'for the friendly attitude it had adopted in regard to the action taken by the Football Association in view of the formation of the Amateur Football Association'.[53] The defectors quickly discovered that their room for manoeuvre was extremely limited. Matches with Queen's Park ceased, the governing body in Scotland falling into line with its English counterpart. This was a 'further blow inflicted on the Corinthians, who consequently find themselves with a very meagre list of fixtures'.[54] When the Sheriff of London Charity Shield Committee inquired 'if they might still be free to select the competing clubs whether affiliated to the Football Association or not', it was made clear that the FA would only sanction a match 'between two teams of this Association'.[55] The competition entered a new phase with professional clubs representing the Football League and the Southern League competing for the Shield.

One of the first shots fired by the FA in the direction of the rebels had observed that the Corinthians were 'notorious' for seeking 'large guarantees' for matches against professional clubs. Without this money, it was argued, 'its position could not have been maintained'.[56] It seems likely that this source of revenue was already drying up, even before the split. They were not the attraction they once had been. 'Their matches during the past few seasons', noted Gibson and Pickford in 1906, 'have on the whole been scantily attended and very few League clubs would be prepared to offer them the guarantees they were able to ask [for] and obtain ten or twelve years ago'.[57] It is clear that this situation could only have deteriorated further after 1907, thus enhancing the incentive to travel abroad. Certainly they could not expect to draw crowds at home or away on a regular basis to compare with most Football League clubs. London's *Football Evening News* had reported in September 1908 that Second Division Clapton Orient's reserve team had attracted 'quite four thousand spectators' to see them play Woolwich Arsenal reserves on the same day that Tottenham Hotspur, only a few miles away, had been watched by 22,000 in a Football League match against Barnsley.[58] In comparison, AFA soccer was barely a spectator sport. When Ipswich Town went to London to play Norsemen in the Southern Amateur League, only twelve spectators turned up; when they hosted an AFA international match, the gate was much higher but still only 2,000.[59] Matches involving the Corinthians were better supported than most, but when they travelled to Oxford University in 1908 with 'a splendid team', just 200 enthusiasts were present, leading the 'Amateur Affairs' columnist in the *Evening News* to conclude that 'amateur football as a spectacle does not attract the public'.[60] A gate of 1,000 for a Christmas fixture at Ramsgate generated £25, 'a good result for a Ramsgate match'.[61] But, even if they covered their travelling expenses, it was hardly sufficient to keep the Corinthians in the manner to which they had once been accustomed.

An Oxford University player writing to his club's secretary in November 1912 had met a Corinthians official who had mentioned they were still owed their share of the gate from a match played a year previously. He added: 'I told him that I would let you know but I didn't encourage him to hope for very much'.[62] No doubt it would have helped, however small the cheque. By this time, the Corinthians had effectively ceased to be a touring side in England and were playing only nine or ten matches a season. It was clear that the FA's policy had made little impact on the AFA's minnows whose fixture lists were generally unaffected, but its impact on the Corinthians and on Oxford and Cambridge Universities, who had also played high-profile matches against professional clubs, was both disproportionate and disadvantageous, and they became anxious to find a compromise that would bring the split to an end. In 1912, the Corinthians took the initiative, voting to pursue reconciliation with the FA by establishing a committee to draft proposals that would enable the AFA to open negotiations. English soccer's great schism duly came to an end in February 1914. The authority of the FA had been preserved; the AFA flag was lowered; it was admitted to the FA as the Amateur Football Alliance with membership intact and some recognition that it represented a separate constituency.[63] As for the Corinthians, it was clear that after almost seven years away from English soccer's mainstream, they 'might at first experience some difficulty in getting matches with the best professional clubs owing to the extended league programmes'.[64] Thus, it was reassuring when West Bromwich Albion and West Ham United found time to play them at the end of the 1913–14 season. They won the first of these matches and then lost at West Ham in a match played for a local charity, but at least the attendance, estimated at 3,000, was more than they had been accustomed to of late and there was, according to the ever-loyal *Sportsman*, 'plenty of "brainy" football' for discerning spectators to enjoy.[65] The Corinthians were unfortunate in that the outbreak of war then intervened, effectively deferring their re-entry into soccer's mainstream until the 1919–20 season. By then it was too late to reclaim the elite status that had been forfeited when it had joined the secessionist movement in 1907.

Realizing their limitations: the Corinthians and English football in the interwar years

Whoever wrote the football notes for *The Cholmeleian*, Highgate School's magazine, in the first full season of post-war soccer summed up his first team's prospects in one word: 'Bad'. What else was there to say? Nothing except that they were without 'a single first eleven colour to fall back upon, and only four of last year's very mediocre 2nd XI'. He could 'scarcely hope for a successful season'. The Corinthians, who came to visit in October, may or may not have raised his spirits by winning 16-0, scoring eight goals in each half, 'all the result of beautiful combination and passing'.[66] Yet, though they showed no mercy on the field, the Corinthians may well have sympathized with the school. Their own prospects were also uncertain after suspending activities for four years not least on account of those who had lost their lives for King and country in the recent conflict. They had a little more in the way of experience to fall back on – rather too much as four or five key players were pre-1914 veterans – but 'the material available in 1919 was poor both in quantity and quality'.[67] This would make it difficult for the club to resurrect itself as a serious touring side, to re-affirm its status as an elite amateur club with a reputation for sporting excellence and to offer a brand of soccer that was both distinctive and attractive. There was also the question of how best to respond to the new challenges of the post-war era with the limited resources then available to the club. The Corinthian Football Club was unique in English football, as Morris has observed, because its mission, above all else, was 'to maintain the sporting prestige of an elite and exclusive social class'.[68] As a middle-class or, more specifically, an upper middle-class club playing what was now essentially 'the people's game', the Corinthians, emerging from the relative obscurity into which they had strayed in 1907, were in a position where they could use soccer either to reinforce the existing cultural hegemony or to build bridges across the class divide. They attempted to achieve both but with limited success.

Touring in the North, the Midlands and Scotland had been a defining feature of the club's identity in the late nineteenth century facilitating co-operation for mutual benefit across class, regional and even national boundaries. Tours to other parts of the country continued thereafter but had disappeared altogether in the last years of the split. Cheap victories over weak opposition tended to diminish rather than enhance the Corinthian's reputation. 'In short', noted *The Times*, after a tour in which various AFA sides had been soundly defeated, '... the Corinthians have gained their successes over sides which a few years ago they would never have thought of meeting'.[69] That the club's first tour, when they were revived after the First World War, was to soccer-playing public schools therefore requires some explanation, especially as it became a Corinthian tradition that continued well into the mid-1930s. In part, it reflected the social exclusivity that had characterized the club since its formation. It was abundantly clear by the 1920s that the very best players had mostly been educated elsewhere, usually in elementary schools, but the club adhered to its unwritten rule restricting membership to gentlemen amateurs who had attended public schools or Oxbridge. This meant that Vivian Woodward, probably the finest amateur soccer player of his generation, could play no part in the Corinthian story, despite being impeccably middle class and very much a gentleman in his behaviour. He had been educated near his home at Clacton-on-Sea before training as an architect and had to be satisfied with Tottenham Hotspur, Chelsea and England, missing out on public school, university and soccer's 'Order of Garter'.[70] Clearly, the Corinthians deemed it imperative to honour the commonly perceived link between public-school education and gentlemanly status even when it was to their disadvantage.[71] It helps to explain why the annual schools tour, usually undertaken in early November, came to feature so prominently in their programme.

One factor, however, which became particularly important just after the First World War, helps to explain the decision to undertake these tours. They were an initiative aimed at halting the 'rush to rugby' in the public schools and in the grammar schools that sought to emulate them. Ross McKibbin has argued convincingly that this was an example of 'deliberate class-differentiation', a middle-class response to the perceived threat emanating from organized labour, which culminated in the General Strike of 1926.[72] There was, no doubt, an element of snobbery too, predisposing those seeking to achieve upward social mobility to spurn the game of the people. Those public schools that remained loyal to soccer were clearly in need of encouragement, not least because their fixture lists were shrinking.

54 Decline and fall

It was this worrying situation that prompted the Corinthians secretary, G.N. Foster, to write to a number of public schools in June 1919, indicating that the club 'would do all in its power to try to create new interest in the game'.[73] Some one-off matches were played early in the season, and a four-match tour was arranged for November taking in four schools – Aldenham, Repton, Shrewsbury and Malvern – in four days. Though it varied slightly from year to year, a pattern was thereby established. The initiative was, no doubt, welcomed by those schoolmasters who favoured soccer and the schoolboy enthusiasts in their care. Malvern College was delighted to inform *The Times* at the start of the 1919–20 season that it had arranged 'a good fixture card ... including a match against the Corinthians'. If its school magazine is a reliable guide, its soccer followers were not about to be disappointed. 'In the opinion of most people', it reported later, 'the match against the Corinthians was the best we have witnessed so far this season'. The first eleven 'did itself full credit', despite being well beaten.[74]

Match reports tended to tell much the same story as the post-war seasons unfolded, even though the Corinthians began to compartmentalize this activity, sending out an 'A' team for these fixtures. 'The visitors had a strong side which included seven Old Blues'; the school, though defeated, produced 'an excellent performance'. So ran a report from Shrewsbury; it was not untypical. From Malvern, after a 7-1 defeat: 'The display by the School side was very pleasing, the game being not nearly so one-sided as the score suggests'.[75] For the Corinthians, public-school matches, especially on tours when dinners could be taken together, were congenial events. Teams selected often included old boys of the schools visited, and there was a chance to enjoy the company of former players who had taken up appointments as schoolmasters, such as Kenneth Hunt at Highgate and Morgan-Owen at Repton. Personal connections seem to have played a very important part in the club's affairs. That Creek should have devoted a separate chapter of his official history to these autumnal ambles around the playing fields of England suggests that he considered them to have been an important aspect of the club's activities. Lessons were still being handed out as late as February 1938. Charterhouse, in a complacent frame of mind having just trounced their rivals Westminster, were beaten 6-2: 'the Corinthians showed them that they still had something to learn'.[76] In terms of stemming the stampede towards rugby union, however, the tours appeared to have little impact. After the FA had appointed a sub-committee in 1925 to investigate the problem and suggest solutions, Wall wrote a powerful letter to the pubic-school headmasters in an effort to secure their co-operation, but he received only the blandest of replies and the rush continued unabated.[77] There was a lesson here for the Corinthians. In visiting only those schools that still played soccer, they were preaching to the converted; they needed to relate to a wider public.

The Christmas-New Year tours to the provinces and Scotland were revived for a few seasons through to the mid-1920s, but the reluctance of clubs battling for league points or cup glory to take on additional fixtures at what was already a busy time of year changed the nature of the Corinthians' schedule. Whereas, in what were now regarded as the club's halcyon days, matches with professional clubs had featured prominently, the Corinthians now preferred to assemble at a London venue, playing an Isthmian League representative team before travelling north to meet opponents such as Northern Nomads and Yorkshire Amateurs, 'clubs established by gentleman amateurs ... in an attempt to solve that old provincial problem of getting enough gentlemen together to run a club on an ambitious and viable basis'.[78] When they moved on to Scotland, the Scottish Universities and a Scottish Amateur League XI awaited before the Corinthians played their New Year fixture with Queen's Park. This tradition had been re-invented in 1920 and for a few years drew impressive crowds, who 'went along to see amateur football at its best'. Yet it proved to be unsustainable now that Queen's Park were in the Scottish League. The Corinthians tended to arrive in Glasgow at a rather awkward time when their opponents were heavily engaged in 'the traditional New Year orgy of [Scottish] football with three games in five days'. The home side could not have relished the prospect of an additional friendly whatever its historical significance.[79] A match report from the early 1930s suggests that Corinthians had won because the home team failed to show 'the fire and sparkle which they do in League competition'. Not surprisingly, the Glasgow public lost interest. 'In former days', the *Scotsman* observed in 1932, 'the meeting of Queen's Park and the Corinthians attracted a crowd of at least 30,000, but at Hampden Park yesterday there was an attendance of only 5,000'.[80] The Corinthians would have to look beyond their traditional programme of tours and friendlies if they were to make a significant impact.

In 1922, they acquired a permanent home ground for the first time when they became joint-tenants at the Crystal Palace with the Casuals, another team of gentlemen amateurs, who played in the prestigious Isthmian League. The trustees welcomed their new tenants primarily because soccer promised to add something to the package already on offer. 'Much had been done to provide additional features for entertainment and amusement', it was claimed, and this included elite amateur soccer.[81] Providing 'occasions' to attract spectators to the vast arena became a priority, and the FA Cup offered a way to achieve this, albeit occasionally. The Corinthians entered the competition for the first time in 1922–23, losing to Brighton after three closely contested matches, but attracting a record home crowd of 20,000. In the following season, watched by an even bigger crowd, Blackburn Rovers were defeated, and it seemed for a short time that the decision to change the club's constitution to facilitate 'pot-hunting' had been entirely justified. 'It was courageous of the Corinthians to depart from their traditions ... to take a ground for home matches and to enter the [FA] Cup', observed the *Athletic News*, but it had been necessary 'for the sake of the club and the sake of amateur football'.[82] The only problem was that it could all be over so quickly, the famous victory over Blackburn being followed by a 5-0 defeat at West Bromwich Albion in the next round. Advancing beyond the third round – the stage at which they were allowed to enter the competition – proved difficult despite some brave performances. Yet, on looking back in 1933, Creek argued that FA Cup-ties, even though the Corinthians lost more often than they won, had resulted in valuable media exposure. A 'magnificent contest' with Newcastle United in 1927 had attracted a crowd of 56,000, and a match commentary had been broadcast by the BBC leading to an 'increased interest in amateur football'.[83] Less than a year after the crowds had flocked to the match with Newcastle, the Corinthians hosted a team representing the Royal Navy. 'On a bitterly cold afternoon', it was reported, 'not more than 500 people were present'.[84] The last Saturday before Christmas was notorious for poor gates, but there were too many instances when 'a small attendance' was reported to be complacent about the club's future.

Creek may have been partially correct in that press coverage, at least until the mid-1930s, was extensive and generally sympathetic. In 1928, the third round draw took them north to New Brighton, then members of the Football League Third Division North, where they were beaten. The 'Corinthian gallants' had tried to play 'the true classical game', claimed the *Athletic News*, but this had proved impossible on account of 'the deplorable ground conditions'.[85] When they achieved an unexpected and remarkable 5-0 victory at Norwich City a year later the reporter who covered this match for the *News* was ecstatic: 'Let me tell the story of this superb and glorious win; how the amateurs overcame the handicap of being a player short for the best part of the game; how they played football as it should be played'.[86] It seemed that the team that knocked Norwich out of the Cup were worthy successors to 'the famous amateurs of old' – W.N. Cobbold, 'the prince of dribblers', C.B, Fry and, inevitably, G.O. Smith. This performance generated interest at the time and even eighty years later when D. J. Taylor wrote about it at some length in his essay *On the Corinthian Spirit*, drawing on an account of the match in the *Eastern Daily Press*.[87] 'How far the Corinthians will be able to carry the amateurs' banner through the present competition will depend a great deal on the luck of the draw', it had observed astutely, thus pointing to the fundamental weakness of an awareness-raising exercise based on winning matches in a knock-out tournament. There was too much that could go wrong, as it did when the 'gallant amateurs' were beaten at West Ham in the next round. At least, according to the *Athletic News*, they had 'DIED LIKE GENTLEMEN', which was some kind of consolation.[88] It was a fate to which they became increasingly accustomed as the 1930s progressed.

In the early 1930s, especially at the time of the club's fiftieth anniversary in 1932, there was much brave talk. At the 'Jubilee Dinner', held characteristically at the upmarket Dorchester, the guest of honour, 'Pa' Jackson, spoke of the importance of remaining true to the principles on which the club had been founded before declaring 'that never would he grant himself an even conscience should they join the Football League'.[89] It was an unlikely prospect. An amateur club, the Argonauts, organized on less socially exclusive lines by ex-Corinthian Dick Sloley, had by then made unsuccessful applications to join the Football League Division Three South in 1928 and 1929.[90] The idea of amateurs taking on professionals week by week in England appealed to some sections of the sporting press who transferred their attention to the Corinthians after the Argonauts foundered. However, that Sloley found it necessary to form a new and rather different kind of organization to pursue this project suggests that the idea of the Corinthians flying the flag for amateurism in the Football League would have encountered significant resistance. Thus, they continued to rely almost entirely on the FA Cup to keep their version of amateur football in the public eye. Their resources stretched to the limit and no longer exempt from the early rounds they sent a hastily assembled side to Reading in November 1935 and lost 8-3. Under the ominous headline 'ECLIPSE OF THE CORINTHIANS', the once sympathetic *Morning Post* suggested that the club was no longer fit for purpose. 'If these Sir Galahads of football', it argued, 'are quixotic enough to think that they can assault the citadels of professionalism with no more training than that entailed in turning out a succession of scratch sides ... they must be prepared for defeat'.[91] Other amateur clubs, more pragmatic and less exclusive, were now better equipped than the Corinthians to make the case for amateurism, not least the Casuals, who won the FA Amateur Cup a few months later.

There were other indications that the Corinthian sun was setting. The Sheriff of London Shield match was revived, but Corinthian participation ended after two defeats by Arsenal in 1931 and 1932, their performance in the second match, which they lost 9-2, attracting severe criticism.[92] A few years later, the annual match with Queen's Park in Glasgow was played for the last time. It could no longer be regarded as a significant test of gentlemanly strength now that their opponents prioritized their Scottish League commitments. The Queen's Park team, it was reported, 'differed in several respects from that which beat Third Lanark on New Year's Day'.[93] Even the varsities could no longer be relied on to give more than lukewarm support. Reviewing the 1936–37 season, the Oxford soccer captain noted that the Corinthians had offered only one match instead of two, which had previously been the custom, thus giving the Dark Blues a spare Saturday to watch a professional match. 'This I think was a much better arrangement in every respect', he explained.[94] Abandoned by their friends and reliant on an increasingly fragile understanding with the Casuals to field any side worthy of the Corinthian heritage, the club was forced to accept the logic of its reduced circumstances.[95] After briefly considering and then quickly rejecting the impractical notion of applying for membership of the Football League's Third Division South – Jackson would have been horrified – the club ceded control of its affairs to a joint committee of Corinthians and Casuals in June 1937, before limping through two anti-climactic pre-war seasons in which it failed to advance beyond the first round of the FA Cup. For the Corinthians, it seemed, the game was up.

By 1939, the club that Jackson had founded fifty-seven years earlier had ceased to tour regularly in the United Kingdom. Its annual Easter tour had been abandoned as early as 1904 in favour of visits to Europe; its Christmas tours, much reduced in scope during the Great Split, did not survive the Great War. There were no 'A' team tours to the soccer-playing public schools after 1931, though some fixtures continued to be played on a one-off basis. As we have seen, the expansion of the English and Scottish League programmes from the late nineteenth century onwards made it progressively more difficult to arrange fixtures with professional clubs. Moreover, when such matches were arranged, it became more obvious, season by season, that the priorities of the professionals lay elsewhere, and even by 1914, the Corinthians were rarely confronted by opponents at full strength. However, we should not underestimate the favourable reputation that the Corinthians had established in their early tours when they gained some spectacular and well-publicized victories. This was occasionally reinforced in later years by creditable performances in the Charity Shield and the FA Cup. Though this could not be sustained, they had, in effect, created a sporting commodity that for a time continued to find a market overseas even as the club's reputation at home diminished.

Notes

1 *Sunday Times*, 9 January 1916.
2 Tony Mason, 'Sporting News, 1860–1914', in Michael Harris and Alan Lee, (eds), *The Press in English Society from the Seventeenth to Nineteenth Centuries* (London: Associated University Presses, 1986), pp. 184–85.
3 Kennedy Jones, *Fleet Street and Downing Street* (London: Hutchinson & Co., 1919), pp. 200–1.
4 Andrew Walker, 'Reporting Play: The Local Newspaper and Sports Journalism, c. 1870–1914', *Journalism Studies*, vol. 7, no. 3, 2006, 455–56.
5 *Pall Mall Gazette*, 31 December 1894; for the media's importance in constructing the Victorian sporting world, see Mike Huggins, *The Victorians and Sport* (London: Hambledon and London, 2004), pp. 141–67.
6 *Portsmouth Evening News*, 17 March 1900.
7 Record Office for Leicestershire, Leicester and Rutland, [LRO], 796.334, Ephemera – Football 1892–2009, Loughborough Corinthians, Menu and Programme, Annual Dinners 1903, 1906; *Leicester Chronicle*, 9 June 1900.
8 Glamorgan Archives, [GA], Cardiff Corinthians Association Football Club MSS, D 751/9/10, Cardiff Corinthians A.F.C.: A Short History, [n.d.].
9 *Western Mail* (Cardiff), 27 November 1899.
10 GA, Cardiff Corinthians AFC MSS, D 751/1, Minutes of Annual General Meetings, 22 July 1898, 2 August 1900, 25 August 1902, 16 August 1905.
11 GA, Cardiff Corinthians AFC MSS, D 751/9/10, A Short History [n.d.]; Martin Johnes, *Soccer and Society: South Wales 1900–1939* (Cardiff: University of Wales Press, 2002), p. 94.
12 *Dundee Evening Post*, 15 September 1900.
13 *Pall Mall Gazette*, 30 April 1900.
14 *Sportsman*, 27 April 1903.

15 Alfred Gibson and William Pickford, *Association Football & the Men Who Made It* (London: The Caxton Press, 1906), vol. 3, p. 66.
16 F.N.S. Creek, *A History of the Corinthian Football Club* (London: Longmans, Green & Co., 1933), p. 38; see also Terry Morris, *In a Class of Their Own: A History of English Amateur Football* (Sheffield: Chequered Flag Publishing, 2015), pp. 170–71.
17 B.O. Corbett, (ed), *Annals of the Corinthian Football Club* (London: Longmans, Green & Co., 1906), p. 22.
18 *Sportsman*, 17 April 1900.
19 *Sportsman*, 28, 29, 30 December 1904.
20 Everton Collection @evertoncollection.org.uk, Board of Directors Minutes, 22 December 1906. The end of season list of results includes the fixture with the Corinthians on 27 December as both a first team and a reserve team match.
21 *Sunday Times*, 15 March 1903; 17 January 1904.
22 Robert Crampsey, *The Game for the Game's Sake. The History of Queen's Park Football Club 1867–1967*, (Glasgow: Queen's Park FC, 1967), p. 40.
23 *Sports Illustrated* (Sheffield), 16 March 1898.
24 *Sheffield Daily Telegraph*, 5 April 1898.
25 *The Times, Sheffield Daily Telegraph*, 6 April 1898. Ernest Needham, *Association Football* (Cleethorpes: Soccer Books Ltd., 2003, first published 1901), p. 17; first published in 1901.
26 *Birmingham Daily Post*, 9 November 1899.
27 *Daily Argus* (Birmingham); *Athletic News* (Manchester), 4 March 1901.
28 *The Times*, 2 March 1903; see also Creek, *History of the Corinthians*, pp. 40–1.
29 *Athletic News*, 2 March 1903.
30 Creek, *History of the Corinthians*, p. 41; Colin Weir, *The History of Cambridge University Association Football Club 1872–2003* (Harefield: Yore Publications, 2004), pp. 22–3.
31 Edward Grayson, *Corinthians & Cricketers* (London: Sportsmans Book Club, 1957), pp. 137–39.
32 *The Times*, 7 March 1904.
33 *Bury Guardian*, 12 March 1904.
34 Geoffrey Green, *Soccer the World Game: A Popular History* (London: Pan Books Ltd., 1953), p. 74.
35 *Athletic News*, 7 March 1904.
36 *Newcastle Daily Chronicle*, 11 March 1907.
37 Gibson and Pickford, *Association Football & the Men Who Made It*, vol. 3, p. 66.
38 For the split see Dilwyn Porter, 'The Revenge of the Crouch End Vampires: The AFA, the FA and English Football's "Great Split", 1907–14', *Sport in History*, vol. 26, no. 3, 2006, pp. 406–28; also Morris, *In a Class of Their Own*, pp. 173–88.
39 W.E. Greenland, *The History of the Amateur Football Alliance* (Harwich: Standard Publishing Co., 1965), p. 22; Porter, 'Revenge of the Crouch End Vampires', pp. 413–14.
40 *Sportsman*, 9 July 1907; report of Hughes-Onslow's speech at the first meeting of the AFA.
41 Sir Frederick Wall, *50 Years of Football 1884–1934* (Cleethorpes: Soccer Books Ltd., 2006; first published, London 1935). p. 55.
42 *Sportsman*, 22 June 1907; letter from Mr J.R. Jones (Aylesbury).
43 Morris, *In a Class of Their Own*, pp. 179–80.
44 Geoffrey Green, 'The Football Association', in A.H. Fabian and Geoffrey Green, (eds), *Association Football*, (London: Caxton Publishing Co., 1960), vol. 1, p. 79.
45 Greenland, *History of the Amateur Football Alliance*, pp. 26–8.
46 *Athletic News*, 17 June 1907.

47 Tony Collins, *A Social History of English Rugby Union* (Abingdon: Routledge, 2009), p. 45.
48 *Sportsman*, 18, 19 June 1907.
49 *Sportsman*, 28, 31 December 1906; 1, 2 January 1907.
50 *Sportsman*, 27, 28, 30, 31 December 1907.
51 *Sportsman*, 3 January 1910; John Eastwood and Tony Moyse, *The Men Who Made the Town: The Official History of Ipswich Town F.C. since 1878* (Sudbury: Almeida Books, 1986), pp. 52–4.
52 National Football Museum [NFM], Football Association [FA], Minutes of Council, 4 October 1907, item 9.
53 National Library of Wales (NLW), Football Association of Wales, Minutes of Council, 20 November 1907.
54 *Sunday Times*, 13 October 1907.
55 NFM, FA, Minutes of Council, 4 November 1907, item 20.
56 *Athletic News*, 8 July 1907.
57 Gibson and Pickford, *Association Football & the Men Who Made It*, vol. 3, p. 66.
58 *Football Evening News* (London), 19 September 1908.
59 Eastwood and Moyse, *Men Who Made the Town*, pp. 52–3.
60 *Football Evening News*, 31 October 1908.
61 *Sportsman*, 29 December 1909.
62 Bodleian Library (BOD), Oxford University Association Football Club [OUAFC] MSS, Dep. d.822-824, Correspondence and Papers, Ian Campbell to C.N. Jackson, 10 November 1912.
63 For the AFA-FA reconciliation, see Porter, 'Revenge of the Crouch End Vampires', pp. 421–24.
64 *Sunday Times*, 7 December 1913.
65 *Sportsman*, 28 April 1914.
66 *The Cholmeleian*, vol. XXXIX, no. 209. November 1919, pp. 164, 169–70.
67 Creek, *History of the Corinthians*, p. 48.
68 Morris, *In a Class of Their Own*, p. 166.
69 *The Times*, 3 January 1910.
70 See Norman Jacobs, *Vivian Woodward: Football's Gentleman* (Stroud: Tempus, 2005), pp. 175–83.
71 For this connection, see J.A. Mangan, 'Introduction: Complicated Matters', in J.A. Mangan, (ed), *A Sport-Loving Society: Victorian and Edwardian Middle Class England at Play* (Abingdon: Routledge, 2006), p. 4.
72 Ross McKibbin, *Classes and Cultures: England 1918–1951* (Oxford: Oxford University Press, 1998), pp. 350–51; see also Collins, *Social History of English Rugby Union*, pp. 66–8.
73 Creek, *History of the Corinthians*, p. 143.
74 *The Times*, 21 October 1919, *The Malvernian*, no. CCCLXXIV, December 1919, p. 716.
75 *The Salopian*, vol. XLV, no. 3, 14 November 1926, no. 455, pp. 55; *The Malvernian*, no. CCCCXL, December 1932, p. 9.
76 *The Carthusian*, vol. XVII, no. 5, February 1938, p. 800.
77 NFM, FA, Minutes of Council, 31 August 1925, item 15; copy of letter from Frederick Wall to W.A. Bulkley Evans, secretary of the Headmasters' Conference, 6 August 1925; Minutes of Council, 22 February 1926, item 9, report of reply received in December 1925.
78 Morris, *In a Class of Their Own*, pp. 222–23.
79 Crampsey, *The Game for the Game's Sake*, pp. 41, 204–8.
80 *Scotsman* (Edinburgh), 2 January 1931, 5 January 1932.

81 London Metropolitan Archives [LMA], CPT/001, Crystal Palace Trustees, Minutes of the 8th annual meeting, 1 December 1922. For the arrangement with Casuals, see Rob Cavallini, *A Casual Affair: A History of the Casuals Football Club* (Surbiton: Dog N Duck Publications, 2009), pp. 102–3.
82 *Athletic News*, 12 January 1924.
83 Creek, *History of the Corinthians*, pp. 151–52.
84 *Sunday Times*, 18 December 1927.
85 *Athletic News*, 16 January 1928.
86 *Athletic News*, 14 January 1929.
87 D.J. Taylor, *On the Corinthian Spirit: The Decline of Amateurism in Sport* (London: Yellow Jersey Press, 2006), pp. 5–12.
88 *Athletic News*, 28 January 1929.
89 *The Times*, 27 October 1932.
90 See Matthew Taylor, *The Leaguers: The Making of Professional Football in England, 1900–1939* (Liverpool: Liverpool University Press, 2005), p. 27; also Steve Menary, 'In Search of the Argonauts', *Soccer History*, no. 27, 2011, pp. 7–13.
91 *Morning Post*, 2 December 1935.
92 Rob Cavallini, *Play Up Corinth: A History of the Corinthian Football Club* (Stroud: Stadia, 2007), pp. 183–84.
93 *Morning Post*, 3 January 1936.
94 BOD, OUAFC MSS, Dep.d.824, Annals Book, Captain's Review of Season 1936–37.
95 Rob Cavallini, *A Casual Affair*, pp. 181–82.

3 'Missionaries of Empire'

The Corinthians on tour in South Africa

Figure 3.1 Corinthians v Orange River Colony, Bloemfontein, 24 July 1907.
Karel Schoeman, *Bloemfontein in Beeld, 1860–1910* (Cape Town: Human & Rousseau, 1987).

In 1806, the British replaced the Dutch as the colonial power in the Cape Colony. With the abolition of slavery in 1834, a serious drought and increased British control, *Voortrekkers* from the Dutch/Boer settler community trekked from the British-dominated Cape into the interior of the country. The South African Republic (Transvaal) and the Orange Free State Republic were established. By the 1850s, London recognized the two fledgling Boer Republics. This independence was short-lived, Britain annexing the Transvaal in 1877, though the republic regained control after the Anglo-Transvaal War (1880–81). The discovery of diamonds in 1867 and gold in 1886 changed the political, economic and social landscapes of South Africa and intensified Anglo-Boer rivalry. The South African War (1899–1902) was the most costly war fought by the British between 1815 and 1914. An outcome of the war was the Union of South Africa, which consolidated white control with allegiance to Britain in 1910. Thus, the Corinthians – who visited in 1897, 1903 and 1907 – toured South Africa at an especially critical juncture in its history.

Despite the political independence of the Boer Republics prior to the South African War, British traders and prospectors engaged in commercial activities in both the Orange Free State and Transvaal. The British presence was boosted by a large influx of British soldiers into South Africa from the late 1870s and by traders who travelled from the Cape Colony and Natal Colony into the Boer Republics. Their influence was not limited to commerce alone. In sporting terms, British teams, clubs and associations were established across the Orange Free State and Transvaal, and they helped to popularize, spread and institutionalize soccer among black and white South Africans. Soccer was not only played by rank-and-file soldiers, miners, traders and artisans, but also by military officers, civil servants and by officials and clerks in the mining and banking sectors too. Though rugby was to become the sport of the English-speaking white elite and white Afrikaners more generally after the First World War, a strong soccer presence was evident from the late nineteenth century onwards. Schools were established across South Africa primarily for white children but in certain instances for black children too. These were modelled on the British public-school system, and this helped to popularize both major football codes in winter and cricket in summer.

Soccer was first played in Natal in 1866, and the colony was considered the 'the home of the game in South Africa'.[1] Clubs such as Pietermaritzburg County Football Club and the Natal Wasps Football Club were established in 1880.[2] The Natal Football Association, the first such soccer organization in South Africa, was established in 1882. The discovery of gold on the Witwatersrand in 1886 saw the game spread to the Transvaal. Teams such as the Alpha Club, Nondescripts, All-Comers, Neer-do-Wells and Pretoria Swifts were established. The Transvaal Football Association was established in 1889. Soccer was not restricted to whites in the Transvaal. Indians formed teams such as the Star of India, Moonlighters, Western Star and the Standard. The Transvaal Indian Football Association was established in 1896, while the South African Indian Football Association was formed in 1903. In Cape Town, rugby remained the most popular of the football codes. Military teams such as the Royal Artillery, York and Lancaster formed the Western Province Football Association (WPFA) in 1890. Soccer was played as early as 1877 in Bloemfontein, and in 1894, the Orange Free State Football Association (OFSFA) was formed.[3] Many soccer officials were also involved in the administration of cricket during the summer months. The Cape Colony Prime Minister Cecil John Rhodes was made honorary president of the OFSFA in 1894, and Presidents Paul Kruger of the Transvaal and Francis Reitz of the Orange Free State were patrons of the association.

Several national, whites-only sports organizations were established in the late 1880s and early 1890s in South Africa. These included associations for cricket, rugby and soccer. The South African Cricket Association (SACA) and the South African Rugby Board (SARB) were formed in 1889. The South African Football Association (SAFA) and the South African Cyclists'

Union were established in 1892 and the South African Amateur Athletic Association in 1894. SAFA applied to the English Football Association (FA) for affiliation in 1897, and this was granted. A SAFA representative was based in London, attended FA meetings and canvassed support for tours to and from Britain. White national sports bodies received the patronage of Sir Donald Currie, the shipping magnate, who donated trophies to these organizations for inter-provincial competitions. Sports associations set out to host touring sides and send South African teams to Britain. The aims were to popularize the game at home, to improve the standard of play, to foster and maintain the links between South Africa and Britain and, significantly, to generate profits for local associations.

Sports tours between Britain and South Africa

South Africa became an important destination for touring British sports team from the 1880s onwards. In cricket, an English eleven captained by R.G. Warton toured South Africa in 1888–89.[4] A second English team captained by W.W. Read toured in 1891–92, and Lord Hawke's teams followed in 1895–96 and 1898–99. South African cricket sides toured England in 1894, 1901, 1904 and 1907. In rugby, W.E. Maclagan led a side comprised of English and Scottish players to South Africa in 1891; a second British side toured in 1896 and 1903. In return, a South African rugby team toured Britain and France in 1906. These tours fostered important sporting links that generated profits for the associations. The tourists travelled across South Africa including the Boer Republics. They played a crucial political role in consolidating notions of the British Empire and fostered an emerging white South African identity, particularly after the South African War.[5] Between 1897 and 1907, five soccer tours to and from South Africa took place. These contributed to the development of the game in South Africa among both black and white soccer players. Despite the outbreak of the South African War in 1899, soccer remained popular and grew, particularly after the arrival of thousands of British troops. Prior to the outbreak of war in 1899, a black soccer team from Bloemfontein travelled to Europe under the auspices of the OFSFA.[6] After the war, in 1906, a representative white South African side played in Argentina, Brazil and Uruguay.[7]

In 1895, SAFA wrote to 'Pa' Jackson, assistant secretary of the FA and secretary of the Corinthians Football Club and asked him to arrange for an English team to visit South Africa. He replied that he was keen to bring out a team that would include English internationals, such as G.O. Smith. SAFA discussed at length the merits of bringing out a touring team from England and decided to invite a team of amateurs. This decision was not unanimous, as delegates from the soccer associations of Griqualand West, the Orange Free State and Western Province wanted a professional side visit the country instead as this could potentially bring in more revenues for local coffers. Jackson and SAFA agreed that the Corinthian Football Club would tour South Africa in 1897, the first by a British club outside of Europe. The South African association pledged to pay all travelling and hotel costs, but it was noted that the Corinthian committee 'think it will be better for the members to adhere to the Corinthian rules and pay for their own wines and spirits'.[8] The journal *South Africa* suggested that the tour 'will succeed in greatly enhancing the popularity of the game, which in South Africa is in comparatively backward condition, Rugby being the general favourite'.[9] Rugby was indeed popular in South Africa at this time, but this was primarily limited to the Cape Colony in towns such as Cape Town, Stellenbosch and Kimberley.

The Corinthian Football Club visited South Africa on three occasions. Their tours were instrumental in popularizing soccer in the country, and the visitors were generally well received. The first tour in 1897, which took place shortly after the ill-fated Jameson Raid and before the outbreak of war, was a modest success. The second tour, in 1903, occurred at the height of post-war euphoria and enthusiasm for empire in Britain and South Africa, and large crowds watched the tourists. The final tour, in 1907, saw the South Africans more generally disenchanted by a second-class touring team who were keen to push their own agenda of amateurism, as the crisis leading to English soccer's Great Split developed at home.

The 1897 tour: 'Rhodes's men?'

Prior to the arrival of the Corinthian team in Cape Town, the local press highlighted concerns about the cost of the tour. SAFA proposed that each centre where the matches were to be staged should guarantee a proportion of the projected costs and that centres generating profits should contribute 75 per cent of this to the national body. This money would be used to make up any losses and to pay for South African players' travel expenses in representative matches. The costs of the tour were predicted to be £2200, while guarantees amounted to £1900.[10] The WPFA and other centres 'strongly objected' and suggested 'each centre stand on its own bottom'. SAFA also requested money for the fares of the visiting team, which the WPFA declined to hand any over until financial arrangements had been made. This dispute was eventually resolved through the intervention of Englishman George A. Parker, secretary of both SAFA and SACA, who had secured a guarantee from the former Cape Colony prime minister and mining baron Cecil Rhodes to cover half of the expenses of the tour. Parker stated that the guarantee from Rhodes was to cover the return passage of the team. By the end of the tour, Parker claimed that Rhodes had guaranteed 'the whole expenses of the Corinthians, somewhat over £2,000 but it is satisfactory to know that [SAFA] will in all probability come out satisfactorily as regards finances'.[11]

Typically Jackson, in his autobiography, claimed credit for arranging the Corinthians' first South African tour, though he did acknowledge Parker's 'valuable assistance'.[12] Parker, however, was probably the key figure both in

1897 and 1903. In England, he had been an active sportsman in the 1880s and 1890s. After Chesterfield Grammar School in Derbyshire, he moved to London where he became well known in soccer circles, playing for the Clapton and Polytechnic Clubs, winning London and Middlesex Cup Honours in 1889, and representing Middlesex at county level. He was also keen cricketer and played against the M.C.C. at Lords. Parker moved to South Africa in the early 1890s. He was appointed the honorary secretary of the South African Football and Cricket Associations in 1894. Thus, he was well qualified to edit *South African Sports*, published in 1897. He captained Transvaal in their soccer match against the Corinthians in Johannesburg in 1897 while managing the tourists on their visits to South Africa in 1897 and 1903, respectively.

At the first game against a Cape Town Civilian XI at Newlands, only 800 spectators were in attendance, even though government offices had closed early to permit civil servants to attend the match and the railway department had issued return tickets to Newlands, where the match was played, for the price of singles. The *Cape Argus* reported that 'planks will be laid along the sides of the field so that the ladies attending the match will not have to suffer the discomfort of standing on the damp ground'. It also referred to the Corinthian team as '*Uitlanders*', the Dutch term used to refer to white non-Afrikaner foreigners in the Transvaal.[13] At a banquet in Cape Town, the vice-president of the WPFA, Rev J.W. Leary, thanked the team from the 'Old Country' and remarked that 'they had [by now] doubtless come to know that South Africa was not exactly a land of savages'. Simkins, president of the Western Province Rugby Union, declared that rugby followers were pleased to welcome their 'sister code' to South Africa and claimed that 'there was no ill-feeling between the followers of the rival codes'. As long as professionalism could be kept at bay, both codes would prosper.[14] He was, no doubt, aware that this would be well received by the distinguished visitors who could claim with some justification to be the world's most famous amateur club at this time.

The team then embarked on their journey to Transvaal where they would play a series of five games. Tensions remained high after the abortive Jameson Raid of 1895. Leander Starr Jameson, a close friend of Rhodes, had led an ill-fated party into the Transvaal to overthrow the Kruger government. Rhodes commissioned Jameson to lead the attack, while *Uitlanders* in Johannesburg were expected to revolt against Boer control. The raid was repulsed, and the uprising never materialized. As a result, Jameson was imprisoned, Rhodes was forced to resign as prime minister, and the Transvaal forged closer links with the Orange Free State in anticipation of war with Britain. Against the Old Natalians at the Wanderers Ground in central Johannesburg, the Corinthians, having won all their previous matches in South Africa comfortably, were held to a draw for the first time on tour. The *Star* commented that 'these games should do a great deal to develop the taste for the Association code on the Rand'.[15] Before the game against a Pretoria XI, the tourists were entertained at the exclusive Pretoria Club and visited President Kruger of the Transvaal who asked whether the Corinthians 'were Rhodes's men', in reference to the Jameson Raid. The captain, Robert Topham, diplomatically replied 'No', an answer with which Kruger 'seemed much pleased'.[16] Lord Hawke's cricketers had previously visited Abe Bailey and Lionel Philips, both implicated in the Raid, in their Pretoria jail in January 1896.[17] They had also visited the site of the surrender of Jameson's raiders at Doornkop and collected souvenirs.[18] Later that year, John Hammond's touring rugby team also hunted for souvenirs at Doornkop and visited Sampson and Davis, two more of Jameson's men, in prison.[19] Topham and Kruger discussed soccer in general, but the president declined an invitation to kick-off the match, joking that 'he had still further use for his legs, and did not want them amputated yet'. Kruger informed G. Meintjes, a member of the *Volksraad* [parliament], 'that if any of the boys are harmed he would have them put in *tronk* [prison]'.[20] The final game in the Transvaal was played against a South African representative team comprised of six players from the Transvaal, two each from Natal and Border and one from the Western Province. Over 5,000 spectators saw the tourists win 3-1 against a side that 'had given a very disappointing account of themselves [and] played a poor game'.[21]

The tourists then travelled to Natal to play four games in the Colony. In preparation for their fixture, the Maritzburg District Football Association (MDFA) agreed to charge 2 shillings (2s) per adult for the match. The local population were outraged, even though the association reminded them that for the visit by the British rugby team the year before tickets had been priced at 2 shillings and six pence (2s 6d), 25 per cent more expensive. According to the *Natal Mercury*, the guarantee for the Pietermaritzburg game was withdrawn, 'and it was decided to give the visitors the whole of the gate less expenses'.[22] In the same newspaper two days later, it was reported that gate receipts had amounted to £97 10s and that the original guaranteed amount of £87 10s had been paid over to SAFA.[23] In addition, a collection box was placed at an entrance to the ground to defray expenses, and this had 'afforded the rank-and-file a chance to do their whack'.[24] Thus, despite being an amateur team on tour, the Corinthian side were able to take home good gate receipts. In due course, the question of what the Corinthians did with the money that came their way via gate receipts and guarantees was to become an issue, just as it had been for Arthur Hornby and other critics back in England a few years earlier.

In Pietermaritzburg, a crowd of 1,000 spectators saw the local team restrict the Corinthians to a single goal, sufficient to continue their winning run, but their narrowest victory on the tour to date. The determination of their South African hosts to secure a victory against their prestigious visitors was indicated by the selection of Charles Bennett 'Buck' Llewellyn of the Swifts. Llewellyn, better known as a cricketer who represented South Africa in fifteen tests, 'played cricket in Natal as a white man, although he was employed ... in Durban as a coloured clerk'.[25] His selection was significant as strict segregation based on race was adhered to across all aspects of South African society and in sport in particular. It suggests that on this occasion, his class status and sporting ability trumped his racial classification. While in Pietermaritzburg, the team visited Zulu Chief Teteleku's *kraal* for a native dance and were entertained by British officers at Fort Napier.[26] The Corinthians then moved on to Durban where 5,000 attended a game against Natal at the Lord's ground that ended in a 2-2 draw.[27] Again, there is no doubt that the hosts were determined to achieve a good result against their formidable opponents. The *Natal Witness* reported

> a scene of wildest excitement, the crowd breaking from all parts of the ground and cheering wildly, white hats and sticks were thrown into the air, and an attempts was made to "chair" the principal members of the Natal team.[28]

Despite the result, Topham was unimpressed, claiming that South African teams were no better than English Second Division sides and that he 'did not hold much encouragement for [South African sides] ... visiting England'.[29]

Once again, the tourists were treated as distinguished visitors. They were made honorary gentlemen of the Durban Club, met with the Mayor, Benjamin Wesley Greenacre, and were entertained by prominent Durban business personalities including Marshall Campbell, the sugar industry magnate. In Port Elizabeth, shops closed early so that employees could attend the game. Despite the home side losing 3-0, the *Telegraph and Eastern Province Standard* noted that they had 'made a far better display against a visiting English team than any other local cricket or Rugby team as hitherto done'.[30] While the *Eastern Province Herald* reported

> no one cares to witness a one-sided game, few people will pay the gate fee to do so, ... the match was a tough one ... the Corinthians rather overdid the passing game ... their display will do much to increase the interest in Association football in the Province.[31]

The tourists departed Durban for the Orange Free State Republic where, prior to the game played at the Recreation Ground in Bloemfontein, the *De Express en Oranjevrijstatsche Advertentieblad* billed the game as 'England vs Free State'. At the evening banquet in Bloemfontein, president Steyn was in attendance and the Orange Free State anthem the '*Volkslied*' was sung, followed by 'God Save the Queen'. In Kimberley, an admission price of 3s 6d was charged, and spectators were encouraged to travel from towns such as De Aar and Vryburg, both over 200 kilometres from Kimberley at reduced train fares.

The 1897 tour was a success; large crowds watched the Corinthians go undefeated against opposition of varying standards and ability across South

Africa. The Corinthian's dominance on the field followed an established pattern. During the 1891 British rugby tour of South Africa, the visitors went undefeated too. Jackson claimed the Corinthians 'were much too strong for the colonists, but the latter displayed a capital knowledge of the game, with every prospect of improvement'.[32] The Transvaal FA wrote that the home teams 'had shown some remarkably good play, and proved themselves not to be so far behind as many thought previously'.[33] Despite the large crowds and handsome profits generated for the visiting team, SAFA recorded a deficit of £186 15s 5d for the tour.[34] South Africa represented an attractive touring option for the Corinthians. On the pitch, they dominated – winning twenty-one and drawing only two of their twenty-three matches – and off the field they received first-class treatment, stayed in luxury hotels and were fêted by mayors and town dignitaries at banquets across the country. Unsurprisingly they returned, though the South African War delayed their second visit.

The 1903 tour: 'a very fair representative lot of the best of the "Varsities and public schools"'

The South African War broke out in October 1899 when Boer forces launched pre-emptive strikes against the British in the Cape and Natal. Within a year, the capitals of the Orange Free State and the Transvaal, Bloemfontein and Pretoria, respectively, fell into British hands. The South African War ended in May 1902. During the first two years of the war, SAFA did not meet and the nationally organized Currie Cup competition was suspended. SAFA met in September 1901 and discussed an English team visit in 1902.[35] Parker wrote to SAFA and suggested an English team comprising of players from the Corinthian, Casual and Clapton soccer clubs visit South Africa and receive two-thirds of the gate money.[36] SAFA declined the suggestion and invited the Corinthian team to tour South Africa in 1903 instead. On their arrival in Cape Town in July 1903, captain Wreford-Brown claimed that 'the present Corinthian team may not be the best combination of English amateurs procurable, but they are undoubtedly a very fair representative lot of the best of the "Varsities and public schools"'. He reiterated the point made by Topham during the 1897 tour 'that the club shall not participate in any pecuniary profits of Colonial tours, only personal expenses therein accepted'.[37] Once again, their South African hosts were determined to ensure that the tour was a success. After the poor turnouts for Corinthian games in Cape Town in 1897, all rugby matches were cancelled to encourage large attendances, and the Corinthians were watched by crowds of 5,500 and 8,000 in their two matches.[38] A week later, the soccer authorities reciprocated, cancelling matches so as not to clash with the visit of the British rugby tourists who attracted crowds of 8,000 and 12,000 to their first two games.

In a drawn game in Bloemfontein against the Orange River Colony in front of 4,000 spectators, the locals included four British Army players, one being John McPherson, a Scottish international and former Nottingham Forrest player.[39] A local newspaper, the *Friend*, reported that women attending the match had remarked 'that Soccer was a much superior game to Rugby; there was science in it, as they did not take hold of the ball and run away with it, which anyone can do'.[40] The *Bloemfontein Post* reported that the two games in the town against 'our cousins from the Old Country' had generated gates of £134 and £160, respectively.[41] The tourists progressed to the Transvaal, since the war a colony, where they played five games, the first against a South African XI at the Wanderers Ground in front of 7,000 spectators, including Lord Milner, Governor of the Transvaal and Orange River Colony. Moving on to Natal, the Corinthians played in Ladysmith, Pietermaritzburg and Durban. While in Northern Natal, the team visited various South African War battlefields and viewed a collection of shells from the siege of Ladysmith. In Pietermaritzburg, 3,000 spectators, including Chief Justice Sir Henry Bale and Prime Minister of Natal Sir Albert Hime, watched the game. The *Natal Mercury* reported that

> ... the play of the Corinthians ... it is pretty, neat, and scientifically attractive. Passing is seen of such character as is never seen except in a first-class match [and they] do not appear to be working to any great extent... [they] practically wear down their opponents ... the ball ... is sent to the toe of some particular player for some special purpose. The game as played by the visitors is, of a truth, very like a huge game of chess ... it is amusing often to see the ball sent between the legs of an opponent; in fact, the visitors seem to control the soccer, and place it here and there, just as polished bat will place a cricket ball.[42]

They were, it seemed, perfect ambassadors, ideally equipped to charm a country that had so recently been torn apart by war with their superior soccer skills.

The match report was not entirely uncritical claiming that the referee had stopped play on occasions as the visitors seemed to 'use their weight, and believe in the good old fashioned shoulder-to-shoulder charge'. In Natal, it was noted, '[we] are very strict, and to minimise the chance of accidents ... consider charging unnecessary'. Despite this difference of opinion, goodwill reigned at the post-match banquet held in the Pietermaritzburg Town Hall where Hime declared that 'visits did good, cementing the friendships between them as sportsmen, and also as Colonists'. He argued that the South African War had brought the Colonialists together and that the Corinthian team was doing the same in a 'peaceful manner'. Wreford-Brown noted that Natal seemed to be very in touch with Britain and, perhaps anticipating criticism, made a point of stating that the 'Corinthians were the guests of the country. They had come out to develop the game – the game they loved – and his club would not accept any penny profit, but any profit would be divided amongst the different Associations'. He also defended his team's robust tactics by explaining that 'Public School Boys always maintained that fair and square shoulder-to-shoulder charging was quite legitimate'.[43] On balance, the visit to Natal could be adjudged a great success for both hosts and visitors. In Durban, over forty firms had agreed to close their doors early so that employees could attend the matches, and 6,000 people witnessed the Corinthians lose their first game in South Africa to a Durban XI. The gate generated £300.[44]

The tourists sailed to the Western Cape where they played and won a further eight games.[45] The lavish hospitality continued. After one match at Grahamstown, the team were entertained at a private home, which was 'a great success, in fact during the whole stay in Grahamstown the inhabitants, especially the ladies were most hospitable and kind to the Corinthians so that some were very loth to leave'. Members of the team also went on a hunting trip.[46] At the Beach Hotel banquet in Port Elizabeth after the game against Eastern Province, the Mayor, J.C. Kemsley, stated:

> The visit of the Corinthian team was infinitely more importance [sic] than a series of wins or losses. Football was admittedly the most popular game played to-day in the British Empire, but the magnificent exposition by the visitors ... the visit of an English team would become an absolute education ... to study the latest developments of the science of the game in the Motherland ... brings in to close touch and fellowship the manhood of the Colonies. Friendships are formed, sympathies evoked, and understandings arrived at which will play no unimportant part in that great federation of the Empire which all are so anxious for.[47]

In his speech at their final banquet, Wreford-Brown 'hoped that footballers in South Africa had benefitted by this visit of the Corinthians for he was quite sure that they had themselves benefitted from their travels and experiences'.[48] He suggested that South African soccer had made great progress since their first tour but complained about the great distances the team had travelled across the country and about the state of many of the pitches. He noted that on good pitches their winning margins were much higher. The Corinthian team had played twenty-five matches, winning twenty-two, drawing two and losing only one; seventy-eight goals had been scored and only eighteen conceded. On their return to Britain, they were asked: 'You had a rattling good time I imagine?' The answer:

> rather ... everywhere we went we were treated right royally and wherever there was a municipality the Mayor and Corporation and civic functionaries welcomed us. We were banqueted, fêted entertained at smoking concerts, invited to dances and we had a splendid time.[49]

In 1903, as on the 1897 tour, the Corinthians played against inferior opposition throughout. However, they did lose one match against Durban and drew against Bloemfontein and Johannesburg. In many speeches and public declarations, the Corinthians are portrayed as 'missionaries of Empire', a significant description in a context of a country that was dealing with the aftermath of the South African War and a reminder that the tour inevitably had a political dimension.

The 1907 tour: 'the splendid apostles of amateur football'

In November 1904, SAFA resigned from the FA so as to permit former professional soccer players to play in South Africa's amateur leagues.[50] In 1905, John Bentley, president of the Football League, wrote to SAFA and offered to bring out a team of professional players during the 1906 season.[51] This offer was turned down by SAFA, and it was resolved to invite the Corinthians to tour South Africa again in 1907, a clear indication that their hosts regarded the 1903 visit as a success. The Corinthians indicated to SAFA that the side to tour the country would consist solely of Oxford and Cambridge players. SAFA concluded that this side would not be as strong as had been anticipated and wrote to the Corinthians' secretary, W.U. Timmis, requesting a 'strong combination' equal to the strength of the side that toured the United States in 1906.

In the build-up to the 1907 Corinthian tour of South Africa, the *Cape Times* wrote that

> Socker (*sic*) enthusiasts ... somewhat dispirited by the phenomenal success of the Rugger exponents in the United Kingdom [during their 1906 tour], plucked up their courage, and biding their time cheered with the others when the Springboks beat Wales, and were disappointed when news of the defeats by Scotland and Cardiff came to hand.[52]

The *Cape Times* failed to acknowledge the overwhelming successes of the 1906 soccer tour to South America, revealing their bias and preference for rugby. It revealed its preference for amateurism in sport claiming that soccer was not worth playing when done so to protect professionals who had turned soccer from a '...robust, manly pastime into an exhibition of clever foot-manipulation where a [sic] honest charge is anathema'. The newspaper maintained that rugby and soccer could both prosper in South Africa:

> ... so long as they remain amateur pastimes in every sense of the word. We have no time though, cash or population for professional sport, and young South Africa, imbued with the true amateur sporting spirit, welcomes the splendid apostles of amateur football ... will show us that amateur sport in the Old Country is by no means dead. ... They are fighting for a principle.[53]

There was, it seemed, some sympathy in South Africa for the Corinthians and the gentlemen of the Amateur Football Association.

But touring could be a serious business. The *Cape Times* claimed that the team was 'not in the habit of looking upon their missionary enterprises merely as holiday tours'.[54] In his welcome address to the team on its arrival in South Africa, the Mayor of Cape Town, William Baxter, observed that they were 'visiting a country in which the principles of amateurism which have always guided the Corinthians Club, are very jealously guarded, and in which professionalism plays no part'.[55] Corinthians' vice-captain R.D. Craig addressed the opening function and stated the case for amateur soccer in Britain and requested the support of SAFA in their struggle. It was reported in the *Athletic News* that Craig had made a 'rare fighting speech', claiming that the FA was 'imbued ... with a commercial spirit'.[56] Perhaps significantly, it was reported after the opening match that 'one cannot help notice the different types of spectators we are having today: Racing men, yachtsmen, men of the motor-car ... [while] His Majesty's forces were well represented and men of the cloth'.[57] In view of the stand that the Corinthians were making for gentlemanly amateurism at home in 1907, this was, no doubt, gratifying, and it may have encouraged them to resort to an exaggerated display of gentlemanly behaviour on the field of play. During their second game in the Cape, the visitors were awarded a penalty and Rowlandson 'purposely kicked the ball behind'.[58] Similar incidents occurred during games in the Transvaal and Natal. By the time they returned to Bloemfontein, SAFA had requested the visitors respect the decisions of the referees and 'that no further bursts of chivalry would rouse the gallery to frantic enthusiasm and that the laws and the rulings of the referees would be obeyed'.[59] The Corinthians complied with this request having made their point, but their performances generally were disappointing. The *Sunday Times* (Johannesburg) headed with 'Corinthians badly beaten', and a *Rand Daily Mail* headline posed the question: 'The Corinthians Crumpled?'[60] The *Mail* went on to suggest that Transvaal soccer would be best served if the Corinthians side avoided defeat in their build up to their games on the Witwatersrand so as to maintain maximum interest in the tour and generate profits from matches.

The recent war continued to cast a shadow. In Kimberley, the Corinthian vice-captain, R. D. Craig, declared that they were delighted to be in the town 'which inscribed its name so indelibly on the records of Empire during the war', a reference to the 124-day siege at which Rhodes had been present. He remarked that

> if the battle of Waterloo was won on the playing fields of Eton, he thought the ideals of Empire were just as likely to materialise in the free and healthy environment of the soccer field as in the stuffy atmosphere of a Downing Street office.[61]

In Bloemfontein, the *Friend* drew extensively on B.O. Corbett's recently published *Annals of the Corinthian Football Club* in which he had argued that 'his colleagues are in a small way missionaries of Empire' and praised 'the influence of tours in cementing good relationships between the Mother Country and not only those of her own kith and kin in the colonies, but people who do not come under the Union Jack'. Corbett had also argued that their tours had 'done much to popularise the British idea of true sportsmanship ... [and were] entirely free from any financial objects'.[62] Despite these good intentions and two Corinthian victories in Bloemfontein, a sense of disappointment lingered. The *Rand Daily Mail* claimed: 'they are only a moderate lot and not up to either of the former visiting combinations'.[63]

After the Johannesburg opener, played in front of 9,000 spectators, the *Sunday Times* reported, 'for once the Rugby grounds were comparatively deserted. It was soccer's day out'.[64] The *Rand Daily Mail* suggested that local spectators may have a 'felt a tinge of regret [that the tourists] were not as good as that team of 1903'.[65] Despite their defeats, the social whirl continued, and the Corinthians visited the gold mines of Johannesburg and watched 'Kaffir dances'.[66] The Corinthians of 1907 were inclined to make excuses for their relatively poor performances. Their captain, Thomas Rowlandson, remarked in an interview in Natal that the tour had witnessed 'indifferent referees', and in one match, he felt his side 'was severely handicapped by them, not that they were not impartial, but that they did not exercise enough energy in the discharge of their duties'.[67] He argued that referees needed to be close to the ball and not follow the game from the centre of the field, thus allowing teams that had been granted free kicks to take them quickly before the opposition could regroup. Rowlandson claimed that the refereeing was not as good as during the 1903 tour.[68]

Perhaps stung by these criticisms of South African referees, George Bull, vice-president of the local FA, intervened with 'a note of warning ... on the question of amateurism', pointing out that 'in order to preserve it is behoved by the SAFA to be careful of the amount guaranteed in connection with any tour under taken by an English team'. He claimed that the £160 guarantee for the game in Pietermaritzburg was excessive; it 'laid itself open to the imputation that the amount went into the pockets of the Corinthians'. He acknowledged that the '... imputation was totally ungrounded ... [but] if football was to be encouraged and amateurism preserved, the guarantee must be kept within the lowest possible limit with regard to the poorer centres'. Craig responded that the guarantees had nothing to do with his team and reiterated that they would never take profits from a foreign tour.[69] The *Sunday Times* then added a more sensational dimension to the story by claiming that Bull had suggested the 'wine bills of the tourists were excessive and that the local people were made to foot the costs of periodical orgies'.[70] Bull retorted by strenuously denying having made such claims.[71] For the Corinthians, Rowlandson explained:

> All we receive are our hotel and travelling expenses. Every penny of the profits of the tour go to the funds of the Association giving the

guarantees to help the game along in South Africa. We take nothing and want nothing. Even our own wine bills, which sadly bothered the heads of the Maritzburg sportsmen, we meet ourselves.[72]

It was, by now, a very familiar protestation of innocence, indicating that the allegations first made by Arthur Hornby and others in the 1890s had never been seriously addressed.

Thereafter, controversy continued to dog the tourists. The soccer public in Natal did raise concerns over admission charges, though these were defended as not exorbitant considering as the Corinthians were a 'crack team'. The *Times of Natal* did query the large guarantees required, their journalist observing that 'personally, I think the sum excessive for a team that prides itself upon amateurism'.[73] Rowlandson, on behalf of the tourists, lodged 'a vigorous protest' against the designated referee Mr. J. Kinnear, for the game against a Durban XI. He recalled that the Corinthians had recorded their only loss of their 1903 tour against Durban, when Kinnear had officiated, and he accused him of taking a bribe. The local officials capitulated, and the referee was replaced.[74] The Durban FA lodged a complaint with the Natal FA regarding Rowlandson's comments. These were discussed by SAFA, and it was agreed that the president and honorary secretary would ask Rowlandson to withdraw the allegations and apologize.[75] In Johannesburg, Richard Goldman of the Transvaal FA was more diplomatic, stating that the match just played against South African representative team 'had established a connecting link between those who came from the Homeland and those who were working out here hoping to build a strong Empire'.[76] However, there were limits and these were tested when the visitors sought South African support in the crisis engulfing English soccer at the time. Rowlandson suggested that it would be a mistake for SAFA to affiliate with the English FA – it had affiliated in 1897, but this had lapsed – and suggested that the International Board [FIFA] would be more suitable. He asked SAFA 'to give the amateurs in England their sympathy and support in the struggle they were making to keep the Association game pure in the Old Country'.[77] SAFA official Godbold responded by urging: 'Gentlemen go home, fight your fight; we are amateurs in this country; we don't want to interfere with you; we leave you to arrange your own differences in your own country'.[78] Thus, as an initiative seeking to gain support for their position, the Corinthians' final tour to South Africa was a failure.

Rowlandson also suggested that it was time the hosts sent a side to tour Britain but the response was lukewarm, Godbold saying that South Africa should first win their tests – they had just lost 2-1 to the Corinthians in Johannesburg – before the idea could be considered.[79] This point was also made in the *Sunday Times*, which had reported that a South African team could travel to Britain in 1909 while acknowledging that it would be difficult to choose a team of South African-born players capable of competing.[80] The Corinthians, it alleged, had come to South Africa as self-appointed missionaries 'to show the local product how to play the game, but they found the keenest opponents in the ex-English or ex-Scottish League veterans, who had forgotten more than they at present know'.[81] Indeed, the report suggested, 75 per cent of South Africa's representative team players had been born in Britain. Wilfred Waller, the South African-born goalkeeper who played for Johannesburg, the Transvaal and South Africa against the tourists, had played in Britain for Bolton Wanderers and Tottenham Hotspur among others and had toured Germany with an English FA XI in 1899. Indeed, Rowlandson suggested that playing against Waller was like 'teaching one's grandmother to suck eggs'.[82]

The Corinthians drew their final three matches on tour, and the *Cape Times* reported that they displayed 'wonderful stability and resourcefulness' after the 'constant strain of the past ten weeks', which included 'much banqueting and junketing generally' and had imposed 'severe duties of a social character'.[83] At the farewell banquet at the Mount Nelson Hotel in Cape Town, Governor Sir Walter Hely-Hutchinson remarked that the sportsmen all over the Empire were indebted to the Corinthian team in the manner they had dealt with professionalism in soccer. Rowlandson, perhaps sensing that the hosts were a little disappointed with the tourists' overall performance, claimed that they had been hindered by the number of injuries they sustained and by the high altitude of the Witwatersrand.[84] He then urged the South African association

> to realise the very great difficulties which stood in the way players leaving England on extended tours – far greater difficulties than were experienced in the case of the athletes touring England from South Africa [and that] several well-known players were prevented through their businesses from leaving at the last minute.[85]

Thus, the 1907 tour ended on a rather downbeat note. It had been characterized by indifferent soccer performances by the tourists. They had won twelve of their twenty-four matches, drawing seven and losing five. The tour highlighted the gains South African soccer had made since the previous visits, and the large crowds suggested that the game was popular in many towns even more so than rugby. The 1907 tour was marred by controversies arising from different interpretations of the rules in which the tourists deliberately missed penalty kicks. This not only upset some of the locals, but also SAFA requested the Corinthians respect the decisions of the home referees. Finally, the tour was characterized by suggestions of financial irregularities and the abuse of local hospitality.

Over the ten years from 1897 to 1907, the war of 1899–1902 notwithstanding, South Africa proved to be a popular tour destination for the Corinthian footballers. They visited on three occasions and were instrumental in popularizing soccer in South Africa. Prior to their first visit in 1897, tours by British rugby and cricket teams to South Africa had taken place, firmly establishing these games as popular sporting pastimes, particularly in the Cape Colony. By the turn of twentieth century, soccer was firmly entrenched in South Africa among all ethnic groups. The Corinthians had proved so popular in 1897 that they were invited to tour again in 1903. They arrived in the country devastated by the South African War and saw themselves as 'missionaries of Empire' spreading the popularity of soccer and upholding British hegemony more generally. South African soccer players proved more equal during the 1903 tour as compared to 1897. This was in part due to the large number of British soldiers stationed in the country who actively participated in teams, leagues and associations. Prior to the final Corinthian visit to South Africa in 1907, some local officials were keen to bring out a professional soccer team to the country, but it had been resolved the Corinthians would visit again. They had now become seasoned travellers as they had toured Europe on three occasions and North America since their last visit to South Africa. Due to the heavy touring schedule and overwhelming successes on the field in 1897 and 1903, a relatively weaker Corinthian side toured South Africa in 1907. The tour also took place against the backdrop of the split engulfing English soccer at the time. As a result of indifferent performances, contending interpretations of the laws and spirit of the game and heavy guarantees burdened on local associations, the Corinthians despite playing in front of record crowds, proved to be a disappointment. Suggestions of financial impropriety set against the broader debates on amateurism and professionalism in British soccer marked the tour. Despite the strides made by rugby in South Africa during this period, soccer remained a firm favourite among many of the population. The English FA sent out an amateur representative side in 1910. This was to be one of four such visits before the Second World War. The first professional British soccer teams arrived in the country in the 1920s, while several South Africans played professional soccer in Britain during this time. But the Corinthians did not tour South Africa again.

Notes

1. G.A. Parker, (ed), *South African Sports* (London: Sampson Low, Marston & Co., 1897), pp. 86, 89; L. Hill, 'Football as Code: The Social Diffusion of 'Soccer' in South Africa', in P. Alegi and C. Bolsmann, (eds), *South Africa and the Global Game: Football, Apartheid and Beyond* (London: Routledge, 2010) pp. 12–28.
2. A. Gibson and W. Pickford, *Football and the Men Who Made It* (Cape Town: McConnel & Co., 1906), p. 233.
3. *The Friend of the Free State and Bloemfontein Gazette*, 17 May 1877.
4. See J. Winch, 'Guardians of the Game: The Role of the Press in Popularising the 1888/89 Tour and Establishing the South African Cricket Association', in B. Murray and G. Vahed, (eds), *Empire and Cricket: The South African Experience 1884–1914* (Pretoria: UNISA Press, 2009), pp. 45–60.
5. See for example D.R. Black and J. Nauright, *Rugby and the South African Nation* (Manchester: Manchester University Press, 1998); G. Levett, 'Constructing Imperial Identity: The 1907 South African Tour of England', in B. Murray and G. Vahed, (eds), *Empire and Cricket: The South African Experience 1884–1914*

78 *'Missionaries of Empire'*

(Pretoria: UNISA Press, 2009), pp. 241–259 and D. Allen, 'Tours of Reconciliation: Rugby, War and Reconstruction in South Africa, 1891–1907', *Sport in History*, vol. 27, no. 2, 2007, pp. 172–89.
6 C. Bolsmann, 'The 1899 Orange Free State Football Team of Europe: 'Race', Imperial Loyalty and Sports Spectacle', *International Journal of the History of Sport*, vol. 28, no. 1, 2011, pp. 81–97.
7 See C. Bolsmann, 'South African Football Tours at the Turn of the Twentieth Century: Amateurs, Pioneers and Profits', *African Historical Review*, vol. 42, no. 2, 2010, pp. 91–112.
8 *Sportsman*, 27 March 1897.
9 'Footballers for South Africa', *South Africa*, 3 July 1897.
10 Ibid.
11 *Cape Times*, 15 July 1897.
12 N. Lane ('Pa') Jackson, *Sporting Days and Sporting Ways* (London: Hurst & Blackett Ltd., 1932), p. 176.
13 *Cape Argus*, 21 July 1897.
14 *Cape Times*, 19 July 1897
15 *The Star*, 7 August 1897.
16 Quoted in B.O. Corbett, *Annals of the Corinthian Football Club* (London: Longmans, Green, and Co., 1906), p. 60.
17 B. Murray, 'Abe Bailey and the Foundation of the Imperial Cricket Conference', in B. Murray and G. Vahed, (eds), *Empire and Cricket: The South African Experience 1884–1914* (Pretoria: UNISA Press, 2009), pp. 261–78.
18 I. Wilton. *C.B. Fry: King of Sport* (London: Metro Publishing, 2002), p. 83.
19 *The Yorkshire Evening Post*, 30 September 1896, p. 3.
20 *Standard and Digger News*, 12 August 1897.
21 *Standard and Diggers' News*, 16 August 1897.
22 *Natal Mercury*, 17 August 1897.
23 *Natal Mercury*, 19 August 1897.
24 *Natal Witness*, 11 August 1897.
25 C. Merrett, *Sport, Space and Segregation: Politics and Society in Pietermaritzburg* (Scottsville: University of KwaZulu-Natal Press, 2009) and C. Merrett, 'Sport and Race in Colonial Natal C.B. Llewellyn, South Africa's First Black Test Cricketer', *Natalia* vol. 32, 2002, pp. 19–35. See also Murray and Merrett, *Caught Behind*.
26 *Times of Natal*, 17 August 1897.
27 *Natal Mercury*, 19 August 1897 and *Natal Witness*, 20 August 1897.
28 *Natal Witness*, 23 August 1897.
29 *Natal Witness*, 19 August 1897.
30 *Telegraph and Eastern Province Standard*, 9 September 1897.
31 *Eastern Province Herald*, 10 September 1897.
32 Jackson, *Association Football*, p. 258.
33 *The Star*, 13 September 1897.
34 *Natal Witness*, 27 August 1898, p. 10.
35 Minutes of the General Meeting of the South African Football Association, 21 September 1901, pp. 3–4. Historical papers collection, William Cullen Library, University of the Witwatersrand, AG3827.
36 Ibid.
37 *South African Review*, 10 July 1903.
38 *Sportsman*, 27 July 1903.
39 *Sportsman*, 5 August 1903.
40 *The Friend*, 13 July 1903.
41 *Bloemfontein Post*, 15 July 1903.
42 *Natal Mercury*, 3 August 1903.

43 Ibid.
44 *Natal Mercury*, 4 August 1903.
45 *Sportsman*, 2 September 1903.
46 *Sportsman*, 16 September 1903.
47 *Cape Daily Telegraph*, 25 August 1903.
48 Ibid.
49 Ibid.
50 *The Standard*, 7 December 1904.
51 Minutes of the General Meeting of the South African Football Association, 14 March 1905, p. 1. Historical papers collection, William Cullen Library, University of the Witwatersrand, AG3827.
52 *Cape Times*, 9 July 1907.
53 Ibid.
54 Ibid.
55 *Cape Times*, 10 July 1907.
56 *Athletic News*, 29 July 1907.
57 *Cape Times*, 12 July 1907.
58 *Sportsman*, 5 August 1907.
59 *Sunday Times*, 1 September 1907.
60 *Sunday Times*, 14 July 1907; *Rand Daily Mail*, 15 July 1907.
61 *Diamond Fields Advertiser*, 20 July 1907.
62 *The Friend*, 22 July 1907, citing B.O. Corbett, *Annals of the Corinthian Football Club* (London: Longmans, Green, and Co., 1906).
63 *Rand Daily Mail*, 25 July 1907.
64 *Sunday Times*, 28 July 1907.
65 *Rand Daily Mail*, 29 July 1907.
66 *Rand Daily Mail*, 25 July 1907.
67 *The Times of Natal*, 7 August 1907.
68 *The Times of Natal*, 12 August 1907.
69 Ibid.
70 *Sunday Times*, 1 September 1907 and *Sunday Times*, 8 September 1907.
71 *Sunday Times*, 8 September 1907.
72 Ibid.
73 *The Times of Natal*, 7 August 1907.
74 *Sunday Times*, 15 September 1907.
75 Minutes of the General Meeting of the South African Football Association, 23 August 1907, p. 5. Historical papers collection, William Cullen Library, University of the Witwatersrand, AG3827.
76 *Rand Daily Mail*, 17 August 1907.
77 Ibid.
78 *The Cape Times*, 16 September 1907.
79 *Rand Daily Mail*, 17 August 1907 and *The Cape Argus*, 17 August 1907.
80 *Sunday Times*, 1 September 1907.
81 Ibid.
82 *Sunday Times*, 1 September 1907.
83 *The Cape Times*, 7 September 1907.
84 *The Cape Argus*, 17 August 1907.
85 *The Cape Argus*, 16 September 1907.

4 Communing with continental amateurism
Corinthians in Europe, c. 1904–39

Figure 4.1 Corinthians v Hannover 96, Hannover, 12 April 1936.
Hannover 96.

'There they were in our midst these sons of Albion, the *crème de la crème* of English football'. The famous Corinthians had arrived at last, and *Het Sportsblad*, the weekly publication of the *Nederlandsche Voetbalbond* (NVB), could hardly contain its excitement. They were 'our teachers from overseas', and Dutch soccer enthusiasts could look forward to witnessing some 'real football'.[1] There was much press coverage of this kind when the Corinthians made their first visits to Europe. When considering how they were perceived by their hosts, however, and how this changed over subsequent tours, establishing historical context is important. First, association football was already well known in most European countries before the Corinthians made their continental debut; they may have been early visitors, but they were not true pioneers. Second, responses to the Corinthians, especially before 1914, were determined partly by the predisposition of key sections of the urban *bourgeoisie* in Northern and Central Europe to look favourably on all things English. It helped, of course, that soccer was 'a game of the elite' in the countries that the Corinthians visited.[2] Sports tourism could be an especially congenial experience when the hosts were attentive, flattering and shared a common social background with their guests. Third, the host-visitor relationship was characterized at first by deference in that the tourists were expected to demonstrate excellence, which continental sides could not hope to match. Over the years as the Corinthians declined and their European opponents improved, this became increasingly difficult to achieve, and the mystique surrounding the club – and English football more generally – gradually evaporated. This reduced the influence of the Corinthians abroad, especially in the 1920s and 1930s.

There are other contingent factors to be taken into account. The club's playing record, despite some famous victories, was characterized by inconsistency, even in its much-hyped 'golden age'.[3] By the 1920s, the Corinthian brand no longer signified soccer excellence. Corinthianism, the set of values that the club represented, was thus reduced to its essence as an idealized version of amateurism formulated in the previous century to underpin the status of a section of the English middle class through gentrification in sport. Before English soccer's 'Great Split', the club's unique selling-point was that it represented both effortless superiority on the field alongside a version of amateurism characterized by social exclusivity and moral superiority. After the split – and especially after the First World War – it could supply only glimpses of 'the glory that was Corinth' while playing but could still offer itself as an embodiment of gentlemanly amateurism for which a receptive audience, albeit increasingly of the *niche* variety, could still be found among soccer's *bourgeois* clientele in Europe. The Corinthians were now routinely represented not as masters of soccer but as exponents of an amateur approach to sport. Their match against Bohemians in Dublin at Easter 1932 was 'a typical amateur battle', according to the *Irish Times*. 'The football on display', it continued, damning with the faintest of praise, 'was more direct than scientific but it did not detract from the enjoyment of the game'.[4] Finally, we should remind ourselves that the Corinthians' tours were merely strands in a complex web of cultural interactions that allowed soccer to grow and flourish globally. 'The game', as Matthew Taylor has observed, 'travelled via the transnational networks of education, industry and commerce, with many of the continent's clubs the product of cross-national alliances and cosmopolitan perspectives'.[5] Much the same might be said of amateurism as a global phenomenon.

The discussion that follows is divided into three main sections. The first explores the various contexts of European football with which the Corinthians engaged while touring. There were important differences, for example, between the anglophile *bourgeois* cultures of Scandinavia or the Low Countries and that of Germany, where the diffusion of English sports – soccer was denounced in some quarters as 'the English disease' – was regarded as a threat by the dominant *Turnen* movement, which favoured gymnastics.[6] The second section focuses on the transnational connections established by the Corinthians on tour between 1904 and 1914 and reflects on how the club's impact on soccer in Europe was compromised by the decision to join the Amateur Football Association (AFA) in 1907 and by the further disruption caused by the First World War. Finally, as Koller and Brändle have argued persuasively, European soccer was transformed in the early twentieth century from an elite recreation to 'what it had been in Great Britain since the *fin-de-siècle*, namely the people's game'.[7] In Germany, for example, in the 1920s, association football had advanced 'with the speed of a spring tide'.[8] As soccer became more popular and the primacy of amateurism was undermined by the rise of professionalism, the Corinthians and what they brought to the game seemed increasingly anachronistic, though some of the old guard of European football were still inclined to look to them for inspiration, even as they were progressively marginalized.

Touring in Europe

'Year by year', noted the *Sportsman* in 1907, 'tours to the Continent become more and more popular, and this Easter the exodus has indeed been remarkable'.[9] It then named various clubs currently visiting Europe, most of which were to be found in the ranks of the breakaway AFA a few months later. The Corinthians, though not listed here, were already experienced overseas travellers having undertaken two tours of South Africa in 1897 and 1902. They had also made their mark in Europe, visiting Austria-Hungary, Bohemia, Germany, France, Sweden and Denmark in 1904 and Germany and the Netherlands two years later. As Mike Huggins has observed, 'better-off amateur sides' were especially well placed to take advantage of expanding opportunities to travel.[10] Short 'continental' tours, usually at Easter, were an established feature of the season for many middle-class amateur clubs by this time. When applying unsuccessfully to join *Fédération de Football Association* (FIFA) in 1907, the AFA's secretary pointed out that 'at least 90 per cent of all the matches that have hitherto been played by English clubs on the Continent have been organised by clubs now affiliated to my Association'. Various 'distinguished clubs', which had 'helped to improve football on the Continent', were mentioned. These included Oxford and Cambridge Universities, the Casuals, Civil Service, and – most distinguished of all – the Corinthians.[11] By 1907, some professional teams, notably Southampton, were also touring, usually at the end of the season when league fixtures had been completed. English middle-class amateurs, however, featured prominently in early tours, and their influence on continental football should not be discounted.

The Corinthians were not the first English soccer club to play in Europe. Clapton, then noted for gentlemanly rather than working-class connections, claimed this distinction, having visited Antwerp in 1890 to take on a Belgian XI.[12] English clubs from the coastal ports of Harwich and Felixstowe visited Rotterdam in 1893 and 1894, and the English Wanderers, 'a scratch team consisting of well-known southern players', completed four tours of the Netherlands between 1896 and 1899.[13] Contacts established by Surrey Wanderers encouraged Oxford University 'to penetrate the fastnesses of Bohemia in search of adventurous football'.[14] In 1899, the Football Association (FA) was persuaded to send a team to play in Berlin, Prague and Karlsruhe where they won all their matches, though by progressively diminishing margins. A Berlin journalist attributed this to 'traditional' post-match drinking sessions with university students to which the tourists were unaccustomed.[15] English accounts of early continental tours routinely emphasized the enthusiasm with which they were welcomed, the hospitality extended by their hosts, the naiveties of opponents and the eccentricities of referees. They were undoubtedly very sociable affairs, not least when the costs were covered by guarantees. Oxford University's four-match tour at Easter 1899, which saw them play twice in Prague and twice in Vienna, scoring forty goals without reply, had been 'authorized on minimum guarantee of £200 to be handed over in Oxford before starting'.[16] Though other important factors, such as pre-existing trade links and the presence of expatriate football enthusiasts in some European cities, also have to be taken into account, these early tours were significant events as far as European football was concerned and this was reflected in local press coverage.

'Better-off amateur sides' from England were especially welcomed because European soccer in the late nineteenth century, along with English sports generally, signified a model of modernity, which bedazzled the *bourgeoisie* from Berlin to Budapest and from Paris to Prague. 'It was a time', recalled Willy Meisl, who grew up in Vienna, 'when the label "Made in England" sufficed to make anything fashionable'.[17] At the turn of the century, even in the remotest parts of the Habsburg Empire, the English love of sport 'was a matter of common knowledge for educated Serbs'.[18] Closer to home, in *fin-de-siècle* France, as Richard Holt has observed, the cult of athleticism prevailing in English public schools was much admired because 'it taught young men to be good competitors in a world where the competitive principle reigned supreme in business and political life'. With confidence in French institutions shaken after defeat in the Franco-Prussian War in 1870–71, it was 'the sons of the Parisian *bourgeoisie* of the 1880s and 1890s [who] suddenly became ardent *footballeurs* and *rugbymen*'.[19] Visits from what was seen as the home of football were welcomed because they signified contact with an attractive and useful aspect of modernity. When Richmond Town Wanderers, a newly formed touring club, announced an intention to visit France in 1905, 'invitations began to flow in from all quarters'.[20] By then, a similar pattern had begun to emerge elsewhere, especially in countries with well-established cultural and commercial links to England. 'German soccer', Willy Meisl noted, 'owed much to the sporting sons of well-to-do families'.[21]

In the Netherlands, where soccer had been taken up alongside cricket in the late nineteenth century, enthusiasm for modern sports was indicative of the Aglophilia to be found among those who 'because of their origins, profession, or education, were part of larger networks than the local and regional structures within which most people's lives were confined'.[22] Similar conditions applied in Belgium, Denmark and Sweden, nation states lacking 'Great Power' pretensions. Here, it has been argued, the urban middle class 'could comfortably exhibit an Anglophilia that bordered on Anglomania'.[23] The Corinthians mainly followed paths that others had marked out a few years previously, benefiting from connections already established. Tours, by Oxford and Cambridge Universities, for example, paved the way for their visit to Austria-Hungary at Easter 1904. Club secretary Timmis, credited with arranging the 1906 tour to the Netherlands, had been there before with the English Wanderers.[24] The arrival of the Corinthians signified international recognition and implied that soccer was a respectable recreation that could be practised safely by *bourgeois* youths without compromising their social status. This may have been especially important in Hungary where there had been an attempt to proscribe this 'sport for wild men' after a very physical encounter between a Hungarian and a German team in 1900.[25] One underlying message of a Corinthians' tour was that if soccer was good enough for the products of England's famous public schools and universities, then it was good enough for their counterparts elsewhere.

In the early years of the century, as the margins of victory often suggested, there was much that the Corinthians could teach their European opponents, especially in relation to tactics, technique and teamwork. When the FA's team had played in Berlin in 1899, it was noted that the visiting forwards 'very rarely kicked the ball with their toes, but nearly always with the inside and outside of their boots'. Moreover, the English passed the ball to each other, whereas the Germans appeared to have played a version of 'kick and rush'.[26] Five years later, in Sweden, the Corinthians encountered 'an abundance of thew and muscle' when playing against a team of university students, but this physical strength was not 'scientifically applied' and the tourists won 11-0.[27] The standard of opposition – not to mention the playing conditions – varied from country to country even from match to match, but the Corinthians, while still running up the occasional 'cricket score', soon began to encounter opponents who had abandoned 'kick and rush' and demanded to be taken seriously. In 1904, the contrast between Sweden and Denmark, for example, where the visitors considered the soccer to be 'of a distinctly higher order' was noticeable. Similarly, in 1906, they found the Netherlands at 'a much more advanced stage' than Germany. Timmis, the Corinthians' secretary, who also played on the tour, when interviewed by the Dutch press, even predicted that 'the Dutch will beat the best English amateurs in a couple of years'.[28] He was proved correct in 1913 when the national team achieved 'the *rite de passage* of beating the English'.[29] The 1908 Olympic tournament, when Denmark reached the final and the Netherlands performed creditably, suggested that European football was set on an upward trajectory.

Soccer enthusiasts in major European cities were kept well informed about the Corinthians, and journalists were often predisposed to see the best in their performances. One Hungarian newspaper in 1904, announcing the imminent arrival of 'the best amateur football team in the world', was well aware of the significance of the recent 10-3 victory over FA Cup-holders Bury. A few days later, it was complimenting the Corinthians on the style of their victory over Budapest's MTK (*Magyar Testgyakorlók Köre*): 'the combination play of the forwards was always exemplary', the half-backs were 'resolute and precise'.[30] It was clear from *Sport und Salon*, published in both Budapest and Vienna, that the Corinthians had more than fulfilled *bourgeois* expectations on their appearance in the Austrian capital. 'Although, from the reputation of the guests, much was expected, this was exceeded by the wonderful team play of the English and their great ball skills'. They could dribble 'like no other team in the world'.[31] In France, where a match was played at the end of the first tour, an 11-4 victory for the visitors was greeted with unbounded enthusiasm in the weekly sporting press. The Corinthians had arrived in Paris wearing 'two crowns': they were 'the best amateurs in England'; they were also 'the most genuine amateurs', utterly beyond reproach. *La Vie au Grand Air* went on to make connections between class and sport. The tourists were

> people of private means who can undertake long journeys to demonstrate the best of association football and everywhere they are welcomed like bearers of good news who come not to preach to deaf ears but to satisfy the sporting passions of the already converted.[32]

Hyperbole characterized much European coverage of the Corinthians at the time. In the Netherlands, prior to their arrival in 1906, the sports pages depicted the English tourists as a model to be emulated, as 'a seductive blend of social superiority and winning ways'.[33] Publicity of this kind likely to backfire in the long run.

Later, problems dating from the split and the First World War were compounded by the soccer politics of the immediate post-war period, which saw the British associations withdrawing from FIFA and refusing to sanction matches against teams from former enemy countries and neutrals. It was not until 1922 that the Corinthians played in Denmark and the Netherlands, while Germany and Austria were not visited until 1925. The United Kingdom's difficult relationship with post-independence Ireland helped to ensure that they did not make the short trip to Dublin until 1932. When tours to the continent recommenced in earnest, the Corinthians discovered that much had changed. Soccer no longer belonged exclusively to the elite, it had been taken up by the masses and had become a secondary battleground of the class warfare then breaking out across the continent. In these conditions, amateurism came under increasing pressure as professionalism emerged in various forms, beginning in Austria, Hungary and Czechoslovakia in the mid-1920s and spreading to Spain, France and Switzerland in the early 1930s. Even in Germany, where the *Deutscher Fussball Bund* (DFB) remained committed to amateurism, so-called 'shamateurism' prevailed at the highest levels of the game.[34] In these conditions and in view of their declining fortunes at home, the Corinthians became progressively less influential in continental Europe, though they kept touring until 1938.

The Corinthians and Europe: before and during English soccer's Great Split

It is important not to overburden accounts of the Corinthians' tours with knowledge of what came later. These early transnational inter-club matches are best understood by referring to the immediate historical context in which they occurred rather than as forerunners of the pan-European competitions with which we have become familiar.[35] When the Corinthians began touring in Europe in 1904, they were finding it increasingly difficult to secure prestigious fixtures at home, especially around Easter when the domestic season was reaching its climax. The Corinthians were a famous club – *the* most famous amateur club – and they could still beat professional opposition in one-off friendlies. Yet, from the mid-1890s, their Easter schedule mainly comprised undemanding fixtures against amateur clubs in the South of England. In 1903, for example, though one match was played against professionals at Southampton, the other fixtures were with Eastbourne, Tunbridge Wells, a Sussex County XI and Hastings. Thus there was much to be gained by responding positively to invitations from continental Europe. Here, the Corinthians would be welcomed because they were from England, because they had a formidable reputation, and because they were middle-class gentlemen committed to amateurism whose arrival would help underpin the status of their *bourgeois* counterparts overseas. There was a demand for English soccer tourists, and private sponsors were available to supply the necessary guarantees. An unsuccessful bid to bring the Corinthians to Austria-Hungary had failed in 1902, but a year later, MTK in Budapest was being congratulated on 'attracting the best amateur team in England ... to come to the Continent'.[36] It was a major *coup*, not least because the Corinthian brand had not previously been exposed in Europe.

The club's first continental tour was probably the most ambitious. They played in Budapest, Vienna, Prague and Leipzig and then 'a scratch match, not on the official card' in Paris. Much was achieved in three weeks. The Corinthians 'were in fine form throughout'; anglophiles and soccer enthusiasts would not have been disappointed by their performances. As the

Athletic News noted after the main part of the tour had been completed, 'They were practically all conquering, and returned with the splendid record of played seven matches, won seven, and a goal score of 50-7'.[37] It helped that their reputation preceded them as they made their way across Habsburg Europe. 'In Vienna', a local sports newspaper observed that '[the] very name "Corinthians" was enough to attract a large crowd'.[38] According to reports sent to the *Sportsman* in London by 'Our Special Correspondent', almost certainly a member of the touring party, G.O. Smith was a particular favourite. The five goals he scored before half-time in the third match were 'a source of intense enjoyment to the Hungarians watching'; later, at a reception in Prague, he was 'draped with the Slavia flag and carried round the room shoulder high, amidst tremendous cheering'.[39]

The English press failed to cover the final 'unofficial' fixture against a team representing the *Union des Sociétés Françaises de Sports et Athlétiques* (USFSA) clubs in Paris. *La Vie au Grand Air*, however, after exhausting its supply of superlatives in describing the Corinthians' performance, featured an illustrated report of a post-match banquet at which *La Societé d'Encouragement du Football Association* had entertained its dinner-jacketed English guests in some style.[40] When, a few months later, the Corinthians toured in Scandinavia, the welcome was similarly enthusiastic. After winning their final match in Sweden by 15-0 in front of 'a record gate', they dined at a fashionable open-air restaurant, enjoying speeches, dancing and music. 'This was our last night in Stockholm', the *Sportsman*'s special correspondent reported, 'where we had been so very hospitably entertained, and, as we all agreed, had spent the best time of our lives!' As on the earlier tour, the Corinthians returned unbeaten, despite meeting awkward opposition in Copenhagen where the Academicals were being coached by an English professional.[41] 'The Corinthians appear to have had a very enjoyable time during their tour in Sweden and Denmark', observed the *Athletic News*, 'where they were entertained right royally by the local sportsmen and bigwigs'.[42] A pattern was being established, which was to last as long as the Corinthians could sustain a reputation that justified the provision of 'right royal' hospitality by their hosts.

'Bertie' Corbett, compiler of the club's first in-house history in 1906, insisted that 'these tours are entirely free from any financial objects'. Expenses were guaranteed, but 'beyond that, not a penny goes into the coffers of the club'.[43] Players' expenses were covered, and if they profited from these tours, it was primarily because they were able to enjoy the advantages of foreign travel, comfortable hotels and the hospitality lavished on them at banquets, dinners, receptions and other events. Sight-seeing was very much part of the experience – they were often driven around in motor-cars – and it would be unwise to underestimate its attractions. At 'Buda Pest' (*sic*), they spent their first morning taking in 'some of the magnificent buildings … notably the Houses of Parliament, situate on the river's edge, and reminding one immediately of Westminster'. The clichéd guide book prose is unmistakeable.

In Leipzig (*Tannhauser*) and Stockholm (*Cavalliera Rusticana*), they were taken to the opera. Whether retreating from stifling Victorian domesticity or the terrors of the Edwardian 'New Woman' much pleasure was taken in the company of team-mates, many of them friends from school or varsity, and a good deal of exclusively male socializing was enjoyed – or endured, according to taste. At a banquet given in their honour in Budapest, 'Curwen gave an exhibition of the cakewalk', a dance popular in England at the time; at a café in Stockholm, 'there was an excellent band and Norris gave us some whistling, apparently much appreciated by our hosts'.[44] The 'social element' of touring was one of its main attractions.

Germany and the Netherlands were visited at Easter 1906. Two matches were played in Berlin, against Germania and Victoria Hamburg, who were trounced 11-0 and 12-1, respectively. Transnational goodwill reigned off the field at 'a very pleasant dinner' given by the hosts. The transition to the Netherlands was seamless. At The Hague, Corbett recalled, 'we put up at the Bellevue, a most comfortable hotel overlooking a deerpark'; again motor-cars were available, and there were opportunities for sight-seeing.[45] Followers of soccer in the Dutch press had been well prepared. As Nicholas Piercey has noted, Dutch newspapers at this time could generally be relied upon to provide favourable coverage and showed particular interest 'where there was involvement with teams from abroad'.[46] *Het Nieuws van de Dag*, some weeks before they arrived, offered a description of the direct attacking style for which the Corinthians were noted and anticipated 'plenty of hard charging'; *Algemeen Handelsblad* supplied an outline history emphasizing the club's public-school/varsity connections.[47] Readers were left in no doubt about the club's past achievements, the style of soccer with which it was associated and the socially exclusive version of amateurism that it professed. 'Advertising for this game is unnecessary', claimed *De Telegraaf* on the morning of their first match in the Netherlands. 'Everyone who has been involved in football knows who the Corinthians are ... Everyone wants to see these English masters play'.[48] As in Austria-Hungary and Scandinavia two years earlier, the Corinthians did not disappoint and HVV (*Haagse Voetbal Vereniging*) were defeated 5-1. 'The team play of this elite of amateur football was stunning'. A day later, the Corinthians played against what was effectively the Dutch national eleven, 'a side that would have extended many a First league team', according to Corbett.[49] They won a hard-fought contest 2-1, their narrowest victory on the continent to that date.

A few weeks before they left England, the Corinthians had trounced the Belgian national side 12-0 in London. When the Dutch press reflected on how close their representative team had come to beating the famous tourists, they anticipated victories in the forthcoming international matches against their closest rivals. This happy outcome failed to materialize – Belgium beat them twice within a fortnight – leading to a crisis of confidence at the NVB and within Dutch soccer more generally. The idea that Dutch players, primarily middle-class amateurs attached to 'Old Boys' or 'Cricket and Football' clubs founded in the late nineteenth century at the height of 'Anglomania', should train systematically was resisted. They were, according to *Het Sportsblad*, far too attached to the idea of soccer as a recreational activity for young men who merely wanted to be sociable, 'far too attached to their glass of beer and to their cigars'.[50] In these circumstances, their recent visitors, the celebrated Corinthians, seemed to offer a more acceptable solution to the problem of an underperforming national team. 'Pa' Jackson, after all, had formed the club with a view to helping England beat Scotland. What was needed, the NVB's international selection committee eventually decided, was 'a club in the spirit of the English Corinthians'.[51] At first referred to in the press as the *Hollandsche Corinthians*, it was envisaged that the Swallows (*De Zwaluwen*), founded in 1907, would operate outside any league system and play a limited number of matches each season against club sides and touring teams. This would allow the NVB, which remained resolutely committed to the principle of amateurism, to bring the best players in the Netherlands together more often in the hope that they would combine effectively when selected for the national side.[52] The English Corinthian influence was palpable; the original model had been adopted and then adapted to meet the particular requirements of the NVB.

As we have seen in Chapter 2, the Corinthians inflicted serious damage on themselves by deciding in 1907 to leave the FA and join the AFA rebels. Denied fixtures with FA-affiliated clubs until the split was healed in 1914, they retreated into the contracting world of middle-class amateur football.[53] The governing bodies of European soccer were aware from the start that they would probably have to take sides. 'As far as our relationship with England is concerned the further development of events is for us of the greatest importance', the NVB noted nervously in its yearbook for 1907–08.[54] Significantly, the FA, having joined FIFA in 1905, became an active influence, determined to protect its position as '*The* Football Association' by denying legitimacy to the AFA secessionists at home and abroad. In June 1908 when FIFA's congress considered the AFA's application for membership, the FA argued that the new association represented 'only a very small section of English football' and the rebels were denied the international legitimacy that would have allowed the Corinthians to continue touring on the continent without restriction. The AFA had some allies, notably the USFSA, whose remit covered a number of sports in France and which claimed to share the same 'principles of amateurism'. However, when the USFSA proposed that FIFA should permit matches between their clubs and AFA members, they were rebuffed.[55] These developments impacted heavily on the Corinthians, and their continental touring between 1908 and 1914 mainly comprised furtive trips to France for matches with USFSA-affiliated clubs and visits to Bohemia, which was not in membership of FIFA. This helps to explain why they looked to the United States and Brazil when arranging major tours in the years before the First World War. Access to most of the soccer nations of continental Europe was effectively denied.

The difficulties soon became apparent. A four-day, three-match excursion to Paris went ahead at Easter 1908. It was reported that the *Comité de Paris* eleven beaten in the first match had been chosen from USFSA clubs in and around the capital. Of all the FIFA-affiliated national associations, the USFSA was the most sympathetic to the AFA's stance. Before returning unbeaten to London, the Corinthians took on the self-styled 'Outcasts', a rather inferior version of themselves as it transpired, comprising players from various Old Boys teams, no less than three of whom had played *for* the Corinthians against *Comité de Paris* a few days earlier. *Le Matin* appears to have been especially anxious to promote this curious event – it was staged at the *Stade du Matin*, which suggests that the newspaper may well have had an interest – claiming disingenuously that two first-class English clubs were playing each other in France for the first time. Its report heaped extravagant praise on 'an excellent exhibition of association football from which everyone would benefit'.[56] A few years later, *Le Matin* announced the imminent arrival of the Corinthians who were 'coming to Paris, having just made a tour of Brazil'. On this occasion, however, it became necessary to explain to readers that 'the famous Corinthians' had chosen to play as the 'the Outcasts'. They may have been even more confused a year later when it was reported that the 'Corinthians Outcasts' were about to play in Paris.[57] The USFSA, which remained out of sympathy with FIFA's policy, appears to have judiciously averted its gaze, though it could hardly have been unaware that these matches had been arranged.

Le Matin had made much of the amateur credentials of their visitors and their impeccable social standing. The Corinthians were 'pillars of amateurism' who played the game 'not for money but for the sole pleasure of beneficial and healthy exercise'.[58] The Easter 1909 tour – an awkward ten-day perambulation from England to Bohemia and back via Switzerland – suggested that they were now primarily intent while on the continent on communing with those who shared their view. Perhaps, on account of FIFA's support for the FA, there was no alternative. Their performances against Slavia in Prague disappointed some local critics who claimed that the Corinthians had been adversely affected by the split. Denied 'more difficult matches against English professionals' and flattered by 'imperialistic tours' to South Africa and North America, their game was 'becoming weaker, especially their team work'. There were some other indications that standards were slipping. When Slavia were awarded a 'soft' penalty in the last minute of the first match with the scores level the Corinthians challenged the referee's decision, Braddell defiantly seizing the ball and holding on to it until the perplexed official brought the game to an end. Thus, as Creek observes, the Corinthians preserved their unbeaten record in Europe, 'but only by something suspiciously like subterfuge!'[59] Reports filed for the *Sportsman* by 'One of the Team', however, confirmed that this incident had been forgotten by the time of the farewell banquet at which Slavia's president made it clear that the Corinthians would 'always be welcome in Prague, where football existed only as a sport' and predicted that they and other AFA members would soon 'be free to meet any and all clubs on the continent'.[60]

This may have seemed at the time a rather distant prospect. If so, it receded further after the Swiss leg of the tour had been completed. The Swiss Football Association (ASF), founder members of FIFA, declined to authorize a fixture that had been arranged with the Servette club in Geneva. This had been promoted privately and guaranteed by the enterprising owner of the *Hotel d'Angleterre*, where the Corinthians were to stay. A compromise was reached, and an alternative match was arranged with a hastily assembled team representing '*la Suisse romande*' (French-speaking Switzerland) who were beaten 6-0, though this proved a less satisfying spectacle than might have been expected if the famous visitors had played the local favourites.[61] At the inevitable post-match 'complimentary banquet', the Corinthians 'were glad to hear that in Switzerland, too, amateur football was likely to advance by leaps and bounds'. However, the ASF had made their point, and after a final match in Lausanne, the Corinthians departed, not to return to Switzerland until 1930. At the time, the tourists may have been unaware of these complications – one of the club's historians refers only to the dates of matches being changed.[62] The episode, however, was indicative of the difficulties that could arise when playing in FIFA-affiliated countries. A pleasant trip to Spain to play in an international tournament at San Sebastian in 1911 saw them take home winner's medals supplied by the Grand Casino, but proved to be less than exotic in that it involved only one match against foreign opposition and two against London Nomads, a scratch team composed of familiar faces from various Old Boys clubs.[63] Travelling to Spain to play a team that they could have met in London simply underlined the increasing isolation to which the AFA's leading clubs had consigned themselves in 1907. Thereafter, the Corinthians made only one trip to the continent before 1914, returning to Bohemia in 1912. At least the gentlemen amateurs could always be assured of a warm welcome in Prague.

After the AFA and the FA settled their differences in 1914, the Corinthians – in the vanguard of the movement for reconciliation – were again free to tour on the continent without restriction and to reconnect with Austria-Hungary, Germany, Scandinavia and the Netherlands, unvisited for six seasons, though this possibility was thwarted by the outbreak of war. As we have seen, relations with France had been maintained after a fashion, mainly because of the USFSA's ambivalence towards the FIFA embargo. As in the Netherlands, the Corinthian model had some appeal there, particularly among those who had taken up British sports with enthusiasm in the 1890s. There were press reports in 1912 that some elite players had formed a new club, 'to demonstrate the beauty of the game as practised by amateurs'; '*Les Corinthiens*' (*sic*) would even adopt the same strip as their English counterparts – white shirts with a blue 'C' badge and dark blue shorts. Significantly, this news was picked up by *De Telegraaf* in Amsterdam, which noted that the new club would have the same aims as the

Dutch Swallows.[64] In January 1914, just as the Split was coming to an end in England, it was reported that a club calling itself *Les Lions de Flandres* had been started in the North-East, drawing its players from USFSA clubs around Lille, and would be run on Corinthian lines. A few weeks later, the French Corinthians (*Les Corinthiens Françaises*) comprising players drawn from eight USFSA clubs finally made its debut at Rouen and went on to play at least two more matches before the end of the season.[65] The AFA-FA split had weakened Corinthianism both in England and on the continent, but it was far from extinct when overtaken by the locomotive of history a few months later.

Flying the flag for amateurism in interwar Europe

Four years of warfare in Europe precluded any possibility that the Corinthians might encourage these initiatives by visiting the continent. By 1917–18, the British Army in France was actively encouraging soccer 'as an effective means of fostering *esprit de section* and *esprit de platoon*', and many officers were committed to 'an ideology of amateurism' fostered by their schools and universities.[66] Beyond these generalities, any specifically Corinthian influence is indiscernible. The club, after playing a few matches at home as the 'Corinthians-under-Arms' in 1914–15, suspended its activities for the duration. When the war ended, it proved difficult to pick up the threads. Many Corinthians had been killed or wounded, or were now simply too old to take up soccer again. As for continental touring, conditions were difficult. The FA had established a 'very excellent alliance' with FIFA before 1914. Now 'the feeling was so strong against playing games, or joining with, the Central Powers, that the British Associations declined to resume membership'.[67] Thus, it was not until September 1921 that the Corinthians returned to the continent, playing two matches in Paris and Lille. The French sporting press was generous, *L'Auto* claiming that the Corinthians, in beating Red Star 2-1, had played 'with an elegance unknown in our country'. Much was made of a sporting handshake offered by a Corinthians defender after he had tripped an opponent.[68] It was reassuring to know that pre-war standards still applied. During the 1920s and early 1930s, as it became difficult for the Corinthians to demonstrate excellence in their play, being seen to behave like gentlemen became very important. When, in 1927, a Red Star Olympique player protested vehemently after a goal had been disallowed in a match against the Corinthians, *L'Auto* criticized him, arguing that 'he should have been inspired by the calm of the British players who were our guests'.[69] In the increasingly embattled, shrinking world of European *bourgeois* soccer, such gestures were important signifiers of class and status.

It was a little longer before soccer relations with former neutrals were restored, the Corinthians touring Denmark and the Netherlands at Easter 1922. They returned to the Netherlands in 1923, after playing two matches in Belgium, and in 1924, when they played a single match of some importance that has been overlooked until recently. Though there was some awareness that they were not the power that they once had been, the welcome they received and the media interest they generated indicated that the arrival of England's celebrated gentlemen amateurs was still an event of some significance in the early 1920s. They were entertained – and entertained themselves – in a style that would have been instantly recognizable to a veteran of pre-war tours. Easter Monday 1922, as the players recovered from the second of their two fixtures in Copenhagen and the obligatory postmatch banquet, was free for 'visits to picture galleries, the Zoo, and a *thé dansant*'. In Belgium, a year later, there was time for 'a very serious golf match' at the Royal Belgian Golf Club and a visit to a Brussels night club where one of the players, Miles Howell, gave 'a perilous juggling exhibition' and then went around with a hat, repeating his act later at a British Embassy reception in The Hague.[70] There was still much amusement to be had when touring with friends from school and university at minimal personal expense. Behind the social whirl, however, was a more serious purpose. When the Corinthians toured in Europe, it was generally at the invitation of people like themselves who were anxious to shore up the ramparts of socially elite amateur soccer. In the immediate post-war period, the *bourgeois* elite who had taken up the game in the late nineteenth century, along with the clubs, institutions and governing bodies they had founded, were under increasing pressure as participation expanded. At the same time, soccer's popularity as a spectator sport brought with it the additional challenge of professionalization. This threatened to undermine the primacy of amateurism, the organizing principle on which upper middle-class control of the game rested.

In the Netherlands, for example, the original 'cricket and football clubs' of the 1890s were now outnumbered by newer clubs whose membership and support was distinctly lower middle or working class in character. Professionalism had already surfaced as 'shamateurism', forcing the NVB to tighten its rules regarding the payment of expenses. In 1921, just a year before the Corinthians' first post-war visit, a group of well-known players, including several Dutch internationals, had attempted to form a professional club. In these circumstances, a visit from the most famous amateurs in the world represented a highly significant intervention, especially as they had been invited to tour by the Swallows, a club run on very much the same lines. They were welcomed as 'not only good players, but sportsmen in the best sense of the word'.[71] As it transpired the 1922 tour left a significant imprint in that a new club emerged, the *Nederlandsche Corinthians*, aiming to uphold 'amateur views and principles' and to 'make the case for soccer in the circles that are gradually withdrawing from active participation'.[72] It quickly became clear, however, that it was the flagship of a movement that was simultaneously reactionary, elitist and socially exclusive; its supporters, largely based around the HVV club, one of the oldest in the country, seem to have been largely motivated by a desire to avoid contact with those they deemed socially inferior. Critics, both inside and outside the NVB, accused its promoters of wanting to start a 'class war' in Dutch soccer. The new club was thwarted when it attempted to arrange a fixture with the Corinthians on their 1923 tour. This did not deter 'a team of Corinthians' from making an unofficial visit to play them in The Hague a year later, an episode that has eluded the attention of the club's historians to date. Thus, the English Corinthians, or at least some of them, had been persuaded to lend respectability to a movement that represented the most conservative elements in Dutch soccer. Though the separatist threat represented by the *Nederlandsche Corinthians* quickly faded, it was an instructive episode.[73]

When relations with Germany and Austria were normalized in the mid-1920s, the Corinthians were among the first English clubs to tour. In both countries, they were welcomed as representatives of an idealized version of the amateur game, but they were only one of a number of English clubs – amateur and professional – who seized the opportunity to renew pre-war contacts. In Germany, visited in 1925 and 1928, they were routinely referred to in the press as 'England's famous amateur football club'. In Austria, visited only once, in 1925, they were 'amateurs who have proved themselves equal to the best English professionals', which made the 2-0 victory achieved by a Vienna Select XI seem all the more significant. 'In terms of pure ability', one Vienna weekly declared, 'we have caught up with our football masters, the English'.[74] By now, however, the significance of a visit from the Corinthians was less likely to be seen as an opportunity to play against the best as a public relations exercise on behalf of amateurism in soccer. In Germany, the DFB was finding it increasingly difficult to hold the line for amateurism as soccer grew in popularity after the war, appealing especially to working-class players and spectators. 'The issue of professional football', according to Koller and Brändle, '... became the main topic of conversation in political discussions about sport in the Weimar Republic'.[75] In these conditions, a Corinthians tour was always likely to have a political dimension. This was especially evident in Austria where a professional football league had been established in 1924. When the Corinthians arrived, they were greeted as 'the most prominent representatives of the amateur idea in sport' and 'true champions of fair play and high-class scientific football'.[76] Some, however, viewed the event from a different perspective. *Illustriertes Sportblatt* pointed out that the Corinthians represented the class of 'English gentlemen' who had invented amateurism 'in order to separate itself and its sport from the common people'. Thus, the Corinthians were not 'what one might have hoped', especially as they had demanded a £300 guarantee to cover their expenses, 'not much less than the professionals of Notts County who come here in a few weeks'.[77] They left Vienna never to return. Not only had they been beaten by a team of Austrian professionals, but doubt had been cast on their amateur credentials as well.

In France, there were similar tensions in the years before professional soccer was sanctioned in 1932. As in Germany, where 'shamateurism' was an open secret, the 1920s – the era of *amateurisme marron* – saw players rewarded via generous payments to cover expenses and industrial companies finding paid employment for star signings.[78] Corinthianism still had some purchase. A team referred to as the *Corinthiens de Paris* was playing friendly matches in 1926–27, but old-style *bourgeois* amateur football was in retreat. Thus, a visit from the English Corinthians provided opportunities for amateur idealists to make themselves heard. When they played Red Star in Paris in 1927, the crowd estimated at 12,000–15,000 had assembled, according to *L'Auto*, 'to pay homage to the famous British amateurs' and one of the speakers at the post-match dinner concluded 'by exalting the spirit of amateurism that the Corinthians embodied so perfectly'. By Easter 1929, when they returned to France, concerns were being raised regarding the poor performances of English teams touring abroad and the Corinthians discovered that they were not above criticism. Playing in Paris against *Club Français*, they disappointed not simply because they were defeated 3-2 but because they had fielded 'a very ordinary team whose composition left much to be desired'. The Corinthians, *L'Auto* concluded bluntly, 'owe the Parisian public another match'. A correspondent signing himself 'Britisher' was so incensed that he wrote a letter of complaint to the *Athletic News* on behalf of British residents in Paris who had been exposed to ridicule as a result of the Corinthians' inept display.[79] The tourists then moved on to the South of France, where they had been invited to play two matches promoted by a fashionable hotel in Cannes to celebrate the 25th anniversary of the *Entente Cordiale*. The won the first match but lost the second – perhaps the hospitality was overwhelming – leading to the conclusion that they were now but a 'pale shadow' of the club that they once had been.[80]

By the early 1930s, as the reputation of the Corinthians faded at home, the club appears to have reached a watershed in its connections with soccer on the continent. In Austria, probably the most advanced soccer culture in continental Europe at this time, Hugo Meisl's famous *wunderteam* was setting standards that the Corinthians could not hope to match and they did not play there after 1925. In the Netherlands, though the NVB retained its commitment to amateurism, the Corinthians reputation had been somewhat compromised by the *Nederlandsche Corinthians* episode; moreover, improving standards meant that they could no longer be relied upon to demonstrate the effortless superiority on the field that had made them so useful to the gentlemanly element within Dutch soccer in their struggle to uphold amateur principles. Visiting in 1933, they lost all three matches, 'the first time the club had ever failed to win a single game on a proper tour'.[81] Invited to France in 1932 to play Sochaux, the club bankrolled by Peugeot, they found themselves involved in a symbolic encounter as the proxy representatives of an increasingly embattled minority in French soccer. Their matches still attracted 'great crowds of amateurs', but they were well beaten by the club then spearheading the drive towards professionalization. 'The Corinthians surprised us', observed *Le Petit Journal*, 'but not in a good way'.[82] When they returned to play *Stade Français* two years later, the *Fédération Français de Football* had recently sanctioned professional soccer, albeit in a rather compromised form. The game had been staged, *L'Auto* suggested drily, in an effort to prove that 'French amateur football still exists'.[83] After 1932, soccer enthusiasts in France who still believed that they could learn from the English game turned to the professionals rather than the amateurs, to Arsenal rather than the Corinthians.[84] In the 1920s, the Corinthians could still, to some extent, live on a reputation derived from an earlier era when touring the continent but, as they moved along the shifting fault-line separating amateurism from professionalism, their options were narrowing. In the 1930s, the final decade of the club's existence, as its pretensions to soccer excellence were stripped away, it focused most of its efforts in Europe on Switzerland and Germany.

Association football in Switzerland, as in other industrialized European countries, experienced rapid expansion in the years following the First World War and followed a similar path towards professionalization, which finally arrived in 1932. The names of some of the oldest clubs – Young Boys of Bern and Zurich Grasshoppers, for example – were suggestive of the late nineteenth-century Anglophilia in which they were rooted. The rapidity with which soccer expanded in the 1920s both under the aegis of the ASF and the workers' sports movement generated similar structural pressures to those encountered elsewhere at this time.[85] Thus, the arrival of the Corinthians in 1930, making their first visit since 1909, especially as their two matches were against Young Boys and the Grasshoppers, represented a significant intervention, especially as the prowess of English professional teams was known and admired. In these conditions, the Corinthians – though praised in extravagant language for their performances – offered an appealing version of amateurism which found a receptive audience. 'The English played an intelligent game, which enormously pleased the public', it was noted after they had defeated both Young Boys and Grasshoppers in 1930.[86] Their appeal as amateurs was enhanced by the particular circumstances in which they toured. English professional clubs touring Switzerland had been criticized for their lack of enthusiasm and the *joie de vivre* that the Corinthians showed was much appreciated in some quarters. 'We prefer them by far to the professionals ... who, for obvious reasons, never take their Continental matches seriously', ran one report.[87] There was life in the Corinthian brand yet though, within a few years, it had suffered reputational damage as news of the club's dismal showing at home filtered through. Whereas 14,000 had attended their match at Zurich in 1931, only 6,000 attended the corresponding fixture in 1935.

So, in the end, as the club staggered towards its demise, it was left with Germany, principally because the DFB remained committed to amateurism in soccer. It was not, of course, unique in that respect, and one match was played in Denmark in 1936, but the Corinthians' preference for Germany was clear and they visited at Easter in 1936, 1937 and 1938. Given the massive popularity of association football and Germany's status as a highly urbanized advanced industrial state, the DFB's attachment to amateurism was not unproblematic. There were rules, but they were easily circumvented. Miscreants were safe as long as they avoided 'acting so blatantly that the DFB could no longer look the other way'.[88] This culture was underpinned by both ideology and pragmatism – officials were reluctant to abandon amateurism because their clubs might lose subsidies and tax exemptions – and persisted into the Nazi era when 'a camouflaged professionalism continued'.[89] Yet, in as far as the Corinthians were communing with fellow amateurs, Germany was an unproblematic destination. For many, playing soccer in Nazi Germany would have been difficult, but there is no evidence that this troubled the Corinthians, collectively or individually. It seems likely that they would have taken the same line as the club's founder 'Pa' Jackson in 1935 when the appearance of the German national team in London provoked left-wing protests. 'I am sure all good sportsmen will agree with me', he wrote to *The Times*, 'that politics should never be associated with sport'. After all, he added, the development of the association game in Germany had been 'materially assisted by the Continental tours of the Corinthians'.[90] As club historian Rob Cavallini has pointed out in mitigation, 'there is no record of any pro-Nazi activity by the Corinth' and as far as can be ascertained, though it does appear that they were compliant guests. The official history of the Karlsruher club recalls their visit in April 1938 and cites a local newspaper report claiming that the Corinthians gave 'the German greeting', and that this had been 'greeted with joy' by the 3,000 spectators.[91] Thus, it seems highly probable that they anticipated the England team's infamous salute before the international match played in Berlin a few weeks later. In further mitigation, however, it might be added that the Corinthians were by now a spent force. These final tours were no doubt enjoyable for those who participated in them, even if the hospitality was on a more modest scale than it had been in the glory days, but they generated little media attention either at home or abroad.

Notes

1 *Sportsblad* (Amsterdam), 19 April 1906.
2 See Christian Koller and Fabian Brändle, *Goal! A Cultural and Social History of Modern Football* (Washington, DC: Catholic University of America Press, 2015), pp. 24–38.
3 See Terry Morris, 'The Corinthian Spirit: Lies, Damned Lies and Statistics', *Soccer History*, vol. 21, no. 40, 2016–17, pp. 12–15.
4 *Irish Times* (Dublin), 29 March 1932. See also *Irish Press* (Dublin), 29 March 1932: 'If ball control had been added to pace we would have seen a real thriller'.
5 Matthew Taylor, 'The Global Spread of Football', in Robert Edelman and Wayne Wilson, (eds), *The Oxford Handbook of Sports History* (Oxford: Oxford University Press, 2017), p. 186.
6 David Goldblatt, *The Ball is Round: A Global History of Football* (London: Viking, 2006), pp. 160–62; Dilwyn Porter, 'Sport and National Identity', in Robert Edelman and Wayne Wilson, (eds), *Oxford Handbook of Sports History* (Oxford: Oxford University Press, 2017), p. 482.

7 Koller and Brändle, *Goal!* p. 42.
8 Willy Meisl, *Fussball der Weltsport* (Zurich and Leipzig: Orell Füssli Verlag, 1930), p. 5.
9 *Sportsman*, 4 April 1907. For details of early tours, see the useful list compiled by Javier Garcia, 'British and Irish Clubs – Overseas Tours 1890–1939', available at www.rssf.com/tablesb/brit-ier-tours-prewwii-html, accessed 3 May 2016.
10 Mike Huggins, 'Sport, Tourism and History: Current Historiography and Future Prospects', *Journal of Tourism History*, vol. 5, no. 2, 2013, p. 124.
11 E.L. Holland (AFA) to C.A.W. Hirschman (FIFA), 19 October 1907, in E.L. Holland, (ed), *The Amateur Football Association Annual 1907–08* (London: The "Marshalsea" Press, 1908), pp. 20–21.
12 Reginald A.J. Ward, *Clapton Football Club: Seventy-Five Years of Football History, 1878–1953* (London: C.E. Fisher Ltd., 1953), p. 9.
13 See Nicholas Piercey and Dilwyn Porter, 'Transnational Connectivity, Cultural Interaction and Selective Adaptation: English Corinthians and Amateur Football in the Netherlands, 1906–1939', *Sport in History*, vol. 37, no. 2, 2017, pp. 127–28, citing the *Morning Post*, 14 February 1899.
14 E.L. Holland, 'Continental Football', in E.L. Holland, (ed), *AFA Annual 1907–08*, pp. 14–16.
15 Heiner Gillmeister, 'The First European Soccer Match: Walter Bensemann, a Twenty-Six-Year-Old Student Set the Ball Rolling', *The Sports Historian*, no. 17, 1997, pp. 1–2.
16 Bodleian Library [BOD], Oxford University Association Football Club MSS, Dep. d. 822, Honorary Secretary's Minute Book, 25 January 1899.
17 Willy Meisl, 'The FIFA', in A.H. Fabian and Geoffrey Green, (eds), *Association Football* (London: Caxton Publishing Co., 1960), vol. 4, pp. 297–98.
18 Dejan Zec, Filip Baljkas and Miloš Paunović, *Sport Remembers: Serbian-British Sporting Contacts during the First World War* (Belgrade: Britanska Ambasada, 2015), p. 23.
19 Richard Holt, *Sport and Society in Modern France* (Basingstoke: Macmillan, 1981), pp. 62–64; see also Geoff Hare, *Football in France: A Cultural History* (Oxford: Berg, 2003), pp. 16–17.
20 R.B. Alaway, *Football All Around the World* (London: Newservice Ltd., 1948), p. 14.
21 Willy Meisl, *Soccer Revolution* (London: Phoenix Sports Books, 1955), p. 84.
22 Marteen van Bottenburg, *Global Games* (Urban: University of Illinois Press, 2002), pp. 101–4; see also Piercey and Porter, 'Transnational Connectivity', p. 126.
23 Goldblatt, *The Ball Is Round*, pp. 119–25.
24 B.O. Corbett, (ed), *Annals of the Corinthian Football Club* (London: Longman, Green & Co., 1906), pp. 85, 111.
25 Gyozo Molnar, 'Hungarian Football: A Socio-historical Overview', *Sport in History*, vol. 27, no. 2, 2007, pp. 295–97.
26 Gillmeister, 'First European Soccer Match', pp. 2–3, citing *Sport im Bild*, 8 December 1899.
27 *Sportsman*, 8 September 1904.
28 Corbett, *Annals of the Corinthian Football Club*, pp. 109, 116, Timmis quoted in *De Telegraaf* (Amsterdam), 22 April 1906.
29 van Bottenburg, *Global Games*, p. 111.
30 *Pester Lloyd* (Budapest), 1, 5 April 1904.
31 *Sport und Salon* (Vienna and Budapest), 9 April 1904.
32 *La Vie au Grand Air: Revue Illustrée de Tous les Sports* (Paris), 21 April 1904.
33 See Piercey and Porter, 'Transnational Connectivity', pp. 131–32.
34 See Koller and Brändle, *Goal!* pp. 81–95.

35 See Geoff Hare, 'What Is an International Match? French Football Clubs and the Earliest "International" Matches', *Sport in History*, vol. 35, no. 4, 2015, pp. 497–98, 501.
36 Corbett, *Annals of the Corinthians*, p. 85; *Allgemeine Sport Zeitung* (Vienna), 4 October 1903. Meisl, *Soccer Revolution*, p. 57, claims that his brother Hugo 'managed to get rid of a small fortune' organizing matches for English touring sides in Austria-Hungary at this time.
37 *Athletic News* (Manchester), 18 April 1904.
38 *Allgemeine Sport Zeitung*, 10 April 1904.
39 *Sportsman*, 9, 16 April 1904.
40 *Le Petit Journal* (Paris), 16 April 1904; *La Vie au Grand Air*, 21 April 1904.
41 *Sportsman*, 12 September 1904.
42 *Athletic News*, 19 September 1904; see especially 'Wreford-Brown's Team in Scandinavia' by 'One of the Team'.
43 Corbett, *Annals of the Corinthians*, p. vii.
44 *Sportsman*, 7, 9, 13, 16 April 1904; 5, 12 September 1904. For brief accounts of these tours, see F.N.S. Creek, *A History of the Corinthian Football Club* (London: Longman, Green & Co., 1933), pp. 71–75; Rob Cavallini, *Play Up Corinth: A History of the Corinthian Football Club* (Stroud: Stadia, 2007), pp. 76–80.
45 *Sportsman*, 21 April 1906; *Athletic News*, 23 April 1906; see also the account of this tour in Corbett, *Annals of the Corinthians*, pp. 111–17.
46 Nicholas Piercey, *Four Histories about Early Dutch Football 1910–1920* (London: UCL Press, 2016), pp. 109–10.
47 *Het Nieuws van de Dag* (Amsterdam), 20 February 1906; *Algemeen Handelsblad* (Amsterdam), 10 March 1906.
48 *De Telegraaf*, 18 April 1906.
49 *De Telegraaf*, 19 April 1906; Corbett, *Annals of the Corinthians*, p. 116.
50 *Het Sportsblad*, 17 May 1906.
51 *Het Sportsblad*, 18 April 1907.
52 Piercey and Porter, 'Transnational Connectivity', pp. 132–33.
53 Dilwyn Porter, 'Revenge of the Crouch End Vampires: The AFA the FA and English Football's 'Great Split', 1907–14', *Sport in History*, vol. 26, no. 3, 2006, pp. 422–23.
54 *Voetbal Almanak 1907–08* (Amsterdam: Nederlansche Voetbalbond, 1907), p. 245.
55 National Football Museum [NFM], Féderation Internationale de Football Association, Minutes of 5th Congress, Vienna, 7–8 June 1908; these are included with the FA's Minutes of Council.
56 *Le Matin*, 6, 15, 17, 18, 19 20 April 190; *Le Petit Journal*, 18 April 1908; Creek, *History of the Corinthians*, p. 81.
57 *Le Matin*, 19, 31 December 1910; 2 January 1911, 7 April 1912.
58 *Le Matin*, 17 April 1908.
59 *Prager Tageblatt* (Prague), 13 April 1909; Creek, *History of the Corinthians*, p. 82.
60 *Sportsman*, 22 April 1909; Creek, *History of the Corinthians*, p. 86.
61 *Le Journal de Genève*, 9, 11, 15, 16 April 1909; see also Cavallini, *Play Up Corinth*, p. 103.
62 *Sportsman*, 26 April 1909.
63 *Sportsman*, 21, 22, 26 April 1911; Creek, *History of the Corinthians*, pp. 85–86.
64 *Le Petit Journal*, 18 October 1912; *De Telegraaf*, 18 October 1912; *Le Matin*, 2 November 1912.
65 *Le Matin*, 10 January 1914; 25 January 1914; *Le Petit Journal*, 25 January 1914.
66 See James Roberts, '"The Best Football Team. The Best Platoon": The Role of Football in the Proletarianization of the British Expeditionary Force, 1914–1918', *Sport in History*, vol. 26, no. 1, 2006, pp. 37, 42–43; Tony Mason

and Eliza Riedi, *Sport and the Military: The British Armed Forces 1880–1960* (Cambridge: Cambridge University Press, 2010), pp. 93, 119.
67 William Pickford, *A Glance Back at the Football Association Council 1888–1938* (Bournemouth: Bournemouth Guardian, 1938), pp. 56–57.
68 *L'Auto* (Paris), 4 September 1921.
69 *L'Auto*, 5 March 1927; see also Zec, Baljkas and Paunović, *Sport Remembers*, p. 127, for a sporting handshake by a Corinthian that was 'greeted with cheers' by spectators in Paris.
70 Creek, *History of the Corinthians*, pp. 91–96.
71 *Nieuwe Rotterdamsche Courant*, 6 April 1922.
72 *Nieuwe Rotterdamsche Courant*, 3 December 1922; statement outlining the aims of the new club.
73 For the Corinthians and Corinthianism in the Netherlands in the 1920s, see Piercey and Porter, 'Transnational Connectivity', pp. 134–38.
74 *Berliner Tageblatt*, 9, 19 April 1924; 12 April 1925; 3 April 1927; *Die Buehne* (Vienna), 30 April 1925.
75 Koller and Brändle, *Goal!* pp. 88–90.
76 Creek, *History of the Corinthians*, p. 105, citing 'the foremost Austrian daily paper of April 16th, 1925'.
77 *Illustriertes Sportblatt* (Vienna), 11 April 1925.
78 Hare, *Football in France*, pp. 20–21.
79 *L'Auto*, 29 March, 1 April 1929; *Athletic News*, 8 April 1929; Creek, *History of the Corinthians*, p. 112, concedes that this was 'one of their worst exhibitions on the continent'.
80 *L'Auto*, 1 April 1929.
81 Cavallini, *Play Up Corinth*, p. 192; Piercey and Porter, 'Transnational Connectivity', pp. 138–39.
82 *L'Auto*, 17 April 1932; *Le Petit Journal*, 18 April 1932.
83 *L'Auto*, 15 April 1934.
84 For French attitudes to Arsenal in this period, see Michaël Delépine, 'The Racing Club vs. Arsenal Matches, 1930–1962: A Franco-British Ritual, European Games or Football Lessons?', *Sport in History*, vol. 35, no. 4, pp. 602, 607–608.
85 See Christian Koller, 'Sport Transfer over the Channel: Elitist Migration and the Advent of Football and Ice Hockey in Switzerland', *Sport in Society*, vol. 20, no. 10, 2017, pp. 1396–98.
86 *Feuille d'Avis de Neuchâtel*, 22 April 1930.
87 Cited in Creek, *History of the Corinthians*, pp. 118–19. Professionals were less enthused by touring than amateurs, see Tony Mason, 'Middle-Class Wanderers and Working-Class Professionals: The British and the Growth of World Football 1899–1954', in E.V.J. Griffiths, J.J. Nott and W. Whyte, (eds), *Classes, Cultures and Politics: Essays on British History for Ross McKibbin* (Oxford: Oxford University Press, 2010), pp. 129–30, 134.
88 Ulrich Hesse-Lichtenberger, *Tor! The Story of German Football* (London: WSC Books Ltd., 2002), p. 63.
89 Holler and Brändle, *Goal!* p. 94; see also Nils Havemann, *Football under the Swastika: The Influence of Sport, Politics and Commerce on the German Football Association* (Frankfurt: Campus Verlag GmbH, 2005), pp. 6–7.
90 Jackson's letter in *The Times*, 30 November 1935.
91 Cavallini, *Play Up Corinth*, pp. 209–11; http://karlsruher-fv1891.de/chronik3.html, citing *Badische Press*, 19 April 1938.

5 'Joy the Corinthians are coming!' The Corinthian Football Club on tour in Canada and the United States

Figure 5.1 Corinthians v Fore River, Boston, 14 September 1906.
National Soccer Hall of Fame.

British and North America sporting tours date from the late 1850s onwards. The first was undertaken by an English cricket eleven who visited Canada and the United States in 1859.[1] A Canadian lacrosse team visited Britain in 1867, 1876 and 1883.[2] In soccer, as we shall see, the first tour took place in 1905. Different forms of football with agreed rules were played at colleges along the east coast from the mid-1850s, including Harvard and Yale.[3] Intercollegiate football was played from 1869, and by the 1870s, major colleges on the east coast had adopted 'American versions' of rugby football, abandoning soccer.[4] In May 1874, two football matches were played between Harvard and McGill University at Cambridge, the first according to Harvard's rules and the second according to McGill's.[5] The following year, the Football Association of Canada adopted rugby union rules, as the game had taken hold in Toronto and Montreal. Soccer was played in Toronto during this period too, and teams included the Carlton Cricket Club, the School of Medicine, the Toronto Lacrosse Club and University College. In 1876, these clubs founded the Toronto Football Association (TFA), renamed the Dominion Football Association (DFA) the following year. In 1878, the DFA introduced a Challenge Cup competition, only seven years after the Football Association (FA) Challenge Cup had been first played for in England.[6]

At the same time, soccer was growing in the north-eastern industrial centres of the United States, primarily Kearny and Harrison in New Jersey, Fall River and New Bedford in Massachusetts and Pawtucket in Rhode Island. In 1884, the American Football Association (AFA), the first of its kind in the United States, was established in Newark and comprised teams from New Jersey, New York, Connecticut and Massachusetts. The AFA Cup was contested from 1885 onwards.[7] In Philadelphia, a soccer league was formed in 1889. Soccer was not restricted to the northeast of the United States during this period. In the mid-1870s, soccer was being played in St. Louis, Missouri, and by the 1890s, organized youth and professional leagues were in existence.[8] In Chicago, Illinois, soccer was played from the early 1880s onwards.[9] Leagues were also formed in Milwaukee and Detroit in the 1890s.[10] Along the Pacific coast, soccer was played from the 1880s.[11] In 1894, a short-lived American League of Professional Football was established in which six teams competed for honours.

In November 1879, the *Glasgow Herald* reported that William Dick, secretary of the Scottish FA, and David K. Brown of the *Toronto Evening Telegram* had plans for a Scottish soccer team to tour Canada and the United States in April 1880.[12] This team known as the Scotch Canadians, comprised players from leading Scottish clubs including Glasgow Rangers' Captain Tony Vallance, played matches in Scotland and England to raise funds for the tour and to supplement the guarantees required in North America.[13] They defeated Rangers (3-2), Tyne and District (5-0), Blackburn Rovers (8-1), Darwen (7-3) and Nottingham Forest (2-0), among others. Dick then visited Canada and was finalizing arrangements for the tour when he died in April 1880 at the age of twenty-nine.[14] The plans were abandoned, though the team continued to play matches after the death of Dick.

A Canadian touring side came to Britain in 1888, playing twenty-three games in sixty-one days, winning nine and drawing five. Opposition included well-known clubs such as Glasgow Rangers, Sunderland, Blackburn Rovers, Newton Heath and the Swifts. The touring team was made up of seventeen players, all bar one of who were born in Canada. A second, more extensive tour from North America to Britain took place in 1891 when twenty-one players visited, of whom nine were American citizens. They played an impressive fifty-eight games in 137 days, of which they won thirteen and drew thirteen.[15] The first international football match in the United States was played in Philadelphia in October 1901 in front of 2,000 spectators. An English cricket eleven captained by Bernard Bosanquet defeated the Belmont Cricket Club 6-0. The *New York Times* reported that 'the Englishmen are all experts at the game and outclassed the Belmonters'.[16]

The *American Cricketer* noted that the game highlighted the possibility of soccer becoming the winter sport for cricket clubs in Philadelphia.[17]

In January 1893, a San Francisco newspaper reported that the Corinthians would tour North America, yet nothing came of this, and it was another decade before a British soccer team would tour.[18] A Vancouver newspaper, in late 1904, reported that the Corinthians were coming, and this was confirmed a few months later when the *Manitoba Free Press* reported that a letter had been received from George A. Parker, who had managed the club's tours to South Africa in 1897 and 1903, confirming the arrangement.[19] After the 1903 trip to South Africa, Parker had returned to London and was employed by *The People*, a London Sunday newspaper. He visited Canada and the United States in 1905 to finalize arrangements for a Corinthians tour later that year. The *Boston Evening Transcript* reported that discussions were held with the Metropolitan Association Football League in New York and Harvard University in the hope of pitting the tourists against a combined intercollegiate team.[20] In August 1905, however, it was announced that the tour had been cancelled. The *New York Times* reported that the English FA 'did not look with too much favour upon the trip and probably feared that it would not be conducted on the principle of pure amateur sport for which the Corinthians team are so well known'.[21] Within days, it was reported that an English soccer team, promoted by Charles M. Murray, would visit North America from Britain.[22] The Pilgrims, as the team was to be called, were an 'all-star' selection picked specifically to make the trip. The English FA sanctioned the tour, and John J. Bentley, president of the Football League, accompanied the team. The visitors were captained by Sheffield United's Fred Milnes and included players from Derby County and Notts Forest (*sic*), among others.[23] The tour was to be funded by publishing tycoon Sir Alfred Harmsworth, owner of the *Daily Mail*.[24] The Pilgrims played seventeen matches in Canada and the United States losing only twice and drawing once. The selection, as the *American Cricketer* observed, 'was not absolutely first-class [but] it is undoubtedly a strong one'.[25] Significantly, the tourists were all amateurs.

A range of newspaper reports suggested that the Pilgrims' tour to North America was 'to popularize the English style of game' and that its purpose was 'a distinctly missionary one'.[26] Captain Milnes suggested that 'our idea was to come over and start a boom for it, which would result in popularizing it and produce teams which could visit England for international matches'. Milnes extolled the virtues of the amateur spirit by saying 'of course we play to win, but this is not our principal purpose. What we particularly desire to accomplish is to impress Americans with the manner in which we play the game'.[27] As it happened, their arrival in the United States coincided with the 'crisis' in American college football.[28] During the 1905 season, a number of deaths and injuries had been recorded, prompting President Theodore Roosevelt to raise concerns about brutality and unethical behaviour in the college game.[29] Harvard President Charles Eliot went so far as to suggest removing the game from campuses.[30] *The New York Times* reported that the Pilgrims' tour was part of 'the project [of] planning a systematic invasion of American college football field with the hope of firmly establishing the English popular Winter sport in this country'. Moreover, Milnes was quoted as saying: 'I cannot see much merit in the football game as played by the American colleges. It is involved, unscientific and puts a premium on brute strength'.[31] In his account of the tour, Milnes was to say of American football that 'the way it is played is below the standard of gentlemanliness'.[32]

The Pilgrims team met with Harvard's president and offered to take the team to Washington to play an exhibition match for Roosevelt.[33] It was suggested that Fred Milnes and Vivian Woodward met with President Roosevelt in Washington, although Milnes makes no mention of this in his recollection of the tour.[34] Sir Ernest Cochrane, chairman of Cantrell and Cochrane, at that time the world's largest soft-drinks manufacturers, visited New York while the Pilgrims were in the city and donated a trophy to be contested by college teams from Canada, England and the United States. The Pilgrims' promoter Murray claimed that Sir Alfred Harmsworth had offered to send over professional soccer coaches to train college teams.[35] The *American Cricketer* compared American football unfavourably with the rival code from England:

> ... the American public is becoming weary of a game which undoubtedly possesses the strongest elements of professionalism. The Englishmen have shown us a sport which must not necessarily be confined to college undergraduates, but may be continued indefinitely after graduation. The game itself impresses us particularly on account of its fairness and on account of the absence of "dirty work" ... it is action from beginning to end and undoubtedly possesses more real skill, generalship and headwork (in more sense than one) than what we are ashamed to call our own game.[36]

The Pilgrims attracted reasonable crowds while on tour, and they contributed to the further development and popularity of the game in North America, but they were unable to dislodge the dominant college winter sport in the United States.[37] Wangerin, drawing on Milnes' post-tour recollections, argues that this would have been an unlikely outcome, claiming that the Pilgrims tour had been 'a sightseeing expedition rather than a mission to change America's sporting predilections'.[38] Nevertheless, in the first half of 1906, a number of American papers reported that the Pilgrims would return later that year.[39] In April, the *New York Times* noted that the Pilgrims' visit of the previous year,

> ... which was an experimental one, proved to be an unqualified success ... The missionary work of the first Pilgrim team has left its mark on association football in this country. Several new leagues have been organized in New York, while many clubs have sprung up all over the country.[40]

Soon, however, it was reported that the Pilgrims would not tour in 1906 but that the Corinthian Football Club, 'stronger in point of talent' and 'thoroughly representative of the best of English play', would come instead.[41] Parker had returned to North America and reported that the *People* newspaper of London would provide the guarantee for the tour and donate a shield to be contested by Canadian soccer teams. The *People's* Shield was contested in Canada until 1912 when Parker severed all ties with Canadian football and returned to Britain.[42] On their departure from Euston Station in London, the Corinthians' Captain B.O. Corbett was full of missionary zeal:

> We are going in the hope of being able to popularize association football in America as a result of the recent controversy upon the merits of the American game. We are strong in every department of the game and it will take a really good team to beat us. I regard the tour as an educational mission for the benefit of the American public, and I believe the American football authorities have invited us with the object of studying the game and perhaps eventually adopting our game.[43]

While Corbett does not explain who the authorities were, it is evident that the tour is partly seen as an attempt to align soccer as oppositional to American football.

'They have come to spread the gospel of Association Football': missionaries and educators and the 1906 Corinthian tour[44]

The *American Cricketer* reported: 'Joy, the Corinthians are coming!' They would 'be undertaking a great missionary work'. 'We shall be truly grateful', it noted deferentially, for what 'they can but teach us'.[45] The *Washington Post* observed that there were a number of schoolmasters on the visiting team and 'if the mission of the tourists is to introduce the game to American colleges it is well a clever team coming'.[46] The *Inter Ocean* ventured to say the Corinthians were expected to be better than the Pilgrims.[47] While they were coming primarily to play soccer, the *New York Times* noted that 'the social features of the Corinthians' visit will be on an elaborate scale'.[48] This was a feature from the outset of the tour as reported by Corinthians' player Morgan-Owen in his regular dispatches to *The People*. On the trip from England, the team engaged in daily runs and 'various deck games, with musical evenings, and the companionship of pleasant people'.[49] Meanwhile, their hosts were preparing seriously. In April 1906, at the general meeting of the New York State Football Association, it was recorded that trial matches would be played between New York, Staten Island and Brooklyn football clubs to select 'the strongest possible team' to face the visitors.[50]

The Corinthians opened their tour in Canada with a victory against a Montreal XI in front of 3,000 spectators. Corbett noted that 'the game scarcely provided a scientific exhibition of football, for our side had obviously not gained their land legs, and the Montreal team indulged in far too much lofty kicking. The weather, too, was extremely hot'.[51] In Toronto, the tourists visited the Canadian Exhibition Ground and Congress House and watched a game of lacrosse. It was reported that Walter Woodward, the secretary of the TFA, had negotiated financial terms with Parker, who was now president of the Canadian Amateur Football Association in 'his private capacity "and" not as secretary of the association'.[52] TFA President F.H. Brigden observed: 'I don't think Mr. Woodward's course is entirely in the interest of the football game' and regretted that 'the affair has devolved into a purely private venture'.[53] This, however, was quickly resolved, and it was agreed that the match in Toronto would take place under the auspices of the TFA. It was noted that the Corinthian players were staying at the King Edward, the city's luxury hotel built three years earlier and that they had visited the Niagara Falls as guests of Sir Henry Pellatt, the Canadian financier. The visitors convincingly defeated Canadian opposition in their first four matches and were offered the opportunity of facing stiffer opposition in the form of Galt Football Club. Galt had drawn with the Pilgrims the previous year 3-3 and in 1904 had been crowned Olympic champions in St. Louis when they represented Canada. Galt's secretary, John Brady, offered the tourists two-thirds of the gate money for a match to be staged in September, but the Corinthians preferred a date in August and a match could not be agreed. Brady remarked that having watched the Corinthians play, 'they are not by any means the equal of the Pilgrims, who were here last year'.[54] While it was clear Parker had negotiated gate money and guarantees for the tourists, the *Washington Post* reported that the team accepted no 'expense money' or prizes.[55]

Before they left Canada, the Corinthians met stronger opposition in Seaforth in front of 6,000 spectators where they were held by reigning Ontario Cup champions Hurons. Corbett reflected on the game and recalled:

> but once more we found a ground little suited to our game. It was rough and very narrow, and eminently suited to the dashing tactics of the Hurons ... the conditions prevented anything like a scientific game being played. Our forwards seemed to feel the heat, and were frequently hustled off the ball.[56]

In his summary of the match for the *People*, Morgan-Owen complained that in Seaforth, they had to 'double-up' as there were not sufficient rooms in the hotel. He noted that the opposition 'were demons for energy and pluck, who had been training hard'.[57] Of their final match in Canada against All Kents, which they won 5-2, Corbett again remarked on the state of the pitch, claiming that 'the ground was again exceedingly rough, being covered in places by a thick growth half-way up to one's knees... The game was therefore little more than a scramble'.[58] This was by now already a familiar feature of Corinthian accounts of overseas touring.

The Corinthians opened the next leg of their tour in Chicago. Local football in the city had seen an expansion from one to three leagues since the visit of the Pilgrims a year earlier and the sport had been introduced in universities and colleges. A crowd of 5,000 watched the tourists beat an almost identical side to the one that faced the Pilgrims the previous year. In attendance at the Chicago game was the University of Chicago's football coach, Amos Alonzo Stagg, who had granted permission for the match to be staged at the University's Marshal Fields.[59] Stagg was diplomatic, remarking that

> Soccer football is a good sport ... it more than comes up to my expectations ... offers possibilities that our American Rugby does not, and certainly seems to be a decidedly skilful game. It requires wind, endurance, and great strength to play it, probably as much as it does in our Rugby. Yet it gives a chance for the small man.[60]

The Corinthians continued their tour with resounding victories in Cincinnati, Cleveland, Philadelphia and other cities. In New York, they defeated an All New York side 18-0 watched by a crowd of 5,000 comprised mostly of British spectators who 'cheered the British team as goal after goal was scored with painful regularity to the home eleven'.[61] However, the tourists met their match in the industrial North-East at Fall River, losing 3-0 in their penultimate game on tour. Wreford-Brown suggested that the loss was due to the exceedingly hot weather they encountered, while his players had played too many matches and were tired.[62] As ever, they were inclined to look for excuses when they were beaten. Corbett suggested that the field was the worst they had played on while on tour, which made the passing game impossible.[63]

In their final match, the Corinthians were held to a draw by Fore River in Boston. Despite the poor showing at the end of the tour, Corbett was to claim that they were 'certainly the best Corinthian team ever taken away from these shores, and probably one of the strongest Association sides ever engaged in a foreign tour'.[64] Manager Parker was scathing in his criticism of Fore River. He suggested that the club had 'tampered with the playing field [and] deliberately shortened in order to embarrass the Corinthians'. He further complained that his team 'felt sore at the way they had been treated in Boston' as no effort had been made to entertain them; 'this was more surprising because our men included the best Oxford and Cambridge players, who naturally expect some welcome from the great American university town, the more after the magnificent reception given the Harvard men at Cambridge'. Though they had won most of their seventeen matches, drawing two and losing only one, this first tour of North America in 1906 by the Corinthians was deemed by Parker to have been a financial failure with losses of $2,000.[65] Yet, soccer in the United States was on an upward trajectory. In Chicago, soccer continued to grow, league membership increasing from eighteen clubs to twenty-five in the 1906–07 season, while the local universities continued to play matches.[66] By 1907, there were over thirty teams in Chicago and at least nine separate soccer leagues in St. Louis.[67] Soccer had also gained a foothold in the Northwest of the United States too, with a senior league in the state of Washington. The tour appears to have generated interest in the game. In Cleveland, five teams had been formed after the visit of the Corinthians.[68] Further south in Oakland, California, the Bay Counties Foot Ball League included a team called Corinthians. The name also appealed to clubs playing in Vancouver, Chicago, Pennsylvania and Buffalo, New York. As in England and Wales, the choice of a club's name almost certainly signified something, if only a wish to be identified with the illustrious tourists.

The Pilgrims returned to North America in 1909 but skipped the Canadian leg of the tour after accepting an offer of $10,000 from a consortium in St. Louis. *The New York Times* suggested that the tour was 'under the auspices of the International Soccer Football Association of America, a party of St. Louis capitalists, and the team is under the sponsorship of Sir Ernest Cecil Cochrane, the donor of the international soccer cup'.[69] Moreover, they accepted 25 per cent of the tour gates or a £200 guarantee.[70] The Pilgrims played twenty-two matches in a six-week period in which they drew on four occasions and lost twice. Rather than adopting the missionary zeal of their 1905 tour in which they promoted soccer as a replacement for American football, the tourists 'intended to showcase soccer to the players and public, especially native-born players'.[71] Fred Milnes, again the captain of the side, remarked: 'who knows but we may have something to learn from out trans-Atlantic cousins?'[72] Logan suggests that the 1909 team were stronger than their 1905 counterparts and the Corinthian team of 1906. Milnes was so confident of the ability of his side that he promised to pay $100 per goal scored by St. Louis players against them.[73] The *Chicago Daily Tribune* claimed that 'getting goals against the Pilgrims is about as hard a job as penetrating the insular nature of the average Englishman, but both may be accomplished if the right approaches are made'.[74] Despite the growing popularity of football in St. Louis, only 9,000 spectators watched the four games played in the city.[75] Towards the end of their tour, injuries had taken their toll and they were defeated by Hibernian in Philadelphia and Fall River Rovers in Massachusetts in front of 8,000 spectators.[76] While the Pilgrims performed well on the pitch, their 1909 tour, like that of the Corinthians three years earlier, resulted in a financial loss.[77] It was reported, however, that it had 'reinvigorated collegiate varsity soccer enthusiasm' and helped in developing home grown talent. For a city like Chicago, the tours by the Pilgrims and Corinthians had helped grow the number of leagues, assisted in defining the semi-professional and amateur ranks and saw football taken up in high schools, colleges and universities.[78] It was also evident by now 'that the need of soccer missions has passed away and the Englishmen had better prepare to beat America's best on their next trip, rather than bring over teams organized for purposes of instruction'.[79]

'Outlaws', the 'American dollar' and the reconfiguration of football in the United States

In early 1910, the *Manitoba Free Press* reported that Parker, now a resident in Toronto, had met with Wreford-Brown in London and agreed that the Corinthians would tour Canada later that year. The same newspaper reported three months later that the Corinthians would not tour the Dominion account of the death of King Edward VII. It was hoped that they would come in 1911. The *Manitoba Free Press* was scathing: 'what a ridiculous and lame excuse ... it can only be believed that the Corinthians have found the death of the King as the best way of saying that "no guarantee has been forthcoming and we cannot go" ... a big guarantee was what was wanted'.[80] The excuse of the King's death was unconvincing, not least because the Corinthians visited Brazil in August 1910, at the same time that they would have toured Canada. They did, however, return to North America in 1911 and played twenty-one matches, sixteen in Canada and five in the United States. The Vancouver press accused Parker of asking for 'rather steep guarantees of $500 [which] verge on the absurd', though Parker claimed the terms offered to him there 'were the worst terms offered anywhere in Canada'.[81] The Corinthians were characterized as middle-class amateur gentlemen by club sources and press sympathizers, yet, as we have seen, Parker's demands could be seen as part of a broader pattern dating from the 1880s, which had led to pointed criticism from Arthur Hornby and others. It was often said that the expenses were paid to the amateur Corinthians that surpassed the wages paid to professionals.[82]

In 1911, however, in the midst of English soccer's Great Split, Parker's concerns over guarantees were only one of his problems. Soccer officials in the United States objected to playing against the Corinthians as they were no longer members of the English FA.[83] The AFA was recognized by the FA, paid a subscription to the English body – as did the Argentinian, New Zealand and South African associations – and would not allow its members and affiliates to play against the Corinthians on their North American tour. The secretary of the FA, Frederick Wall wrote describing the Corinthians as 'outlaws' and requesting no games should be arranged with them.[84] Moreover, Wall alleged that Parker was 'running the tour personally and a business proposition'.[85] As a consequence, the secretary of the American association, Andrew N. Beveridge, ordered that no AFA affiliates were to shun the tourists, suggesting that Parker was only concerned with chasing the 'American dollar'.[86] Beveridge claimed that Parker thought 'he would have more chance to make more money for himself' if he negotiated directly with clubs rather than through his association.[87] Despite this intervention, the Board of Governors of the New York State Amateur Association Football League comprised of 1,000 players vowed to continue with their preparations for the visit of the Corinthians. Teams such as Newark FC and the Howard and Bullough FC stated that they intended to play against the tourists.[88]

The Corinthians kicked off their 1911 tour by beating an All-Ontario XI in front of 10,000 spectators. Lieutenant-Governor Gibson offered to present silver medals with gold centres to the 'first Canadian side to beat the Corinthians'.[89] On arrival in Toronto, the local press hailed the arrival of 'the world's greatest soccer players'.[90] In front of 7,000 spectators, the tourists lost to an All-Toronto team and whose 'class surprised the tourists'.[91] The visitors, reporting to the *Sportsman* back in London, explained that 'the standard of play is considerably higher than before'.[92] Again, they were entertained by local dignitaries such as Sir Henry Pellatt and accommodated in luxury hotels. In Winnipeg, they resided in the Royal Alexandra, the 'most luxurious of the Canadian Pacific Railway's hotels'.[93] Despite the hospitality the Corinthians enjoyed, Parker raised concerns regarding the division of gate takings. On his insistence, copies of all receipts were provided to the tourists.[94] The 1911 tour included matches in the west of Canada in Winnipeg, Regina, Saskatoon, Edmonton, Calgary, Ladysmith, Victoria and Vancouver. The Corinthians were beaten once in Canada and drew against Ladysmith after scoring a last-minute equalizer.

In the United States, they won all their matches, which included their record-setting 19-0 against members of the Philadelphia cricket club league. The *American Cricketer* suggested that 'the men were out of practice and decidedly out of training'.[95] It was disappointing, but soccer's popularity in the city was increasing with seven leagues contested by fifty-four clubs.[96] In Chicago, the English gentlemen amateurs embraced modernity, playing an evening match under electric lights at the White Sox baseball ground.[97] In New York, watched by 5,000 spectators at the Polo Grounds, they played against a New York State League XI, comprised of players from nine different clubs.[98] The visitors were taken to Brighton Beach after the match, and a banquet was held in their honour at Reisenweber's Casino on Coney Island. The tourists went on to defeat the Newark FC two days later in front of 2,000 spectators. In the aftermath of the New York and Newark matches, Bronx United were expelled from their AFA-controlled league, the Newark FC was banned from the National League and individual players who participated in the match were suspended for twelve months.[99] The Philadelphia cricketers were deemed 'outlaws' by the AFA. According to Wangerin, the 1911 Corinthian tour 'served as a catalyst for the reorganisation of soccer in the United States'.[100] Some of the AFA affiliates suggested that they were being governed by a 'foreign body' in terms of their relationship with the FA.[101] After the punishments meted out by the AFA, the Southern New York State Association 'withdrew from the AFA' and declared itself to be 'a national governing body in its own right: the American Amateur Football Association'. It applied for recognition from FIFA in 1912 but was rejected, the AFA being preferred.[102] In 1913, a new national body, the United States Football Association was established and affiliated to FIFA in the same year.

Prior to the outbreak of the First World War, the Corinthians visited Bohemia and Brazil in 1912 and 1913, respectively. The club continued with its international tours in 1921 with a visit to France, Denmark and Holland in 1922 and Belgium and Holland in 1923. The Corinthians returned to North America in 1924, which would be the club's last tour outside of Europe before its merger with Casuals Football Club in 1939. The first North American tours of the Pilgrims and Corinthians in 1905/6 were ground breaking, but by the mid-1920s, teams from the United States – the All-American Soccer Football Club in 1916, Bethlehem Steel in 1919 and St. Louis in 1920 – were themselves touring abroad and a Canadian team went as far as Australia and New Zealand in 1924.

'We are having a wonderful time': the Corinthians on tour in 1924

In the 1920s, though barely justified by their performances at home, the Corinthians reputation abroad, based largely on what they had been able to achieve in their heyday, was sufficient to ensure that they continued to be an attraction overseas, at least for a few years. Canadian and US newspapers reported in 1924 that negotiations were underway for another visit. The vice-president of the Dominion of Canada Football Association, Tom Mitchell, had received 'assurances that the Corinthians will be well up to their usual high standards of play'.[103] It was by now a tired cliché, but the *Lethbridge Daily Herald* proclaimed prior to the team's arrival in Canada that they 'are missionaries of the association football game'.[104] The 1924 Corinthians, however, could not live up to this billing however, failing to win more than half of the matches they were to play in Canada and the United States. They were something of a scratch side; their party did not include a recognized goalkeeper, and three different players were used as stopgaps.[105] Initially, explanations for their poor performances focused on the warm weather and insufficient preparation time.[106] Towards the end of the Canadian leg of the tour, however, it was obvious that the Corinthian team were rather weak. As the *Daily Colonist* remarked:

> Although it is pleasant to see one's own side winning most of the time it is disappointing to the football officials who arranged for the Corinthians' tour of Canada to see them defeated as often and regularly ... A team which almost always loses does not draw the crowd and the box office receipts suffer accordingly ... The principal object of the Corinthians tour was intended to be an educational one and that it probably has been though perhaps hardly in a way expected. The old country people have undoubtedly been educated into a better knowledge of the class of football now played in Canada.[107]

112   *'Joy the Corinthians are coming!'*

Some aspects of the tour would have been familiar to an earlier generation of Corinthians. As the *Daily Colonist* acknowledged, '[they] had to play their matches in the intervals of almost continuous travel and entertainment'.[108] The visitors were fêted and entertained in all the cities and towns they visited. The *Lethbridge Daily Herald* noted caustically: 'the famous Englishmen have perhaps overlooked St Paul's training rules while enjoying Canadian hospitality'.[109] Tour manager G.C. Bambridge was suitably grateful: 'the people of Canada are really too good to us ... we have been having a wonderful time'; while Oxford undergraduate V.E. Morgan confessed that 'Canada was a marvellous place particularly the girls ... [who] compare very favorably with the English girls ... I am very fond of dancing, for dancing is prohibited at Oxford'.[110] Another Oxford student in the Corinthian party remarked: 'I have never seen so much ice in my life as in Canada. You have iced water, iced tea, iced butter and ice cream. In England we train on beer, not on ice'.[111] The Canadian press raised concerns over the standard of play and warned that the tour would lose money if the team did not win more matches.[112] Despite some poor performances, local organizing committees busily prepared for the arrival of the team in towns across the country. In Lethbridge, Alberta, appeals were made to ensure the guarantee was raised as organizers wanted to give the team 'a royal welcome, a welcome they will long remember'.[113] Yet, despite the prediction that over 4,000 spectators would watch their match in Lethbridge, only 1,200 turned up to see them. The Corinthians concluded their tour with five games in the North-East of the United States and managed two draws against American Soccer League sides Philadelphia FC and Brooklyn Wanderers. At the end of the tour conclusion, there was press comment claiming that it had been 'a dismal failure' financially as far as the hosts were concerned.[114] The *Daily Colonist* reported that the tour had lost $2,630 with only Quebec paying their guarantee in full, while Ontario paid less than $800 of the $7,000 that they had guaranteed.[115] Of the total $24,450 that had been guaranteed prior to the arrival of the team, just over half of the amount – $12,692 – had been paid.[116]

The Corinthian Football Club visited North America on three occasions between 1906 and 1924. Before the First World War, they were inevitably compared with the FA-approved Pilgrims who also became familiar visitors. In the case of the first tour in 1906, the Corinthians were portrayed as soccer missionaries who were to proselytize the virtues of the most popular British sport. This visit has to be seen in the context of contemporary concerns about the safety of American football. While the Pilgrims in 1905 and the Corinthians in 1906 may have demonstrated excellent soccer skills, their comments in the press on the virtues of association football may in the circumstances have seemed arrogant and patronizing. By the first decade of the twentieth century, though soccer was popular on certain campuses, American football was well established in colleges throughout the United States. However appealing or skilful the English gentlemen amateurs in their white shirts, it was unlikely that soccer would dent this hegemony.

While the Corinthians were superior to most of the opposition they encountered at this time, when they did meet more accomplished teams, a range of excuses were used to justify disappointing performances, especially when they were beaten. These ranged from hot weather to poor playing surfaces and unfair play by opposing teams. As we have seen, they accused some teams of cheating by deliberately shorting the length of pitches. On their 1911 tour, they played most of their games in Canada rather than against more challenging opposition in the United States. This was due to split between the Amateur Football Association, to which they belonged, and the English FA. The governing body in the United States was closely aligned to its English counterpart and refused to sanction matches against the visitors, punishing clubs and players who took the field against the 'outlaws'. In 1924, it was soon patently clear that the Corinthians were not the force they had been over a decade previously and that the standard of soccer played in the United States and especially in Canada was much improved. In many respects, it seemed that nothing had changed. The Corinthians, even in 1924, continued to be fêted on all their tours around the world, enjoying luxury transportation and accommodation in pre-war style. They were shown the attractions of the cities they visited and entertained at civic functions. However, as was the case in their final tour of South Africa in 1907, the local press now asked awkward questions about their lack of performance on the field in relation to their extensive social programme.

While the Corinthians were ostensibly an amateur team, their extensive travels were costly. Local football officials and associations footed the bill by providing guarantees for the visitors who were also able to take a percentage of the profits from the gates. George Parker, the Corinthian manager in South Africa in 1903 and North America in 1906 and 1911, was able to negotiate handsome guarantees for the gentlemen tourists. The Corinthians were initially a profitable draw card for local sport promoters, but by 1924, it was evident that they no longer captured the public imagination and their tours were loss making.

Notes

1 F. Lillywhite, *The English Cricketers' Trip to Canada and the United States* (London: F. Lillywhite, 1860).
2 D. Marrow and K. Wamsley, *Sport in Canada: A History* (Oxford: Oxford University Press, 2013).
3 *Globe*, 5 October 1858, M.I. Smith, *Evolvements of Early American Football: Through the 1890/1 Season* (Bloomington, IN: AuthorHouse, 2008) and L. Jones, *Soccer: Canada's National Sport: 150 Years of the Memorable, Unexpected and Controversial* (Toronto: Covershots, Inc., 2013), p. 24.
4 D. Wangerin, *Distant Corners: American Soccer's History of Missed Opportunities and Lost Causes* (Philadelphia, PA: Temple University Press, 2011), p. 1, Smith, *Evolvements of Early American*, p. xiii.
5 *Boston Post*, 16 May 1874.
6 Jones, *Soccer*, p. 24.

7 R. Allaway, *Rangers, Rovers and Spindles Soccer, Immigration and Textiles in New England and New Jersey* (Haworth, NJ: St Johann Press, 2005).
8 D. Lange, *Soccer Made in St. Louis: A History of the Game in America's First Soccer Capital* (St. Louis, MO: Reddy Press, 2011).
9 G. Logan, 'Pilgrims' Progress in Chicago: Three English Soccer Tours to the Second City, 1905–09', *Soccer & Society*, vol. 11, no. 3, 2010, pp. 198–212.
10 Smith, *Evolvements of Early American Football*.
11 D. Van Rheenen, 'The Promise of Soccer in America: The Open Play of Ethnic Subcultures', *Soccer & Society*, vol. 10, no. 6, 2009, pp. 781–94.
12 *Glasgow Herald*, 12 November 1879.
13 *Glasgow Herald*, 2 December 1879.
14 *The Athletic News*, 14 April 1880.
15 Jones, *Soccer* and David Brown, 'Canadian Imperialism and Sporting Exchanges: The Nineteen-Century Cultural Experience of Cricket and Lacrosse', *Canadian Journal of the History of Sport*, vol. 20, no. 1, 1987, pp. 55–66.
16 *The New York Times*, 9 October 1901.
17 *The American Cricketer*, October 1904.
18 *The Morning Call*, 22 January 1893.
19 *Daily Colonist*, 26 November 1904; *Manitoba Free Press*, 7 March 1905.
20 *Boston Evening Transcript*, 6 July 1905.
21 *The New York Times*, 14 August 1905.
22 *Chicago Daily Tribune*, 20 August 1905.
23 F. H. Milnes, *A Football Tour with the Pilgrims in America* (Sheffield: Greene and Thompson, 1905).
24 *New York Tribune*, 21 August 1905.
25 *The American Cricketer*, November 1905.
26 *Atlanta Constitution*, 3 September 1905; *Chicago Daily Tribune*, 28 September 1905; *Washington Post*, 29 October 1905.
27 *The New York Times*, 21 October 1905.
28 R. Smith, 'Harvard and Columbia and Reconsideration of the 1905–06 Football Crisis', *Journal of Sport History*, vol. 8, no. 3, 1981, pp. 5–19 and John S. Watterson, 'The Gridiron Crisis of 1905: Was it Really a Crisis?' *Journal of Sport History*, vol. 27, no. 2, 2000, pp. 291–98. See also B. Ingrassia, *The Rise of Gridiron University: Higher Education's Uneasy Alliance with Big-Time Football* (Lawrence: University Press of Kansas, 2012).
29 Ying Wu, 'The Pilgrims Come to America: A Failed Mission of British Cultural Imperialism', *Sports History Review*, vol. 29, no. 2, 1998, pp. 212–24.
30 Wangerin, *Distant Corners*, p. 2.
31 *The New York Times*, 10 October 1905.
32 Milnes, *A Football Tour*, p. 57.
33 *The New York Times*, 16 October 1905.
34 Spalding's official association "soccer" football guide 1907 and Milnes, *A Football Tour*, Norman Jacobs, *Vivian Woodward: Football's Gentleman* (Stroud: Tempus, 2005), p. 70, suggests that Roosevelt invited Milnes and Woodward to the White House.
35 Wangerin, *Distant Corners*, p. 6 and *The New York Times*, 10 October 1905.
36 *The American Cricketer*, 1905 April.
37 Logan, 'Pilgrims' Progress in Chicago'.
38 Wangerin, *Distant Corners*, p. 6.
39 *The New York Times*, 14 February 1906 and *Chicago Daily Tribune*, 2 April 1906.
40 *The New York Times*, 3 April 1906.
41 *New York Daily Tribune*, 22 July 1906 and *The Toronto Daily Star*, 28 July 1906.
42 *The Winnipeg Tribune*, 29 June 1912.

'Joy the Corinthians are coming!' 115

43 *The Sun*, 8 August 1906.
44 *The American Cricketer*, September 1906.
45 *The American Cricketer*, April 1905.
46 *The Washington Post*, 12 August 1906.
47 *The Inter Ocean*, 19 August 1906.
48 *The New York Times*, 12 August 1906, p. 5.
49 *The People*, 9 September 1906.
50 Minutes of the General Meeting of the New York State Football Association, 25 April 1906. Hap Meyer Soccer Collection at Southern Illinois University Edwardsville.
51 B.O. Corbett, *Annals of the Corinthian Football Club* (London: Longmans, Green & Co., 1906), p. 120.
52 *The Toronto Daily Star*, 15 August 1906.
53 Ibid.
54 *The Toronto Daily Star*, 16 August 1906.
55 *The Washington Post*, 26 August 1906.
56 Corbett, *Annals of the Corinthian Football Club*, p. 130.
57 *The People*, 16 September 1906.
58 Corbett, *Annals of the Corinthian Football Club*, p. 132.
59 Logan, 'Pilgrims' Progress in Chicago', pp. 198–212.
60 *Chicago Daily Tribune*, 26 August 1906.
61 *The New York Times*, 9 September 1906.
62 *The New York Times*, 16 September 1906.
63 Corbett, *Annals of the Corinthian Football Club*, p. 151.
64 Ibid, p. 118.
65 *The Washington Post*, 30 September 1906.
66 Logan, 'Pilgrims' Progress in Chicago', pp. 198–212.
67 Wangerin, *Distant Corners*, p. 26.
68 *Spalding's Athletic Library Official Soccer Foot Ball Guide* (New York, 1909), p. 67.
69 *The New York Times*, 1 October 1909, p. 10, 'Pilgrim soccer arrive'.
70 Wangerin, *Distant Corners*, p. 27.
71 Logan, 'Pilgrims' Progress in Chicago', pp. 198–212.
72 Quoted in Wangerin, *Distant Corners*, p. 27.
73 Logan, 'Pilgrims' Progress in Chicago', pp. 198–212.
74 *Chicago Daily Tribune*, 24 October 1909.
75 Quoted in Wangerin, *Distant Corners*, p. 29.
76 *The New York Times*, 14 November 1909.
77 Quoted in Wangerin, *Distant Corners*, p. 31.
78 Logan, 'Pilgrims' Progress in Chicago', pp. 198–212.
79 Quoted Wangerin, *Distant Corners*, p. 36.
80 *Manitoba Free Press*, 1 March 1910.
81 *Daily Colonist*, 20 July 1911; *Vancouver Daily World*, 29 July 1911.
82 See Wray Vamplew, *Pay Up and Play the Game: Professional Sport in Britain, 1875–1914* (Cambridge: Cambridge University Press, 1988), p. 346, fn. 109.
83 *The Washington Post*, 30 July 1911.
84 *New York Daily Tribune*, 20 August 1911.
85 *The Newark Evening Star*, 31 July 1911.
86 *The Newark Evening Star*, 11 August 1911.
87 *Association Football News*, 15 August 1911.
88 *The Newark Star*, 8 August 1911.
89 *The Toronto Daily Star*, 3 August 1911.
90 *The Toronto Daily Star*, 5 August 1911.
91 *The Toronto Daily Star*, 8 August 1911.

92 *The Sportsman*, 16 August 1911, p. 7.
93 *Manitoba Free Press*, 19 August 1911.
94 *Lethbridge Daily Herald*, 10 August 1911.
95 *The American Cricketer*, October 1911.
96 *The American Cricketer*, October 1911.
97 *Chicago Daily Tribune*, 7 September 1911.
98 *The New York Times*, 17 September 1911.
99 *The New York Times*, 1 October 1911; *The Globe and Commercial Advertiser*, 25 September 1911; and *The Sunday Call*, 8 October 1911.
100 Wangerin, *Distant Corners*, p. 34.
101 Quoted in Wangerin, *Distant Corners*, p. 38.
102 Quoted in Wangerin, *Distant Corners*, p. 40; National Football Museum [NFM], Football Association Minute Books, Minutes of the 9th Annual Congress of FIFA, 30 June–1 July 1912.
103 *The New York Times*, 27 January 1924.
104 *The Lethbridge Daily Herald*, 1 August 1924.
105 F.N.S. Creek, *A History of the Corinthian Football Club* (London: Longmans, Green and Co., 1933).
106 *Medicine Hat Daily News*, 1 August 1924.
107 *Daily Colonist*, 30 August 1924.
108 Ibid.
109 *The Lethbridge Daily Herald*, 21 August 1924.
110 *Toronto Daily Star*, 6 August 1924.
111 Ibid.
112 *The Brandon Daily Sun*, 11 August 1924.
113 *The Lethbridge Daily Herald*, 9 August 1924.
114 *The Brandon Sun*, 12 September 1924.
115 *Daily Colonist*, 23 November 1924.
116 Ibid.

6 *Noblesse Oblige* and the Corinthian sojourns in Rio de Janeiro and São Paulo

Figure 6.1 Corinthians v Brasileiros, Rio de Janeiro, 24 August 1913.
Fluminense Archive, Rio de Janeiro.

After touring North America in 1906, the Corinthians crossed the Atlantic again in 1910 when they embarked on a six-match tour in Brazil. Argentina, rather than its northern neighbour, might well have been preferred in that its soccer culture was more developed and its playing standards were higher. A football club had been established in Buenos Aires by British settlers as early as 1867, though locals had initially been dismissive of 'the game of the crazy Englishmen'. The Argentine Association Football League had been established in 1893, the first of its kind in South America.[1] In 1903, the name of the fledgling national association was changed to the Argentine Football Association (AFA), and it was affiliated with the Football Association (FA) in

London, as the New Zealand and South African Football Associations had in 1897. It was one way in which the FA could demonstrate a concern 'to help the game overseas'.[2] Delegates from overseas associations attended meetings in London and canvassed for English teams to visit their respective countries.

Thereafter, Argentina became part of the developing network of world soccer. As a result of the AFA's affiliation, Southampton toured Argentina in 1904 and Nottingham Forest in 1905, each also playing a single match in neighbouring Uruguay, whose team competed in the Argentine cup competition at this time.[3] A South African team toured in 1906 and were referred to by the local press as the 'representatives of the Dark Continent'.[4] Everton and Tottenham Hotspur visited in 1909. Argentina was favoured by most of the few British teams that visited South America before 1914.[5] The game was growing in popularity, especially among the urban elite, which, like its counterparts in continental Europe, were much taken with the English at this time, a tendency reinforced by Argentina's place in Britain's informal empire. *Sociedad Sportive Argentina* arranged a one-day tournament for 'small' and 'independent' teams in Buenos Aires in 1904, attracting eighty teams. Significantly, this included one that had adopted the name 'Corinthians'.[6] However, with their fixture list at home in England reduced to just nine games in 1909–10 – some against very indifferent opposition – and opportunities to tour in Europe severely curtailed, the Corinthians were in no position to spurn a very generous invitation to visit Rio de Janeiro and São Paulo in August and September 1910, respectively. Argentina, as we shall see, was to prove an elusive destination as far as England's famous amateur tourists were concerned.

Soccer in São Paulo and Rio de Janeiro

When the South African team toured in 1906, they met a Paulista XI that included Charles Miller, the 'so-called "founder" of soccer in Brazil'.[7] According to legend, Miller brought two soccer balls and the FA rule book back to Brazil after completing his studies in England in 1894, though this is probably a convenient and unreliable foundation myth. British sailors in port had played various football games in Brazil since the 1860s, and Jesuit schools in Rio were playing soccer in the 1880s. Yet Miller's career is instructive. Born in São Paulo in 1874 to an English-Brazilian mother and a Scottish father, he was sent to school in Southampton where he became a keen athlete. While still a schoolboy, Miller turned out for St Mary's Church of England Young Men's Association Football Club, which later became the Southampton FC. He also played for the Corinthians (once) – and against them – and was involved in local soccer administration. On his return to Brazil, Miller joined the São Paulo Athletic Club (SPAC), established in 1888, and played cricket for the elite British social club. He began arranging soccer matches between SPAC and newly formed clubs in São Paulo, and these formed the basis of a local league that had emerged by the turn of the century.[8] Soccer was taken up by students playing for Associação Athletica Mackenzie College and by immigrants of many nationalities at Sport Club Internacional, Sport Club Germânia, Club Athletico Paulistano and Associação Athletica Palmeiras.[9]

Meanwhile, soccer had gained a foothold in Rio de Janeiro. Three teams regularly contested matches and games often pitted locals against British-born, as was the case in many other cities in Britain's formal and informal overseas empire. Complex webs of connectivity were being spun. Oscar Cox was from an Anglo-Brazilian family; his British father was born in Ecuador and his mother in Brazil, but he had been educated at Lausanne in Switzerland, where he had learned to play soccer. A keen sportsman, like Miller, Cox was responsible for arranging a series of matches between Rio de Janeiro and São Paulo select teams in 1901. Two games were played in São Paulo, and at the post-match banquet, the *bourgeois* soccer enthusiasts toasted both the President of Brazil and King Edward VII.[10] In 1902, the twenty-two-year-old Cox became president of the newly established Fluminense Football Club located in Laranjeiras, a fashionable neighbourhood in Rio. Inevitably, the club was socially exclusive, its members all young men like Oscar Cox, 'sons of rich fathers, educated in Europe, used to spending money'.[11] Cox's Fluminense club mirrored the social standing of the SPAC, and while the social elite of the two cities prospered, floating on a wave of inward investment from Europe, especially Britain, its clubs dominated the emerging soccer leagues. However, following a pattern with which we are already familiar, their place at the top of Brazil's football hierarchy was soon being challenged by factory teams from working-class neighbourhoods, such as Bangu in Rio, where a club was established in 1904 by British employees of a textile company.[12]

Miller was appointed Acting British Vice-Consul in São Paulo in 1904. In the same year, his former club Southampton visited Buenos Aires. Their ship docked in Rio de Janeiro en route to the Argentine capital, but he failed to persuade them to play in Brazil. Efforts by São Paulo soccer officials to persuade Nottingham Forest to make a detour to Brazil were also unsuccessful so that Miller and other soccer enthusiasts had to wait until 1906 for the first match against foreign opposition on home soil when the South African tourists beat his Paulista XI 6-0 at the *Velódromo* in São Paulo.[13] In 1908, select team from Buenos Aires visited Rio, São Paulo and Santos, winning six of their seven games and drawing one, but it was to Europe rather than their neighbours that Brazilians looked for inspiration and recognition. As Cain and Hopkins observed in their magisterial study of British imperialism, it was a country where, if British power was not felt as it was in India and Africa, yet 'British influence was exercised in much the same way as it was in Canada and South Africa'.[14] There was a degree of cultural and economic penetration, which meant that contacts with London were valued. As far as soccer was concerned these were limited, though the FA invited the *Liga Paulista* to send a Brazilian side to England in 1908, a tour that did not materialize.[15]

By this time, however, the impact of the schism in English football after 1907 was becoming relevant, not least because it had cramped the Corinthians' style, restricting the countries they could visit conveniently on overseas tours, especially in Europe. This created conditions in which they responded favourably to an invitation to visit Brazil, especially when it came from the upmarket anglophiles at Fluminense, who had, by 1910, won the Rio state championship four times, and were anxious to test themselves against stronger opposition while basking in the reflected glory that the celebrated English gentlemen would bring with them. It helped, of course, that they could expect generous guarantees and that Fluminense were prepared to pay half the costs involved in travelling to Brazil and make arrangements for hotel accommodation.[16] Whatever problems the Corinthians faced at home, it was clear that their reputation still counted in Rio where players from various clubs began to train together in preparation for the visit. There were some anxieties regarding the paucity of qualified referees, and it was clear that the hosts wanted to make a good impression.[17] The *Brazilian Review*, a weekly English-language newspaper published in Rio, feared that spectators might ruin the party by misbehaving. 'The plain fact', it observed, 'is that the amenities of public school soccer are unsuited to the South American temperament'.[18]

The Corinthians head to South America

The Times announced the departure of the Corinthians from Southampton on the *RMS Amazon*.[19] They were embarking on a short six-match tour, playing three games in Rio de Janeiro and three in São Paulo. On their arrival in Rio de Janeiro, the tourists were received in the manner to which they had become accustomed on their overseas travels, being driven by motor vehicle through the town and visiting the Tijuca forest.[20] British diplomat Ernest Hambloch recalled that 'the enthusiastic Brazilians made almost a national occasion of the first match'.[21] Club secretary Timmis ensured that there would be no refereeing problems with Fluminense by taking the match himself. He was probably taken by surprise when Oswaldo Gomes opened the scoring for the hosts after only twelve seconds but reassured when the Corinthians replied by scoring ten.[22] Before their second match in Rio, the English tourists were taken to the Corcovado mountain and lunched at Paineiras. Their victory by 8-1 against a combined Rio XI was almost as convincing as their trouncing of Fluminense, though one local newspaper, *Folha do Dia*, suggested that the English visitors were not as good as the scoreline suggested.[23] The attendance was much larger than for first match, and for the city's elite, it was somewhere to be seen, a fashionable occasion. A reserved area in the stadium had been set aside for single women who brought a 'chic' atmosphere to the ground. There was a 'waft of perfume in the air representing wealth'. Relishing their role as representatives of the kind of Englishness that Rio's urban elite appreciated, the Corinthians played a cricket match across the Guanabra Bay in Icaraí on the following day, drawing their match against a team of the Rio Cricket and Athletic Association. An evening event followed at the *Clube dos Diarios*.[24]

In their final match in Rio, the Corinthians defeated Brasileiros on a Sunday afternoon at the Fluminense ground. The occasion was notable for many of the features that we have come to recognize as typical of 'international' matches, and there was a 'delirious fever of patriotism' among the estimated 7,000 spectators who were broadly representative of the city's population, an indication of the growing popularity of the game.[25] Brazilian President Nilo Peçanha was in attendance, along with the British envoy William Haggard, the Argentine and Portuguese ambassadors and numerous local and foreign dignitaries. For the newspaper *O Piaz*, the match was 'Inglaterra versus Brazil', and national anthems were played by a navy band prior to kick-off. At half-time, President Peçanha handed out medals to the Corinthian players. Despite the patriotic characteristics of the event, a certain anglophile deference was evident, as the match was refereed Captain G.J. Todd, commander of the British naval ship *HMS Amethyst*, which happened to be in port. The Corinthians beat the Brazilian side 5-2, but the local press, though praising the visitors lavishly, predicted that the São Paulo select side would provide a sterner test. At a farewell banquet, held less than a mile from the Fluminense ground at the Metropole Hotel, the guests were treated to a feast. The printed menus featured the heraldic emblems of the United Kingdom and Brazil, lending the dinner the appearance of a state occasion.[26] As was customary at such events, the Corinthians dined well. The menu offered steak, poultry and pork, along with *fruits européens*, and was accompanied by various French wines, including champagne.[27]

The English tourists then travelled by train to São Paulo where they were greeted by a large and enthusiastic crowd at the station and were transported in cars with floral decorations to the Hotel Majestic.[28] There was considerable interest in their opening match against the local champions Palmeiras with some spectators arriving three hours before kick-off. That some of the 5,000 spectators carried flags suggest that the idea that the fixture was effectively of 'international' status carried some weight. As in Rio, the matches with the Corinthians were very fashionable occasions. Local press reports indicated that 'many beautiful young women' were in attendance at the *Velódromo*; the match with Palmeiras – the strongest team that the Corinthians met on their 1910 tour – was 'sporting event but a social one too'. After achieving a 2-0 win, their narrowest margin of victory on the tour, the teams returned to the Majestic for the official post-match dinner where goodwill appeared to reign and much champagne was consumed.[29] Undoubtedly, the match had been competitive, and the São Paulo newspaper *Jornal do Commercio* subsequently complained of 'excessive violence', almost certainly a reference to the Corinthians use of the shoulder charge, which may have been acceptable in England but was hardly ever seen on the harder grounds to be found in Brazil.[30] It was, of course, not the first or last time that this became a contentious issue when English teams played overseas and encountered different soccer cultures.

Not surprisingly, this theme resurfaced after the Corinthians won their second match in the city by 5-0 against a defeated São Paulo Select XI. The Corinthians were praised for their skilful performance; they were 'professors' of soccer, whereas the São Paulo team were merely 'students'.[31] The English-language *Brazilian Review*, however, complained that the spectators had been hostile and that the game 'was played amidst a continuous roar of taunts, jeers and hisses, directed by the crowd against the visiting team'. Moreover, it accused the São Paulo team of 'utter loss of temper, hacking, fouling and generally unsportsmanlike conduct'.[32] The match was certainly not without incident. Teams from England venturing abroad at this time were often unimpressed with local referees, but the visitors had little to complain of here when they were awarded a controversial goal, much to the annoyance of the home crowd. According to Creek's club history, this led to an incident when '[a] small nigger boy was so incensed ... [and] so evidently stirred by patriotic feelings, [that] he assaulted Timmis in the correct place with his bare foot'.[33] It is possible that the São Paulo locals may have decided that this well-placed kick was no more than Timmis deserved, *Jornal do Commercio* observing that the crowd had been surprised and upset when the Corinthians had shoulder-charged their goalkeeper. It had responded defensively to the *Brazilian Review*'s suggestion that spectators had generally been hostile to England's most famous team of gentlemen amateurs, claiming that only a small section of the crowd, who were 'less educated and illiterate', had misbehaved.[34] Meanwhile, the anglophile *Brazilian Review* stuck with its original story.[35]

It was probably just as well that their third and final match in the city – the last of their Brazilian tour – was virtually an exhibition match against *Extrangeiros*, a cosmopolitan scratch side 'converter at the last minute converted into a team purely English'. That team selection was confined to São Paulo's finest Englishmen was probably significant, as if the hosts were determined to avoid any possible embarrassment. As far as the *Brazilian Review* was concerned, 'the idea was to show the Corinthians a game of clean English "footer", by way of a change from the exotic variety provided to them in previous matches'. Such was the interest that an estimated 10,000 spectators attended to watch the Corinthians win comfortably and to see Charles Miller making an appearance against the distinguished visitors. He missed a penalty, quite possibly deliberately; he had once played for the Corinthians in England and may well have been influenced by the idea that no gentleman would commit a foul deliberately. According to the *Review*, the award of the penalty kick had been 'waived by the S. Paulo Englishmen'.[36]

In summing up the tour, the *Brazilian Review* claimed that the Corinthians had defeated the 'six best Brazilian teams, composed of men fit and trained in league Championship matches'. What was even more satisfactory, however, was that their victories had been achieved in an apparently effortless style, which the Brazilians called *brincando* while seeing the sights, attending the theatres and amusing themselves generally. 'Not a bad record, one thinks nor one easy to equal!'[37] The English-language newspaper continued its strident criticism of soccer and its followers in São Paulo where, it claimed, 'a feeling of antipathy, akin to hatred, is already growing up between Brazilians and Englishmen' and soccer was now 'no more than a simple explosion of Anglophobia, the effect of excessive chauvinism on a weak brain'.[38] If this was so – and it seems highly exaggerated – it does not appear to have registered with the Corinthians, who went out of their way, in a letter addressed to the São Paulo League and published in *O Estado se São Paulo*, to thank their hosts for their kind hospitality, which had left them with 'many happy memories'.[39] Neither does it appear to have deterred those who were determined to emulate the English visitors as Sport Club Corinthians Paulista was formed while they were still in the city, the club's name, according to Hamilton, suggested by Charles Miller.[40]

The return of the Corinthians in 1913

In July 1913, it was reported that the Corinthians would return to Brazil, Oscar Cox having negotiated a return visit while in London.[41] By this time, six seasons into the Split and restricted at home to just ten matches in 1912–13, the club could barely perform its role as the flagship of gentlemanly amateurism, being confined to matches against other members of the Amateur Football Association. There were, however, occasional glimpses of a sporting style that Corinthians of an earlier era would have recognized. One member of the party of fourteen informed the *Sportsman* that 'they had a good side, which included several first-class cricketers, and that they would probably vary the programme arranged by playing cricket matches'.[42] The first match, against a Rio XI, signalled that the tour was not destined to follow quite the same triumphal course as in 1910 when the visitors were beaten 2-1, the winning goal for Rio being scored by another gentlemanly amateur – though not one who would have qualified for the socially elite Corinthians – Harry Welfare, who had played for Northern Nomads and Liverpool. In the report that eventually reached the *Sportsman*, it was noted that '[the] home team played better and the Corinthians worse than in the corresponding match of 1910'. After a comfortable victory against Rio's foreigners (*Estrangeiros*), they then faced a representative Brazilian eleven at Fluminense's stadium in a match watched by an 'extraordinary attendance' of 15,000 enthusiastic and patriotic spectators and also various dignitaries, including the Brazilian minister for foreign affairs and the British and American ambassadors. The game had been publicized as if it were a full-fledged 'international' match, according to *O Paiz* a 'Foot-Ball Internacional Inglaterra Versus Brazil'.[43] The Corinthians, fielding a slightly stronger eleven than in their first match, achieved a 2-1 victory. For Creek, this established a pattern. For this match and the rest of the tour, 'the Corinthians were definitely superior to their opponents, although they found it harder to win their games than in 1910'.[44]

The three matches played in Rio suggested that the standard of football there had probably improved since the Corinthians' first visit three years earlier. It seemed likely that they would have faced stronger opposition still in São Paulo if some of the city's best players had not been otherwise engaged. The local *Liga Paulista de Futebol* had arranged a five-match tour of Argentina and Uruguay, which coincided with the Corinthians' visit, an indication, perhaps of changing priorities.[45] Teams from Buenos Aires had played in in São Paulo in 1908 and again, earlier in 1912, making a very favourable impression. *O Estado de São Paulo* claimed that their soccer 'was the best we have ever witnessed ... Even the Corinthians were inferior. They may have been more vigorous but they were less brilliant'.[46] Interest in association football was growing in the city where a new league for amateur clubs had been established, partly as a reaction to instances of shamateurism among some of the established *Liga Paulista* clubs.[47] A match between the English and the São Paulo Corinthians was anticipated in some quarters – 'when Greek meets Greek, then comes a tug of war' – but no such clash was scheduled.[48] In some ways, the most significant event of their visit to the city was that they received while there an invitation from Argentina's ambassador to Brazil to visit Buenos Aires in 1914.[49] Clearly, whatever the constraints under which they laboured at home, they remained credible opponents overseas, their visits conferring respectability on soccer as a pursuit and prestige those who played it.

In many ways, the touring experience of 1913 was very similar to that which the Corinthians had enjoyed three years earlier. Arriving in São Paulo, they were met by local soccer officials and driven to the Hotel d'Oeste where they were comfortably billeted for the rest of their stay. Various outings, a visit to the zoo and other entertainments were arranged for their benefit, including a hockey match between 'Scratch Inglez' and 'Scratch Paulista'.[50] The *Brazilian Review*, reviewing the tours, sensed that the hectic socializing expected of the visitors was not conducive to soccer excellence, noting rather sardonically that 'their usual vigorous programme' involved a zoo visit 'to see the snakes', a 'general romp around' on a farm, and then 'theatre every night and sleep – well, there will be plenty of time to do that when they get aboard the steamer'.[51] Despite these distractions, the Corinthians won their first game in the city against a Paulistano XI by 2-1, though it was observed that they were not as good as had been expected and that the team was weaker than the one that had toured in 1910. It was anticipated that their next opponents, Mackenzie College, would be 'more homogenous and disciplined' and would provide a sterner test.[52] In the event, the Corinthians achieved their biggest win of the tour by 8-2, their opponents discipline deserting them in a second half, which would have probably disappointed those who believed that sport could advance the cause of Anglo-Brazilian relations. According to the *Correio Paulistano*, 'Mackenzie completely lost their cool, playing as if they were blind, behaving with brutality and managing to injure several' opposition players.[53] One of the home players was subsequently suspended by the club.[54] As was by now customary, however, there was a dinner in the evening attended by at least some of the Mackenzie players and the tourists appeared to shrug off the afternoon's unpleasantness quite easily.

For their final match in Brazil, played on a Sunday afternoon, the stadium was full half-an-hour before kick-off. Women who arrived late were unable to find seating in the main grandstand, while gentlemen packed the perimeter of the field. A 1-1 draw with Palmeiras seemed an appropriate way for the tour to draw to its conclusion, the report provided by a player for the Sportsman noting that 'the home side had no more than a fair share of the luck in drawing'.[55] At the farewell banquet held at the Hotel d'Oeste, the tourists were joined by the directors and the players of the three teams they had faced in São Paulo, along with several representatives of the press. An orchestra played the national anthems of Brazil and Britain, and this was followed by waltz music. The feast laid on by the hotel included several dishes with one named after the English team: 'Tournedor à la Corinthians'. Several speeches were made, including one by Corinthian captain Morgan-Owen, who expressed his gratitude to the Brazilian hosts and included a few phrases in Portuguese. The customary pleasantries were exchanged, and the Corinthian players each received tie-pins, medals, watches and precious stones including rubies from their hosts.[56]

While the Corinthian results were not as good as on their 1910 tour, they were nonetheless respectable. *O Estado*, however, noted that 'the way they play is always the same', and the idea that they were tactically conservative continued to haunt the Corinthians in the years that followed.[57] An anonymous tourist observed that Brazilian soccer had improved since 1910 and it seems likely that the Englishmen would have been severely tested had the São Paulo players who were in Argentina been available for selection, but he passed no comment on what had happened to the Corinthians over the same period. The Brazilians were said to be practising more regularly and were accustomed to narrow and fast pitches, which did not suit the expansive Corinthian style. However, there was some consolation to be drawn from the observation that their teams would struggle against 'an average English University side ... under English conditions'.[58] Ivan Snell, who had been on both Brazilian tours, who also thought that Brazilian soccer had improved, observed that the 1913 tourists were not representative of the club's true strength – they had travelled without wingers or a recognized centre-forward – and hoped to return in 1914 with a stronger side.[59] The Corinthians' had won four games in Brazil, drawn once and suffered one narrow defeat, yet the rather muted response to what they had achieved suggests that more had been expected of them and an awareness that the club's fortunes were on the wane. It is now clear, of course, that soccer in Brazil was at the start of a period in which it made rapid progress as the sport was effectively creolized, with players of British and European origin being increasingly outnumbered by native Brazilians.[60] However, for the Corinthians, the 1913 tour was to be their last. They had made their mark, but it faded fairly rapidly thereafter, along with British cultural influence in South America. Perhaps it was just as well. As we have seen, they visited both South Africa and North America on three occasions, and it became apparent during the course of the third trip that they were neither the soccer force nor the spectator attraction that they once had been.

Argentina 1914: the tour that wasn't

The immediate context of the Corinthians' ill-fated tour to Argentina in 1914 was supplied by the rather uneasy armistice between the FA and the Amateur Football Association, which brought English soccer's ten-year schism to an end in 1914. No sooner had the Corinthians played against English Wanderers, West Bromwich Albion and West Ham United in March and April 1914, the three matches appearing to signify that they had succeeded in reconciling the warring parties, than it was announced that they would be touring Argentina later in the year. This was problematic in that the tour was arranged by the *Federación Argentina de Football* (Argentine Football Federation),[61] was formed in 1912 after the socially elite *Club de Gimanisia y Esgrima de Buenos Aires* (Buenos Aires Gymnastic and Fencing Club) had persuaded a number of clubs to join it in a breakaway movement, claiming that under the AFA, they were being 'mistreated and underrepresented'.[62] This depressingly familiar scenario seemed likely to undermine the fragile agreement that had been reached at home. The AFA's immediate response was to instruct its secretary to telegram the FA in London asking them to do everything possible to 'avoid the realisation of such a visit'.[63] The *Standard*, an English-language newspaper published in Buenos Aires, claimed that news of the proposed tour had come as a 'bombshell' and that it was unlikely the FA would permit the Corinthians to visit Argentina 'under the auspices of an unaffiliated body'.[64] While the party of fourteen players was on its way to Argentina a further complication arose in that they agreed to visit Uruguay to play in Montevideo under the auspices of the Uruguayan Football Association, also unrecognized by FIFA. Though the Corinthians protested that the arrangements they had made could be honoured because they pre-dated the ending of the Split, the club had put itself in a position where it appeared to be undermining the deal that it had just brokered. It was reported from Buenos Aires that Ivan Snell, who was touring again in 1914, 'greatly deplores the possibility of another split in England, especially as his club had so much to do with the healing of the old one; but he made it clear that the Corinthians could not be permit themselves to be trampled on "like a minor club"'. They 'were at perfect liberty to play with whom they pleased'.[65] It was even suggested that the Corinthians had 'tendered their resignation to the Football Association'.[66]

All this was immaterial in that it was overtaken by events. If the tour had gone ahead as planned, some press comment suggested an awareness that England's football prestige would have been very much at stake. The *Sheffield Daily Telegraph*, for example, delighted that the party included a local player, R.C. Maples, who had captained his school team who was now at Oxford, hoped that the Argentine opposition would 'feel the full weight of their football powers'. The article went on to note that the Argentinian press was predicting that soccer there would soon be superior to soccer played in England, the country that remained convinced that it had given the game to the rest of the world, and that 'patriotic Britons in South America were finding the uppishness of the natives aggravating'. Club sides from other European countries, notably Italy, were by now making their presence felt in Brazil and Argentina. *'Noblesse oblige'* dictated that the Corinthians were honour-bound to uphold the nation's prestige abroad.[67] The idea that international sport was 'war by other means' had taken root, and England's gentleman amateurs could not avoid its implications. Britain declared war on Germany on 4 August 1914 while the Corinthians were at sea. When the tourists landed in Brazil five of the party, all reservists, immediately took the first boat home. The remaining Corinthians re-embarked on the ship that had taken them out and followed a little later. Max Woosnam, whose career as an outstanding amateur was still largely in front of him, reached his home by the end of August and within a day had enlisted in the Montgomeryshire Yeomanry as a Second Lieutenant. 'Woosnam', notes his biographer, 'knew what was expected of him, as it appears, did all of the Corinthians'.[68] The opportunity to tour in Argentina never came again.

Notes

1. Cesar R. Torres, '"If We Had Had Our Argentine Team Here!" Football and the 1924 Argentine Olympic Team', *Journal of Sport History*, vol. 30, no. 1, 2003, pp. 1–24. For a general survey of the development of soccer in South America in this period, see Tony Mason, *Passion for the People? Football in South America* (London: Verso, 1995), pp. 1–26.
2. Peter J. Beck, *Scoring for Britain: International Football and International Politics, 1900–1939* (London: Frank Cass, 1999), pp. 57–58.
3. Cesar R. Torres, 'Tribulations and Achievements: The Early History of Olympism in Argentina', *International Journal of the History of Sport*, vol. 18, no. 3, 2002, pp. 59–92.
4. 'The Arrival of the South African Football Team', *Buenos Aires Herald*, 19 June 1906; Chris Bolsmann, 'South African Football Tours at the Turn of the Twentieth Century: Amateurs, Pioneers and Profits', *African Historical Review*, vol. 42, no.1, 2010, pp. 91–112.
5. *Guide to the Football Field* (Buenos Aires: Argentine Football Association, 1903); Chris Bolsmann, 'White Football in South Africa: Empire, Apartheid and Change, 1892–1977', *Soccer and Society*, vol. 11, nos. 1–2, 2010, pp. 29–45.
6. 'Sports: Football', *El Gladiador*, 30 September 1904.
7. For Charles Miller, see Aidan Hamilton, *An Entirely Different Game: The British Influence on Brazilian Football* (Edinburgh: Mainstream, 1998), pp. 19–78. Matthew

Brown, *From Frontiers to Football: An Alternative History of Latin America, since 1800* (London: Reaktion Books, 2014). See also Alex Bellos, *Futebol: The Brazilian Way of Life* (London: Bloomsbury 2002); Andreas Campomar, *Golazo: A History of Latin American Football* (London: Quercus, 2014); Josh Lacey, *God Is Brazilian, Charles Miller: The Man Who Brought Football to Brazil* (Stroud: Tempus, 2005); John Mills, *Charles Miller: o Pai do Futebol Brasileiro* (São Paulo: Panda Books, 2005); and Chris Taylor, *The Beautiful Game: A Journey through Latin American Football* (London: Phoenix Press, 1998).
8 David Goldblatt, *The Ball Is Round: A Global History of Football* (London: Penguin, 2006), p. 126. For early football in Brazil, see Christopher Thomas Gaffney, *Temples of the Earthbound Gods: Stadiums and Cultural Landscapes in Rio de Janeiro and Buenos Aires* (Austin: University of Texas Press, 2008), p. 43; Fatima Martin Rodrigues Ferreira Antunes, 'The Early Days of Football in Brazil: The British Influence and Factory Clubs in São Paulo', in Paulo Fontes and Bernando Buarque De Hollanda, (eds), *The Country of Football: Politics, Popular Culture and the Beautiful Game in Brazil* (London: Hurst and Company, 2014).
9 Ibid, Reginald Lloyd, (ed), *Twentieth Century Impressions of Brazil: Its History, People, Commerce, Industries, and Resources* (London: Lloyd's Greater Britain Publishing Company, 1913) and José Moraes dos Santos Neto, *Visão do Jogo Primórdios do Futebol no Brasil* (São Paulo: Cosac & Naify, 2002); Antônio Figueiredo, *História do foot-ball em São Paulo* (São Paulo: Secção de obras d' O Estado de São Paulo, 1918).
10 Hamilton, *An Entirely Different Game*, p. 44.
11 Mario Filho, *O negro no futebol brasilero* (Rio de Janeiro: MAUAD, 5th ed., 2010), p. 34.
12 Antunes, 'The Early Days of Football in Brazil'.
13 Tomás Mazzoni, *História do futebol no Brasil 1894–1950* (São Paulo: Leia, 1950).
14 Peter J. Cain and Antony G. Hopkins, *British Imperialism: Innovation and Expansion 1688–1914* (Harlow: Longman, 1993), p. 315.
15 See Hamilton, *An Entirely Different Game*, p. 64.
16 Gregg Bocketti, *The Invention of the Beautiful Game: Football and the Making of Modern Brazil* (Gainesville: University Press of Florida, 2016), p. 123.
17 *Jornal do Commercio*, 31 July 1910.
18 *Brazilian Review*, 30 August 1910.
19 *The Times*, 6 August 1910.
20 Programme of Entertainments August 1910. Fluminense Football Club Archive, Rio de Janeiro.
21 Quoted in Bocketti, *The Invention*, p. 124.
22 *Jornal do Commercio*, 25 August 1910.
23 Quoted in Hamilton, *An Entirely Different Game*, p. 70.
24 *Jornal do Commercio*, 26 August 1910; *O Paiz*, 27 August 1910.
25 *O Paiz*, 29 August 1910 and *Jornal do Commercio*, 27 August 1910.
26 *Jornal do Commercio*, 28 August 1910; *O Paiz*, 29, 30 August 1910.
27 'Banquete em honra dos Corinthians offercido pelo Fluminense Football Club, Rio de Janeiro, 28 de Agosto 1910'. Fluminense Football Club Archive, Rio de Janeiro.
28 Hamilton, *An Entirely Different Game*, p. 70.
29 *O Estado de S. Paulo*, 1 September 1910; *Jornal do Commercio*, 1, 2, September 1910.
30 *Jornal do Commercio*, 3 September 1910.
31 *Jornal do Commercio*, 17 September 1910.
32 *Brazilian Review*, 13 September 1910.
33 F.N.S. Creek, *A History of the Corinthian Football Club* (London: Longmans, Green and Co., 1933), p. 84.

34 *Jornal do Commercio*, 17 September 1910.
35 *Brazilian Review*, 27 September 1910, p. 904.
36 *Jornal do Commercio*, 6 September 1910; *Brazilian Review*, 13 September 1910.
37 *Brazilian Review*, 13 September 1910.
38 *Brazilian Review*, 27 September 1910, p. 904. For the matches played on this tour, see Creek, *History of the Corinthians*, pp. 82–84; Hamilton, *An Entirely Different Game*, pp. 67–78; Rob Cavallini, *Play Up Corinth: A History of the Corinthian Football Club* (Stroud: Stadia, 2007), pp. 106–8.
39 Cited in *Jornal do Commercio*, 19 September 1910.
40 Hamilton, *An Entirely Different Game*, p. 77; see also Cavallini, *Play Up Corinth*, p. 107.
41 *Gazeta de Noticias*, 24 July 1913.
42 Cited in Hamilton, *An Entirely Different Game*, p. 91.
43 *O Paiz*, 25 August 1913.
44 Creek, *History of the Corinthians*, pp. 87–88; for this tour, see also Hamilton, *An Entirely Different Game*, pp. 91–96; Cavallini, *Play Up Corinth*, pp. 113–14.
45 Minutes of the Associación Argentina de Football, 4 June 1913.
46 Mason, *Passion for the People?* p. 25.
47 Hamilton, *An Entirely Different Game*, p. 21 and John R. Mills, *Charles William Miller: 1994–1994. Memoriam Clube Atlético São Paulo* (São Paulo: SPAC, 1994).
48 *The Brazilian Review*, 5 August 1913.
49 *O Estado de S. Paulo*, 29 August 1913.
50 *O Estado de S. Paulo*, 27 August 1913.
51 *Brazilian Review*, 2 September 1913.
52 *O Estado de S. Paulo*, 29 August 1913.
53 Quoted in Hamilton, *An Entirely Different Game*, p. 95.
54 *The Sportsman*, 24 September 1913.
55 Ibid.
56 *Correio Paulistano*, 1 September 1913.
57 Hamilton, *An Entirely Different Game*, p. 95.
58 *Pall Mall Gazette*, 24 September 1913.
59 *The Sportsman*, 24 September 1913.
60 Brown, *From Frontiers to Football*, pp. 108–9.
61 *The Standard* (Buenos Aires), 6 May 1914 and *La Argentina*, 8 May 1912.
62 Torres, 'If We Had Had Our Argentine Team Here!' pp. 1–24.
63 Minutes of the Meeting of the Council of the Associación Argentina de Football, 4 May 1914. Sergio Lodise Collection.
64 *The Standard* (Buenos Aires), 16 May 1914.
65 *The Standard*, 5 July 1914.
66 *La Argentina*, 17 July 1914; *Athletic News*, 3 August 1914.
67 *Sheffield Daily Telegraph*, 25 July 1914.
68 Mick Collins, *All-Round Genius: The Unknown Story of Britain's Greatest Sportsman* (London: Aurum 2006), pp. 64–66; see also Creek, *History of the Corinthians*, pp. 88–89.

Conclusion

Figure C.1 Banquet in honour of the Corinthians, Paris, 1904.
La Vie au Grand Air, pub. Paris, 21 April 1904.

From 'Pa' Jackson onwards, the Corinthians have been very influential in writing their own story. Those who have written histories of the club – Corbett (1906), Creek (1933), Cavallini (2007) – have themselves been Corinthians or closely associated with the Corinthian-Casuals. They lean heavily on each other – Creek on Corbett, Cavallini on Creek and Corbett – and, while useful as guides to the club's playing record, they demand careful and critical reading. Grayson's (1955) *Corinthians and Cricketers* was inspired by an adolescent devotion to G.O. Smith and reflects the author's regret at the erosion of Corinthian ideals in sport. A.H. Fabian and Geoffrey Green, editors of *Association Football* (1960), a four-volume history of the development of the game in the United Kingdom, had both played for the club in its declining years. Green's obituary in *The Times* recalled his career as 'an old fashioned attacking centre half for Cambridge University and the legendary

Corinthians'.[1] It was, perhaps, inevitable that these writers were sometimes less than clinical in their assessment of the club's achievements and inclined to overstate its influence. In mitigation, the Corinthians' disdain for league and cup competitions made objective comparison with the records of other clubs difficult. More recently, some histories of association football have underestimated their importance. Jonathan Wilson's (2008) excellent history of football tactics, *Inverting the Pyramid*, for example, leaves them out of the story altogether. Our intention has been to write the Corinthian Football Club – for many years, *the* most famous amateur club in the world – back into the history of the development of the global game.

One does not have to be an apologist to recognize a discernible Corinthian legacy. The famous name lived on long after the demise of the original club. Curiously, despite the club's aversion to 'pot-hunting', the Corinthians donated a trophy to the London Schools Football Association for an inter-district competition in 1893, and the Corinthian Shield is still awarded annually.[2] The Islington Corinthians, formed in 1937, were socially a more mixed party than their illustrious predecessors but emulated them by touring extensively, 'fraternising with governors, princes, ambassadors, film stars and the like'.[3] Between 1945 and 1963, the Corinthian League provided a competitive framework for senior amateur clubs on the outskirts of London.[4] In England, the Corinthians now live on primarily as the Corinthian-Casuals, currently in the Bostik League South, the eighth tier of England's soccer pyramid. The hyphenated club's mission statement echoes nineteenth-century concerns about how the game should be played. It aims 'to promote fair play and sportsmanship [and] to play competitive football at the highest level possible whilst remaining strictly amateur and retaining the ideals of the Corinthians and Casuals Football Clubs'.[5] The Corinthians name is still favoured by a number of clubs, some more illustrious than others. A club calling itself the Corinthians was founded in Sevenoaks, Kent in 1972 by Ron Billings, successful businessman, soccer enthusiast and 'one of the last great twentieth-century advocates of amateurism'. 'Strictly amateur', it currently competes at a level just below that of the Corinthian-Casuals in the Southern Counties East League.[6] And, of course, we should not forget Sport Club Corinthians Paulista, founded after the English Corinthians' first visit to Brazil in 1910.

What has survived is not just a name but an idea of how the game should be played. For many years, there was a tendency, especially among those who valued the contribution of the public schools and universities to soccer's early development, to measure excellence against standards set by the Corinthians, a highly subjective exercise, especially as it was often based on memory and wishful thinking. When Moscow Dynamo toured Britain in 1945, Sir Godfrey Ince, who had taken a London University team to play in Russia in 1914, described their performance against Chelsea as 'about the finest football exhibition I have seen in Britain since the Corinthians were a great side'.[7] In the late 1940s and early 1950s, middle-class soccer enthusiasts focused on Pegasus, a team of Oxbridge graduates, good enough to win the Football Association (FA) Amateur Cup in 1951 and 1953, seeing them as the Corinthians reborn. Their founder, Dr Harold Thompson of St John's College, Oxford, when making the case for exemption from the qualifying rounds of the competition, claimed that 'the revival of the Corinthian F.C. in its old form is the ardent wish often expressed by many people of widely different connection'.[8] Geoffrey Green, at *The Times*, for whom – along with Manchester United and Real Madrid – Pegasus was one of the outstanding clubs of the 1950s, was in no doubt that 'many people ... looked to them to retrieve the spirit of the Corinthians'.[9] There were still a number of senior amateur clubs that could be described as 'middle class', and references to the Corinthians and their legacy surfaced when they caught the media's attention. This was especially evident when Corinthian-Casuals reached the final of the Amateur Cup in 1956. Green, in his match preview, believed that 'popular sentiment' would be very much on their side 'largely because in that hyphenated title there still lives on the memory, the spirit, and the glory that was Corinth!'[10] This proved sufficient to inspire the underdogs to draw with Bishop Auckland at Wembley, but they were well beaten in the replay. It was very much the last hurrah, though references to the Corinthian spirit occasionally resurface.

Setting this aspect of the Corinthian legacy aside, it becomes easier to address those areas in which the club did make a significant contribution to the development of soccer and we now turn our attention to its impact on the way the game has been and is played, to its role as a flagship for amateurism, and to the importance of touring as a factor in soccer globalization. Despite the millions of words written about the Corinthians, it is still difficult to envisage exactly how they played. Surviving newsreel footage, apart from being in rather short supply, was usually shot from a single standing camera, making it impossible to form an impression of formation, tactics or style. The frame introducing the silent record of their FA Cup match with Blackburn Rovers in 1924 assumes that 'all sporting football lovers' will take delight in a victory for the amateurs over the professionals but the moving pictures that follow fail to capture anything distinctive about the Corinthians beyond the gentlemanly affectation of strolling onto the pitch with hands in pockets, signifying that soccer was for them pleasure rather than business, leisure rather than work.[11] Accounts by those who saw them play, however, often suggest awareness of a particular Corinthian style. Although their robust defensive play, especially when the Walters brothers were at full-back, was admired by some, it was their relentless emphasis on attack that seems to have captured the imagination of observers, both at home and abroad. *Athletics News* columnist John Lewis, who saw them play on their 1906 Christmas tour, observed that, when on the offensive, it was 'their common practice to keep in a line as nearly as possible, so that when the ball is put forward the next man follows it at top speed, draws the defender towards him, and then puts it forward again, and the next man takes up the tale – always going forward'. This was 'in striking contrast' to the game as played by professionals who – points being at stake – were more inclined to play a percentage game with the emphasis on ball retention and minimization of risk.[12] Those who admired the Corinthians expected them to play with 'style', even if its precise definition eluded them. 'What are the characteristics of the Corinthians' game and therefore the best English football?', asked a French football paper in 1922: 'Ball control is excellent, dribbling is superb, but never exaggerated, shooting is sure with left and right foot and teamwork, above all, is the main characteristic'.[13] The adjective 'elegant' was often used by journalists to describe the Corinthians at their best, especially when the gentleman amateurs were able to demonstrate apparently effortless superiority.

What did become apparent was a reluctance to adapt to new conditions. When the Austrian coach Hugo Meisl visited the Netherlands to watch the Corinthians on their return to the mainstream of European soccer in 1922, he was delighted to report: 'Nothing has changed. The Corinthians still represent the highest school of football. Amateurism'.[14] Though this was intended as a compliment, the club's inability to modify its approach eventually became problematic, especially after the introduction of the new offside law in 1925 and the widespread adoption of the 'WM' formation, with the centre-half, previously an attacking player, now assigned a defensive role. In the debate that ensued Corinthians and former Corinthians showed themselves reluctant to abandon the system with which they were familiar. 'Pa' Jackson, intervening from the sidelines, set the tone, convinced that changing the laws in the interests of professional clubs – the new offside rule was intended to make the game more attractive for paying spectators – was inevitably detrimental and 'had deprived the amateurs of much that was delightful in the old times'.[15] Former Corinthian, Kenneth Hunt, in his pamphlet *Football: How to Succeed* (1932), was still making a case for setting up defensively on distinctly old-fashioned lines in order to leave the centre-half free to prompt attacks.[16] Tactical conservatism was certainly not the only reason why the Corinthians began to struggle on the field, but it did not help. There was some disagreement within the club regarding tactics with secretary G.N. Foster having to defend himself against critics like Howard Fabian who regarded him as 'a diehard' regarding forward play. Foster was not prepared to approve a new approach 'merely because the Arsenal and other clubs find it best, or Howard plays it with Derby County'; there was no point in 'seeking to play the pros at their own game'; it was far better to proceed 'on Corinthian lines'.[17] This may have sufficed before 1925, but it is hard to resist the conclusion that the Corinthian approach, however effective it once had been or however aesthetically pleasing, had little to offer thereafter. 'In the past', a Swiss newspaper reflected some years later, 'we knew no better style than that played by the Corinthians of England .... But their time has passed'.[18]

If the influence of the Corinthians persisted on the field of play, it is in relation to establishing the presumption that players would conduct themselves in a 'gentlemanly' fashion. It was assumed that this came naturally to the Corinthians who, being gentlemen, would have an innate sense of how to behave on and off the field. This underpinned an obituary of R.C. Gosling, Corinthian of the 1890s and 'ever a true English gentleman', who was 'never ungenerous in action or unkind in word'.[19] It informed the opening remarks of Hunt's pamphlet where readers were urged to observe 'the spirit of the game as well as the letter of the law', 'to be undiscouraged by defeat' and 'chivalrous in victory'. We should not underestimate the impact of these sentiments. Hunt's advocacy of fair play so impressed Kim Yong Sik, a Korean footballer on tour in China in 1934, that he changed his ways.[20] A search for traces of clubs that modelled themselves on the Corinthians generated a reference to Caldecott Corinthians, a village team playing in Leicestershire after the Second World War. Though referred to in the local press simply as 'Caldecott', their records for 1951–52 indicated an achievement that justified the Corinthian label. Local officials, as Nicholas Fishwick observed in his invaluable work on park football in the interwar period, liked to apply 'Corinthian standards', and Caldecott, having won their league, were duly congratulated on 'something even more [important] – that is playing football in the spirit in which it ought to be played'.[21] 'Ungentlemanly conduct' – since 2007 referred to as 'unsporting behaviour' – remains an offence under the laws of the game. Moreover, though few would now refuse to take advantage of a penalty when awarded, as the Corinthians did on their South African tour in 1907, players learn that they are expected to observe certain sporting conventions, such as kicking the ball out of play when an opponent is injured. Corinthianism, it could be argued, exerts a residual influence that, even sixty or so years after the original club's demise, might still serve as a point of reference. 'When I see the name "Corinthians", I think of gentlemen and sportsmanship', a disgruntled Llanelli supporter observed after a match against Cardiff Corinthians in the 1990s. 'There was little of the Corinthian spirit about this mob, however, who were the worst bunch of cloggers I have seen for years'.[22] Those who professed to be Corinthians, it seems, were still expected to behave like Corinthians.

As we have seen, the relationship between the original Corinthians and amateurism is more complex than we might have expected. It was rooted in their sense of superiority and the idea that the social class and sporting status were indivisible. To use D.J. Taylor's neat encapsulation of the Corinthian mindset, 'An amateur, to put it starkly, was born; a professional made'.[23] Given that the club was formed just as the FA was struggling to come to terms with professionalism, it was always likely that the Corinthians would be cast as backward-looking champions of a lost cause, albeit one that died rather slowly. Some, undoubtedly, had a distaste for professionalism and all that it represented. The author of a biographical sketch of Arthur Dunn, who played for the club in the 1880s and 1890s, claimed that the arrival of professionalism had 'cast a shadow over Arthur's life for he realised what a menace it entailed to his beloved sport'.[24] Yet, in responding to this menace, one that threatened to turn their world upside down each time a team of working-class professionals won the FA Cup, the Corinthians offered not outright confrontation but, by touring and taking on the professionals in the North and Midlands, public demonstrations of their innate superiority. Even when beaten, they could claim a moral victory simply by turning up and behaving like gentlemen. As gentlemen amateurs, they 'were allowed to pursue victory but only within certain limitations of style and excellence'.[25] When these were no longer achievable, they increasingly sought refuge in the company of likeminded sportsmen wherever they could be found at home or abroad.

Amateurism, essentially a reaction against both professionalism and commercialism in sport, leads inevitably to the question of money, not least because playing without expectation of payment or reward has conventionally been regarded as the defining quality of the true amateur. Did the Corinthians fall short in this respect despite their many and frequent protestations of innocence? Some historians are inclined to this view. Mike Huggins, for example, with reference to guarantees demanded and expenses paid, has argued that they very quickly became 'a professional side in all but name'.[26] Awkward questions linger to which the club's officers, Jackson especially, never provided totally convincing answers, but it is misleading, taking the context in which they operated into account, to regard the Corinthians as professionals, even though they would rarely have had to put their hands in their pockets while on tour. In the nineteenth century and for much of the twentieth, a middle-class amateur playing first-class cricket might reasonably expect to be paid more in expenses than a working-class 'pro' would take home in wages. The practice was well established in England long before professionalism became an issue in soccer and the Corinthians arrived on the scene. 'Strict' or 'pure' amateurism was at best a discursive ideal; to be an 'amateur' or a 'professional' was an indication of social status; amateur rules were designed primarily to discriminate unfairly between the classes; that was their purpose. Significantly, Hunt, writing a letter to a fictional public schoolboy who had been invited to sign as an amateur with a professional club, later touched on the possibility 'of losing caste with your fellows if you play with pros'.[27] To be a Corinthian was to belong to a particular social caste. A Corinthian could not be a professional whatever benefits he might derive directly or indirectly from soccer.

Where the Corinthians were probably most at odds with the amateur ideal, however, was in relation to the systematic and profitable exploitation of symbolic rivalries – North versus South, 'Toffs' versus 'Plebs' – whenever they played against professional opposition in London or when touring at home or abroad. Most soccer clubs, even if they professed to be amateurs, were required to operate as businesses to some extent, especially when they took money at the gate, and the Corinthians were no different in that respect. Jackson, moreover, was an entrepreneur who saw the commercial opportunities offered by association football in the late nineteenth century. The brand of socially exclusive amateurism that was the club's unique selling point was also instrumental in enhancing its appeal in emerging soccer markets, securing the sponsorship and guarantees that allowed players to tour overseas in style at little expense to themselves, whatever expenses were paid. Ironically, the club's social exclusivity – it remained essentially a club for public-school/Oxbridge men – eventually undermined its credibility, damaging the brand that had been so assiduously cultivated. If only, Norman Creek lamented in 1937, the Corinthians had widened their outlook to include players who had been to 'smaller universities' in London and the provinces, 'that famous amateur side need never have fallen to its present lowly state'.[28] In the long run, the Corinthians' sporting pretensions were fatally undermined by a narrow social outlook that was distinctly snobbish.

Finally, we have to consider the Corinthian's role as a touring club. Initially, they toured only within the United Kingdom, though we should not underestimate the depth of the social chasm that they traversed as they crossed from one of the 'two nations' famously identified by Disraeli in his novel *Sybil* (1845) to the other. It is likely that the first Corinthians found people they encountered in the mill towns of Lancashire or in Glasgow at least as foreign as those that a later generation met when overseas. When they began to export their particular brand, starting with the South African tour of 1897, the English game of association football had already established a global footprint through empire, education and trade. 'The colonising propensities of the British race', according to FA secretary Charles Alcock, writing in 1891, had 'been instrumental in the diffusion of a love of football to the extreme limits of our possessions'. South Africa, in particular, was 'a fruitful field for the energies of footballers settling there', and the game was spreading from Canada to the United States where it would soon be played 'on a very extensive scale'.[29] Trade and education played their part. In many countries, English football, in its various forms, arrived initially with the merchant fleet and seamen who amused themselves and the locals by kicking a ball about. Free trade and football were inextricably linked.[30] British communities settling abroad in order to conduct business reinforced the connection, not least because they established schools and colleges where the cult of athleticism prevailed just as it did back home. Some of the local *bourgeoisie*, smitten with anglophilia, even sent their boys to England to be educated. From Buenos Aires to Berlin, from Rio to Rotterdam, similar processes of diffusion were evident. When the Corinthians eventually arrived, they were pushing at doors that had already been opened. They were welcomed initially because they were English and because local enthusiasts believed that they could learn from 'a group chosen from the best public school and university players', from an elite club who, as a Paris newspaper later recalled, 'have always retained one of the purest styles with the round ball'.[31]

We are now aware, however, that the process of diffusion underpinning the development of soccer as a global phenomenon was complex. Movement was not only in one direction, from Britain outwards to its formal and informal empire. Globalization rested on a multiplicity of transnational and international connections between soccer enthusiasts who had never heard of globalization. The Corinthians, as they toured overseas, were part of this process, facilitating links between the sport's movers and shakers wherever they were encountered. In Europe, for example, they quickly found that their tours supplied opportunities for those wishing to promote soccer to come together. Playing in Berlin in 1906, the Corinthians who had visited Sweden two years earlier 'were delighted to find that Colonel Balch and Count von Rosen [friends from Stockholm] were at the match'. Walter Bensemann, who knew 'Pa' Jackson and was the prime mover in early Anglo-German exchanges, was there to greet the Corinthians when they arrived in Switzerland in 1931.[32] As we have seen, Hugo Meisl, instrumental in arranging their match in Austria 1904, was everywhere, notably in the Netherlands when the Corinthians played there in 1922 and later in England with his *wunderteam* in 1932. The Corinthians supplied a convenient focal point, but their part in the process of diffusion should not be overstated. In the United States, for example, the impact of the Pilgrims may have been more significant. On tour, the Corinthians were effectively an advertisement for a particular brand of soccer that had flourished under the patrician hegemony established by gentlemen amateurs in Victorian England and was now looking for new markets. Their influence on the development of the game globally depended largely on local conditions. Anglophile hosts were initially inclined to regard them as exemplars of soccer perfection, though later they looked more often to professionals for lessons in how to play the game. By 1932, Arsenal were clearly 'the team best qualified to represent British football in Paris'.[33] Corinthian football, a seductive blend of social elitism and soccer excellence, helped to confer legitimacy on amateurism wherever they went, but their hosts learned over time to adapt or reject English models to suit their own purposes.

Notes

1. *The Times*, 11 May 1990.
2. Colm Kerrigan, *A History of the English Schools' Football Association 1904–2004* (Harefield: Yore Publications, 2004), pp. 11–12; the Corinthians also donated cups to be competed for by amateur clubs in Hungary and Sweden, see F.N.S. Creek, *A History of the Corinthian Football Club* (London: Longmans, Green & Co., 1933), pp. 74–75.
3. R.B. Alaway, *Football All Round the World* (London: Newservice Ltd., 1948), p. 127; for the captain's account of this tour, see pp. 97–126.
4. A Corinthian League had originally been proposed during the Great Split, but the FA refused to sanction it unless its name was changed. National Football Museum (NFM), Football Association Minutes, Leagues Sanction Committee, 24 August 1912.
5. www.corinthian-casuals.com, accessed 1 October 2017.

6 David Bauckham, *The Last Corinthian* (2016), at www.dbauckham.exposure.co/the_last_corinthian, accessed 1 October 2017.
7 Sir Godfrey Ince, 'Thank You Dynamo', in *Dynamo – and All That* (London: Valiant Publications, 1946), p. 27.
8 Thompson's memorandum [May 1948], see Dilwyn Porter, 'Amateur Football in England, 1948–1963: The Pegasus Phenomenon', *Contemporary British History*, vol. 14, no. 2, 2000, pp. 5–6.
9 Geoffrey Green, *Soccer in the Fifties* (London: Ian Allen, 1974), pp. 35–38.
10 *The Times*, 7 April 1956.
11 See britishpathe.com/video/tit-bit-of-the-first round (1924); also britishpathe.com/video/first-time-since the war (1925); britishpathe.com/video/well-played-new-brighton (1928); britishpathe.com/video/bravo-corinthians (1930).
12 *Athletic News* (Manchester), 1 January 1906.
13 *Le Ballon Rond* (Bordeaux), 22 July 1922.
14 *De Telegraaf* (Amsterdam), 21 April 1922.
15 N Lane Jackson, 'The Corinthians', *The Times*, 26 October 1932.
16 See Rev. K.R.G. Hunt, *Football: How to Succeed* (London: Evans Brothers Ltd., 1932), pp. 23–26.
17 Circular letter from G.N. Foster, 28 April 1933, cited in Rob Cavallini, *Play Up Corinth: A History of the Corinthian Football Club* (Stroud, 2007), pp. 190–91.
18 *La Gazette de Lausanne*, 18 July 1946.
19 *Athletic News*, 17 April 1922.
20 Hunt, *Football: How to Succeed*, p. 3; Jong Sung Lee, *A History of Football in North and South Korea c.1910–2002* (Bern: Peter Lang, 2016), p. 73.
21 Record Office for Leicestershire, Leicester and Rutland (LRO), Caldecott Corinthians FC, DE 8161/4/1-5, Match Record Book 1951–52, unidentified press cutting; Nicholas Fishwick, *English Football and Society 1910–1950* (Manchester: Manchester University Press, 1989), p. 73.
22 Glamorgan Record Office [GA], Cardiff Corinthians AFC MSS, D 751/12/4, copy of match report on unofficial Llanelli club website, [nd].
23 D.J. Taylor, *On the Corinthian Spirit: The Decline of Amateurism in Sport* (London: Yellow Jersey Press, 2006), p. 57.
24 Shane Leslie, *Men Were Different: Five Studies in Late Victorian Biography* (London: Michael Joseph, 1937), pp. 167–68.
25 Ed Smith, 'Left Field', *New Statesman*, 28 July–10 August 2017, p. 48.
26 Mike Huggins, *The Victorians and Sport* (London: Hambledon and London, 2004), p. 60.
27 K.R.G. Hunt, 'Captain of Footer: Being Letters from his Uncle to James Macalister Brown, of Severn Side School', *Boy's Own Paper*, November 1922, pp. 34–35.
28 F.N.S. Creek, *Association Football* (London: J.M. Dent & Sons, 1937), p. 193.
29 Charles Alcock, *The Association Game* (London: George Routledge & Sons, 1891), pp. 73–74.
30 See Pierre Lanfranchi and Matthew Taylor, *Moving with the Ball: the Migration of Professional Footballers* (Oxford: Berg, 2001), p. 2.
31 *Le Petit Journal* (Paris), 6 January 1925.
32 Creek, *History of the Corinthians*, pp. 76, 117.
33 *Le Petit Journal*, 31 October 1932.

Bibliography

Archive sources

Bodleian Library, Oxford, Oxford University Association Football Club, minute books and other MSS.
Essex Records Office, Chelmsford, Essex County Cricket Club, minute books.
Everton Collection, evertoncollection.org.uk, minute books.
Fluminense Football Club Archive, Rio de Janeiro.
Glamorgan Archives, Cardiff, Cardiff Corinthians Association Football Club MSS.
Hap Meyer Soccer Collection, Southern Illinois University Edwardsville, General Meeting of the New York State Football Association minute books.
Historical Papers Collection, William Cullen Library, University of the Witwatersrand, South African Football Association minute books.
London Metropolitan Archives, Crystal Palace Trustees, minute book.
National Football Museum Archives, Preston, Football Association minute books; Preston North End FC, Football League player registrations, 1889.
National Library of Wales, Aberystwyth, Football Association of Wales, minute books.
Record Office for Leicestershire, Leicester and Rutland, Wigston Magna, ephemera – football 1892–2009; Caldecott Corinthians FC, match record book.
Sergio Lodise Collection, Asociación Argentina de Football, minute books.
Surrey History Centre, Woking, Surrey County Cricket Club, minute books, match receipt books.

Newspapers and periodicals

Allgemeen Handelsblat (Amsterdam)
Allgemeine Sport Zeitung (Vienna)
American Cricketer (Philadelphia)
Association Football News
Athletic News (Manchester)
Atlanta Constitution
Berliner Tageblatt
Birmingham Daily Post
Blackburn Weekly Standard and Express
Birmingham Mail
Bloemfontein Post
Boston Evening Transcript

Bibliography

Buenos Aires Herald
Bury Guardian
Cape Argus (Cape Town)
Cape Daily Telegraph (Port Elizabeth)
Cape Times (Cape Town)
Chicago Daily Tribune
Correio Paulistano (São Paulo)
Daily Argus (Birmingham)
Daily Colonist (Victoria)
De Telegraaf (Amsterdam)
Diamond Fields Advertiser (Kimberley)
Die Bühne (Vienna)
Dundee Evening Post
Eastern Province Herald (Port Elizabeth)
El Gladiador (Buenos Aires)
Feuille d'Avis de Neuchâtel
Football (London)
Football Evening News (London)
Football Field and Sports Telegram (Bolton)
Gazeta de Noticias (Rio de Janeiro)
Glasgow Herald
Het Nieuws van de Dag (Amsterdam)
Het Sportsblad (Amsterdam)
Illustriertes Spotsblatt (Vienna)
Irish Times (Dublin)
Irish Press (Dublin)
Jornal do Commercio (Rio de Janeiro)
L'Auto (Paris)
La Argentina (Buenos Aires)
La Gazette de Lausanne
La Vie au Grand Air: Revue Illustrée de Tous les Sports (Paris)
Le Ballon Rond (Bordeaux)
Le Journal de Genève
Le Matin (Paris)
Le Petit Journal (Paris)
Leicester Chronicle
Manitoba Free Press
Medicine Hat Daily News (Alberta)
Morning Post (London)
Natal Mercury (Durban)
Natal Witness (Pietermaritzburg)
New York Times
New York Daily Tribune
Newcastle Daily Chronicle
Nieuwe Rotterdamsche Courant
Nottingham Evening Post
O Estado de S. Paulo (São Paulo)
O Paiz (Rio de Janeiro)
Pall Mall Gazette (London)

Pastime (London)
Pester Lloyd (Budapest)
Portsmouth Evening News
Prager Tageblatt (Prague)
Rand Daily Mail (Johannesburg)
Sheffield Daily Telegraph
Spalding's Athletic Library Official Soccer Foot Ball Guide (New York)
South Africa Review (London)
Sports (Illustrated) (Sheffield)
Sport und Salon (Budapest and Vienna)
South African Review (London)
Sports (Illustrated) (Sheffield)
Standard and Digger News (Kimberley)
Sunday Times (London)
Sunday Times (Johannesburg)
Telegraph and Eastern Province Standard (Port Elizabeth)
The American Cricketer (Philadelphia)
The Brandon Daily Sun
The Brandon Sun
The Brazilian Review (Rio de Janeiro)
The Carthusian
The Cholmeleian
The Evening Post (Dundee)
The Friend (Bloemfontein)
The Inter Ocean (Chicago)
The Lethbridge Daily Herald
The Malvernian
The Morning Call (San Francisco)
The New York Daily Tribune
The Newark Evening Star
The Newark Star
The People (London)
The Salopian
The Scotsman (Edinburgh)
The Sportsman (London)
The Standard (Buenos Aires)
The Star (Johannesburg)
The Sun
The Times (London)
The Times of Natal (Durban)
The Toronto Daily Star
The Umpire (Manchester)
The Washington Post
The Winnipeg Tribune
The Yorkshire Evening Post
Toronto Daily Star
Vancouver Daily World
Washington Post
Western Mail (Cardiff)

Bibliography

Primary Sources: books, memoirs and other published items

Alaway, R.B., *Football All Round the World*, (London: Newservice Ltd., 1948).

Alcock, C.W., *The Association Game*, (London: George Routledge & Sons, 1891).

Argentine Football Association, *Guide to the Football Field*, (Buenos Aires: Argentine Football Association, 1903).

Catton, J., *The Story of Association Football*, (Cleethorpes: Soccer Books Ltd., 2006; first published 1926).

Corbett, B.O., (ed), *Annals of the Corinthian Football Club*, (London: Longmans, Green & Co., 1906).

Creek, F.N.S., *A History of the Corinthian Football Club*, (London: Longmans, Green & Co., 1933).

Creek, F.N.S., *Association Football*, (London: J.M. Dent & Sons, 1937).

Figueiredo, A., *Historia do Foot-Ball em São Paulo*, (São Paulo: Secção de obras d' O Estado de São Paulo, 1918).

Fry, C.B., 'Character sketches', in Corbett, B.O., (ed), *Annals of the Corinthian Football Club*, (London: Longmans, Green & Co., 1906). pp. 31–54.

Fry, C.B., *Life Worth Living: Some Phases of an Englishman*, (London: Pavilion Library, 1986; first published 1939).

Gibson, A. and Pickford, W., *Association Football & the Men Who Made It*, vol. 3, (London: Caxton Press, 1906).

Gibson, A. and Pickford, W., *Association Football & the Men Who Made It*, vol. 4, (Cape Town: McConnel & Co., 1906).

Holland, E.L., (ed), *The Amateur Football Association Annual 1907–8*, (London: The "Marshalsea" Press, 1908).

Hunt, K.R.G., 'Captain of footer. Being letters from his uncle to James Macalister Brown of Severn Side school', *Boy's Own Paper*, November 1922, pp. 34–35.

Hunt, K.R.G., *Football: How to Succeed*, (London: Evans Brothers Ltd., 1932).

Ince, Sir Godfrey, *'Thank You Dynamo'*, in *Dynamo and All That*, (London: Valiant Publications, 1946).

Jackson, N.L., *Association Football*, (London: George Newnes, 2nd ed., 1900; first published, 1899).

Jackson, N.L., ('Pa'), *Always Fit and Well*, (London: George Newnes Ltd., 1931).

Jackson, N.L., ('Pa') *Sporting Days and Sporting Ways*, (London: Hurst & Blackett, 1932).

Jones, K., *Fleet Street and Downing Street*, (London: Hutchinson & Co., 1919).

Leslie, S., *Men Were Different: Five Studies in Late Victorian Biography*, (London: Michael Joseph, 1937).

Lillywhite, F., *The English Cricketers' Trip to Canada and the United States*, (London: F. Lillywhite, 1860).

Lloyd R., (ed), *Twentieth Century Impressions of Brazil: Its History, People, Commerce, Industries, and Resources*, (London: Lloyd's Greater Britain Publishing Company, 1913).

Mazzoni, T., *História do futebol no Brasil 1894–1950*, (São Paulo: Leia, 1950).

Meisl, W., *Fussball: Der Weltsport*, (Zurich: Orell FüssliVerlag, 1930).

Milnes F.H., *A Football Tour with the Pilgrims in America*, (Sheffield: Greene and Thompson, 1905).

Nederlansche Voetbalbund, *Voetbal Almanak 1907–08* (Amsterdam: Nederlansche Voetbalbond, 1907).

Needham, E., *Association Football*, (Cleethorpes: Soccer Books Ltd., 2003; first published 1901).
Parker, G.A., (ed), *South African Sports*, (London: Sampson Low, Marston & Co., 1897).
Pickford, W., *A Glance Back at the Football Association Council 1888–1938*, (Bournemouth: Bournemouth Guardian, 1938).
Rahilly, J.J., *Rugby Football*, (London: C. Arthur Pearson Ltd., 1904).
Robinson, R., *A History of the Queen's Park Football Club 1867–1917*, (Glasgow: Hay, Nisbet & Co., 1920).
Smith, G.O., 'The attack', in Montague Shearman (ed), *Football*, (London: Longmans, Green and Co., 1904), pp. 104–119.
Wall, Sir F., *50 Years of Football*, (Cleethorpes: Soccer Books Ltd., 2006; first published, London 1935).
Ward, R.A.J., *Clapton Football Club: Seventy-Five Years of Football History 1878–1953*, (London: C.E. Fisher Ltd., 1953).

Books

Allaway, R., *Rangers, Rovers and Spindles Soccer, Immigration and Textiles in New England and New Jersey*, (Haworth: St Johann Press, 2015).
Allison, L., *Amateurism in Sport: An Analysis and a Defence*, (London: Frank Cass, 2001).
Amery, J., *The Life of Joseph Chamberlain, vol. 5, Joseph Chamberlain and the Tariff Reform Campaign*, (London: Macmillan, 1969).
Bailey, P., *Leisure and Class in Victorian England: Rational Recreation and the Contest for Control*, (London: Routledge and Kegan Paul, 1978).
Bateman, A., *Cricket, Literature and Culture: Symbolising the Nation, Destabilising Empire*, (Farnham: Ashgate, 2009).
Beck, P.J., *Scoring for Britain: International Football and International Politics, 1900–1939*, (London: Frank Cass, 1999).
Bellos, A., *Futebol: The Brazilian Way of Life*, (London: Bloomsbury, 2002).
Black, D.R. and Nauright, J., *Rugby and the South African Nation*, (Manchester: Manchester University Press, 1998).
Bocketti, G., *The Invention of the Beautiful Game: Football and the Making of Modern Brazil*, (Gainsville: University Press of Florida, 2016).
Booth, K., *The Father of Modern Sport: The Life and Times of Charles W. Alcock*, (Manchester: The Parrs Wood Press, 2002).
Bottenburg, M. van, *Global Games*, (Urbana: University of Illinois Press, 2001).
Bragg, M., *12 Books That Changed the World*, (London: Hodder & Stoughton, 2006).
Brown, M., *From Frontiers to Football: An Alternative History of Latin America, since 1800*, (London: Reaktion Books, 2014).
Cain, P.J., and Hopkins, A.G., *British Imperialism: Innovation and Expansion 1688–1914*, (Harlow: Longman, 1993).
Campomar, A., *Golazo: A History of Latin American Football*, (London: Quercous, 2014).
Carter, N., *The Football Manager: A History*, (Abingdon: Routledge, 2006).
Cavallini, R., *The Wanderers F.C.: Five Times F.A Cup Winners*, (Worcester Park: Dog N Duck Publications, 2005).

Bibliography

Cavallini, R., *Play Up Corinth: A History of the Corinthian Football Club*, (Stroud: Stadia, 2007).

Cavallini, R., *A Casual Affair: A History of the Casuals Football Club*, (Surbiton: Dog N Duck Publications, 2009).

Chapman, D.I., *Dubbined Boots and Shin Pads: A History of Leyton F.C.*, (London: Leyton and Leytonstone Historical Society, 2012).

Collins, M., *All-Round Genius: The Unknown Story of Britain's Greatest Sportsman*, (London: Aurum, 2006).

Collins, T., *A Social History of English Rugby Union*, (Abingdon: Routledge, 2009).

Crampsey, R.A., *The Game for the Game's Sake. The History of Queen's Park Football Club 1867–1967*, (Glasgow: Queen's Park FC, 1967).

dos Santos Neto, J.M., *Visão do Jogo Primórdios do Futebol no Brasil*, (São Paulo: Cosac & Naify, 2002).

Dunning, E. and Sheard, K., *Barbarians, Gentlemen and Players: A Sociological Study of the Development of Rugby Football*, (Oxford: Martin Robertson, 1979).

Eastwood, J. and Moyse, T., *The Men Who Made the Town: The Official History of Ipswich Town F.C. since 1878*, (Sudbury: Almeida Books, 1986).

Fishwick, N., *English Football and Society*, (Manchester: Manchester University Press, 1989).

Filho, M., *O Negro No Futebol Brasilero*, (Rio de Janeiro: MAUAD, 5th ed., 2010).

Gaffney, C.T., *Temples of the Earthbound Gods: Stadiums and Cultural Landscapes in Rio de Janeiro and Buenos Aires*, (Austin: University of Texas Press, 2008).

Goldblatt, D., *The Ball Is Round: A Global History of Football*, (London: Penguin, 2006).

Grayson, E., *Corinthians & Cricketers*, (London: Sportsmans Book Club, 1957).

Green, G., *Soccer The World Game: A Popular History*, (London: Pan Books Ltd., 1956).

Green, G., *Soccer in the Fifties*, (London: Ian Allen, 1974).

Greenland, W.E., *The History of the Amateur Football Alliance*, (Harwich: Amateur Football Alliance/Standard Publishing Co., 1965).

Hamilton, A., *An Entirely Different Game: The British Influence on Brazilian Football*, (Edinburgh: Mainstream, 1998).

Hare, G., *Football in France: A Cultural History*, (Oxford: Berg, 2003).

Havemann, N., *Football under the Swastika: The Influence of Sport, Politics and Commerce on the German Football Association*, (Frankfurt: Campus Verlag GmbH., 2005).

Hess-Lichtenberger, U., *Tor! The Story of German Football*, (London: WSC Books Ltd., 2002).

Holt, R., *Sport and the British: A Modern History*, (Oxford: Oxford University Press, 1989).

Holt, R., *Sport and Society in Modern France*, (Basingstoke: Macmillan, 1981).

Huggins, M., *The Victorians and Sport*, (London: Hambledon and London, 2004).

Ingrassia, B., *The Rise of Gridiron University: Higher Education's Uneasy Alliance with Big-Time Football*, (Lawrence: University Press of Kansas, 2012).

Jacobs, N., *Vivian Woodward: Football's Gentleman*, (Stroud: Tempus, 2005).

Johnes, M., *Soccer and Society: South Wales, 1900–1939*, (Cardiff: University of Wales Press, 2002).

Jones, L., *Soccer: Canada's National Sport: 150 Years of the Memorable, Unexpected and Controversial*, (Toronto: Covershots Inc., 2013).

Joyce, M., *Football League Players Records 1888–1939*, (Nottingham: SoccerData, 2002).
Kerrigan, C., *A History of the English Schools Football Association 1904–2004*, (Harefield: Yore Publications, 2004).
Koller, C. and Brändle, F., *Goal! A Cultural and Social History of Modern Football*, (Washington, DC: Catholic University of America Press, 2015).
Lacey, J., *God is Brazilian, Charles Miller: The Man Who Brought Football to Brazil*, (Stroud: Tempus, 2005).
Lanfranchi, P. and Taylor, M., *Moving with the Ball: The Migration of Professional Footballers*, (Oxford: Berg, 2001).
Lange, D., *Soccer Made in St. Louis: A History of the Game in America's First Soccer Capital*, (St. Louis, MO: Reddy Press, 2001).
Lee, J.S., *A History of Football in North and South Korea, c.1910–2002*, (Bern: Peter Lang, 2016).
Lemmon, D. and Marshall, M., *Essex County Cricket Club: The Official History*, (London: Kingswood, 1987).
Lowerson, J., *Sport and the English Middle Classes 1870–1914*, (Manchester: Manchester University Press, 1993).
Markovits, A. and Hellerman, S., *Offside: Soccer and American Exceptionalism*, (Princeton, NJ: Princeton University Press, 2001).
Marrow, D. and Wamsley, K., *Sport in Canada: A History*, (Oxford: Oxford University Press, 2013).
Mason, T., *Association Football and English Society 1863–1915*, (Brighton: Harvester, 1980).
Mason, T., *Passion of the People? Football in South America*, (London: Verso, 1995).
Mason, T. and Riedi, E., *Sport and the Military: The British Armed Forces 1860–1960*, (Cambridge: Cambridge University Press, 2010).
McDowell, M.L., *A Cultural History of Association Football in Scotland, 1865–1902: Understanding Sport as a Way of Understanding Society*, (Lampeter: Edwin Mellen Press, 2013).
McKibbin, R., *Classes and Cultures: England 1918–1951*, (Oxford: Oxford University Press, 1998).
Meisl, W., *Soccer Revolution*, (London. Phoenix Sports Books, 1955).
Merrett, C., *Sport, Space and Segregation: Politics and Society in Pietermaritzburg*, (Scottsville, KY: University of KwaZulu-Natal Press, 2009).
Mills, J., *Charles Miller: o Pai do Futebol Brasileiro*, (São Paulo: Panda Books, 2005).
Mills. J., *Charles William Miller: 1994–1994: Memoriam Clube Atlético São Paulo*, (São Paulo: SPAC, 1994).
Mitchell, A., *First Elevens: The Birth of International Football and the Men Who Made It Happen*, (Glasgow: Andy Mitchell Media, 2012).
Morris, T., *In a Class of Their Own: A History of English Amateur Football*, (Sheffield: Chequered Flag Publishing, 2015).
Nielsen, E., *Sport and the British World, 1900–1930: Amateurism and National Identity in Australasia and Beyond*, (Basingstoke: Palgrave Macmillan, 2014).
Parker, E., *British Sport*, (London: William Collins, 1941).
Piercey, N., *Four Histories about Early Dutch Football 1910–1920*, (London: UCL Press, 2016).
Russell, D., *Football and the English: A Social History of Association Football in England, 1863–1995*, (Preston: Carnegie Publishing, 1997).

Sharpe, I., *40 Years in Football*, (London: Sportsmans Book Club, 1954).
Smith, M.I., *Evolvements of Early American Football: Through the 1890/1 Season*, (Bloomington: AuthorHouse, 2008).
Tabner, B., *Football through the Turnstile ... Again*, (Harefield: Yore Publications, 2002).
Taylor, C., *The Beautiful Game: A Journey through Latin American Football*, (London: Phoenix Press, 1998).
Taylor, D.J., *On the Corinthian Spirit: The Decline of Amateurism in Sport*, (London: Yellow Jersey Press, 2006).
Taylor, M., *The Leaguers: The Making of Professional Football in England, 1900–1939*, (Liverpool: Liverpool University Press, 2005).
Taylor, M., *The Association Game: A History of British Football*, (Harlow: Pearson Longman, 2008).
Vamplew, W., *Pay Up and Play the Game: Professional Sport in Britain 1875–1914*, (Cambridge: Cambridge University Press, 1988).
Walvin, J., *The People's Game: The History of Football Revisited*, (Edinburgh: Mainstream, 1994).
Wangerin, D., *Distant Corners: American Soccer's History of Missed Opportunities and Lost Causes*, (Philadelphia, PA: Temple University Press, 2011).
Weir, C., *The History of the Oxford University Association Football Club 1872–1998*, (Harefield: Yore Publications, 2004).
Wiener, M.J., *English Culture and the Decline of the Industrial Spirit, 1850–1980* (Cambridge: Cambridge University Press, 1981).
Wilton, I., *C.B. Fry: King of Sport*, (London: Metro Publishing, 2002).
Zec, D., Baljkas, F. and Paunović, M., *Sport Remembers: Serbian-British Sporting Contacts during the First World War*, (Belgrade: Britanska Ambasada, 2015).

Journal articles

Allen, D., 'Tours of reconciliation: Rugby, war and reconstruction in South Africa, 1891–1907', *Sport in History*, vol. 27, no. 2, 2007, pp. 172–89.
Benson, J., 'Athletics, class and nation: The Oxford-Cambridge University tour of Canada and the United States of America, 1901', *Sport in History*, vol. 33, no. 1, 2013, pp. 1–18.
Bolsmann, C., 'White Football in South Africa: Empire, apartheid and change, 1892–1977', *Soccer & Society*, vol. 11, no. 1–2, 2010, pp. 29–45.
Bolsmann, C., 'South African football tours at the turn of the twentieth century: Amateurs, pioneers and profits', *African Historical Review*, vol. 42, no. 1, 2010, pp. 91–112.
Bolsmann, C., 'The 1899 Orange Free State Football Team of Europe: 'Race', imperial loyalty and sports spectacle', *International Journal of the History of Sport*, vol. 28, no. 1, 2011, pp. 81–97.
Bottenburg, M. van, 'Beyond diffusion: Sport and its remaking in cross-cultural contexts', *Journal of Sport History*, vol. 36, no. 1, 2010, pp. 41–53.
Brown, D., 'Canadian imperialism and sporting exchanges: The nineteen-century cultural experience of cricket and lacrosse', *Canadian Journal of the History of Sport*, vol. 20, no. 1, 1987, pp. 55–66.
Deléphine, M., 'The Racing Club vs. Arsenal matches, 1930–1962: A Franco-British ritual, European games or football lessons?', *Sport in History*, vol. 35, no. 4, 2015, pp. 604–17.

Gillmeister, H., 'The first European soccer match: Walter Bensemann, a twenty-six-year-old German student set the ball rolling', *The Sports Historian*, no. 17, 1997, pp. 1–13.

Hardy, S., 'Entrepreneurs, organizations, and the sports marketplace: Subjects in search of historians', *Journal of Sport History*, vol. 13, no. 1, 1986, pp. 12–33.

Hardy, S., Norman, B. and Sceery, S., 'Toward a history of sport branding', *Journal of Historical Research in Marketing*, vol. 4, no. 4, 2012, pp. 482–509.

Hare, G., 'What is an international match? French football clubs and the earliest "international matches"', *Sport in History*, vol. 35, no. 4, 2015, pp. 497–514.

Holt, R., 'Amateurism and its interpretation: The social origins of British sport', *Innovation*, vol. 5, no. 1, 1992, pp. 19–31.

Huggins, M., 'Second-class citizens? English middle-class culture and sport, 1850–1910: A reconsideration', *International Journal of the History of Sport*, vol. 17, no. 1, 2000, pp. 1–35.

Huggins, M., 'Sport, tourism and history: Current historiography and future prospects', *Journal of Tourism History*, vol. 5, no. 2, 2013, pp. 107–30.

Koller, C., 'Sport transfer over the Channel: Elitist migration and the advent of football and ice hockey in Switzerland', *Sport in Society: Cultures, Commerce, Media, Politics*, vol. 20, no. 10, 2017, pp. 1390–404.

Lewis, R.W., 'The genesis of professional football: Bolton-Blackburn-Darwen, the centre of innovation, 1878–85', *International Journal of the History of Sport*, vol. 14, no. 1, 1997, pp. 21–54.

Logan, G., 'Pilgrims' progress in Chicago: Three English soccer tours to the Second City, 1905–09', *Soccer & Society*, vol. 11, no. 3, 2010, pp. 198–212.

McDowell, M.L., 'Queen's Park FC in Copenhagen, 1899–1903', pp. 1–18, www.idrottsforum.org/mcdowell 140514, published 14 May 2014.

McDowell, M.L., '"To cross the Skager Rack", discourses, images, and tourism in early "European" football: Scotland, the United Kingdom, Denmark and Scandinavia', *Soccer & Society*, vol. 18, nos. 2–3, pp. 245–69.

Menary, S., 'In search of the Argonauts', *Soccer History*, no. 27, 2011, pp. 7–13.

Merrett, C., 'Sport and race in Colonial Natal C.B. Llewellyn, South Africa's First Black Test Cricketer', *Natalia*, vol. 32, 2002, pp. 19–35.

Molnar, G., 'Hungarian football: A socio-historical overview', *Sport in History*, vol. 27, no. 2, 2007, pp. 293–317.

Morris, T., 'The Corinthian spirit: Lies, damned lies and statistics', *Soccer History*, no. 40, 2016–17, pp. 12–15.

Piercey, N. and Porter, D., 'Transnational connectivity, cultural interaction and selective adaptation: English Corinthians and amateur football in the Netherlands, c1906–1939', *Sport in History*, vol. 37, no. 2, 2017, pp. 124–45.

Porter, D., 'Amateur football in England, 1948–1963: The Pegasus Phenomenon', *Contemporary British History*, vol. 14, no. 2, 2000, pp. 1–30.

Porter, D., 'Revenge of the Crouch End Vampires: The AFA, the FA, and English football's 'Great split', 1907–14', *Sport in History*, vol. 26, no. 3, 2006, pp. 406–28.

Porter, D., '"Coming on with leaps and bounds in the Metropolis": London football in the era of the 1908 Olympics', *London Journal*, vol. 34, no. 2, 2009, pp. 101–22.

Rheenen, D. van, 'The promise of soccer in America: The open play of ethnic subcultures', *Soccer & Society*, vol. 10, no. 6, 2009, pp. 781–94.

Roberts, J., '"The best football team. The best platoon": The role of football in the proletarianization of the British Expeditionary Force, 1914–1918', *Sport in History*, vol. 26, no. 1, 2006, pp. 26–46.

Smith, R., 'Harvard and Columbia and reconsideration of the 1905–06 football crisis', *Journal of Sport History*, vol. 8 no. 3, 1981, pp. 5–19.
Taylor, M., 'Editorial – Sport, transnationalism, and global history', *Journal of Global History*, vol. 8, no. 2, 2013, pp. 199–208.
Torres, C.R., 'Tribulations and achievements: The early history of Olympism in Argentina', *International Journal of the History of Sport*, vol. 18, no. 3, 2002, 59–92.
Torres, C.R., '"If we had had our Argentine team here!" football and the 1924 Argentine Olympic Team', *Journal of Sport History*, vol. 30, no. 1, 2003, 1–24.
Walker, A., 'Reporting play: The local newspaper and sports journalism, c. 1870–1914', *Journalism Studies*, vol. 7, no. 3, 2006, pp. 452–62.
Wu, Y., 'The Pilgrims come to America: A failed mission of British cultural imperialism', *Sports History Review*, vol. 29, no. 2, 1998, pp. 212–24.

Chapters in edited collections

Ackland, N., 'The Corinthians', in Fabian, A.H. and Green, G., (eds), *Association Football*, (London: Caxton Publishing Co., 1960), vol. 1, pp. 386–97.
Antunes, F.M.R.F., 'The early days of football in Brazil: The British influence and factory clubs in São Paulo', in Fontes, P. and Buarque De Hollanda, B., (eds), *The Country of Football: Politics, Popular Culture and the Beautiful Game in Brazil*, (London: Hurst and Company, 2014), pp. 17–40.
Bottenburg, M. van, 'Why are the European and American sports worlds so different? Path dependence in European and American sports history', in Tomlinson, A., Young, C. and Holt, R., (eds), *Sports and the Transformation of Modern Europe: States, Media and Markets, 1950–2010*, (London: Routledge, 2011), pp. 205–25.
Bryant, A.M., 'Jackson, Nicholas Lane [Pa Jackson] (1849–1937)', *Oxford Dictionary of National Biography*, (Oxford: Oxford University Press, 2004), doi:10.1013/ref.odnb/50296.
Carter, N., 'Football's first Northern hero? The rise and fall of William Sudell', in Wagg, S. and Russell, D., (eds), *Sporting Heroes of the North: Sport, Religion and Culture*, (Newcastle upon Tyne: Northumbria Press, 2010), pp. 123–43.
Green, G., 'The Football Association', in Fabian, A.H. and Green, G. (eds), *Association Football*, (London: Caxton Publishing Co., 1960), vol. 1, pp. 47–97.
Hobsbawm, E., 'Mass-producing traditions: Europe 1870–1914', in Hobsbawm, E. and Ranger, T., (eds), *The Invention of Tradition*, (Cambridge: Cambridge University Press, 1992), pp. 263–307.
Hill, L., 'Football as code: The social diffusion of 'soccer' in South Africa', in Alegi, P. and Bolsmann, C., (eds), *South Africa and the Global Game: Football, Apartheid and Beyond*, (London: Routledge, 2010), pp. 12–28.
Levett, G., 'Constructing imperial identity: The 1907 South African Tour of England', in Murray, B. and Vahed, G., (eds), *Empire and Cricket: The South African Experience 1884–1914*, (Pretoria: UNISA Press, 2009), pp. 241–59.
Mangan, J.A., 'Introduction: Complicated matters', in Mangan, J.A., (ed), *A Sport-Loving Society: Victorian and Edwardian Middle-Class England at Play*, (Abingdon: Routledge, 2006), pp. 1–10.
Mason, T., 'Sporting news, 1860–1914', in Harris, M. and Lee, A., (eds), *The Press in English Society from the Seventeenth to Nineteenth Centuries*, (London: Associated University Presses, 1986), pp. 168–86.

Mason, T., 'Middle-class wanderers and working-class professionals: The British and the growth of world football 1899–1954', in Griffiths, C.V.J., Nott, J.J. and Whyte, W., (eds), *Classes, Cultures and Politics: Essays on British History for Ross McKibbin*, (Oxford: Oxford University Press, 2011), pp. 121–38.

Meisl, W., 'The F.I.F.A.', in Fabian, A.H. and Green, G., (eds), *Association Football*, (London: Caxton Publishing Co., 1960), vol. 4, pp. 297–305.

Murray. B., 'Abe Bailey and the foundation of the Imperial Cricket Conference', in Murray, B. and Vahed, G., (eds), *Empire and Cricket: The South African Experience 1884–1914*, (Pretoria: UNISA Press, 2009), pp. 261–78.

Porter, D., 'Sport and national identity'. In Edelman, R. and Wilson, W. (eds), *The Oxford Handbook of Sports History*, (Oxford: Oxford University Press, 2017), pp. 477–89.

Russell, D., 'From evil to expedient: The legalization of professionalism in English football, 1884–85, in Wagg, S., (ed), *Myths and Milestones in the History of Sport*, (Basingstoke: Palgrave Macmillan, 2011), pp. 32–56.

Russell, D., 'Kicking off: The origins of association football', in Steen, R., Novick, J. and Richards, H., (eds), *The Cambridge Companion to Football*, (Cambridge: Cambridge University Press, 2013), pp. 13–26.

Taylor, M., 'The global spread of football', in Edelman, R. and Wilson, W., (eds), *The Oxford Handbook of Sports History*, (Oxford: Oxford University Press, 2017), pp. 183–95.

Winch, J., 'Guardians of the game: The role of the press in popularising the 1888/89 tour and establishing the South African Cricket Association', in Murray, B. and Vahed, G., (eds), *Empire and Cricket: The South African Experience 1884–1914*, (Pretoria: UNISA Press, 2009), pp. 45–60.

Miscellaneous

2014 FIFA World Cup Brazil TM: Television Audience Report, London 2014, available at www.resources.fifa.com/mm/document/affederation/tv/02/74/55/57/2014f-wcbraziltvadience(draft5)(issue date14.12.15)_neutral.pdf, accessed 9 September 2017.

BritishPathé newsreel: britishpathe.com/video/tit-bit-of-the-first-round (1924); britishpathe.com/video/first-time-since-the-war (1925); britishpathe.com/video/well-played-new-brighton (1928); britishpathe.com/video/bravo-corinthians (1928).

Cardiff Corinthians AFC Website, www.clubsite.co.uk/cardiff corinthiansafc/History?id/=17836, accessed 4 October 2017.

Corinthian-Casuals FC Official Website, www.corinthian-casuals.com, accessed 1 October 2017.

David Bauckham, 'The Last Corinthian', www.dbauckham.exposure.co/the_last_corinthian, accessed 1 October 2017.

'How English-schooled-Charles-Miller-set-the-tone-for–Football-in-Brazil', www.theguardian.com/football/blog/2014/jul/05, accessed 20 July 2014.

Javier Garcia, 'British and Irish Clubs – Overseas Tours 1890–1939', www.rssf.com/tablesb./brit-ier-tours-prewwii-html, accessed 3 May 2016.

Ed Smith, 'Left Field', *New Statesman* (London), p. 48, 28 July–10 August 2017.

Index

Ackland, N. 10–11
Alcock, C.W. 8–9, 24, 136
Aldenham School 54
Amateur Football Association 15, 47–52, 72, 82, 89, 91, 94, 126
amateurism 5, 6, 11–12, 72–3, 74, 81, 133, 86, 95, 96–7, 134–5
American Amateur Football Association 110
American Football Association 102, 109
anglophilia 81, 83, 84, 88–9, 96, 120
anglophobia 123, 127
Annals of the Corinthians Football Club (B. O. Corbett) 9, 44, 73–4, 87, 130
Argentina 7, 16, 117–18, 124; thwarted tour of 126–7
Argentine Football Association 117–18, 126
Argonauts 57
Arsenal 36, 57, 96, 133, 137
Association Football & the Men Who Made It (A. Gibson and W. Pickford) 11, 33, 51
Association Suisse de Football (ASF) 91, 96
Aston Villa 4, 36, 44–5, 46
Athletic News 9, 24, 25, 47
Austria 6, 12, 82, 83, 85, 86, 91, 94

Bambridge, G.C. 112
Barbarians 36, 42
Beardshaw W.F. 26
Belgium 83, 84, 88, 92–3, 11
Bensemann, W. 137
Buenos Aires 117, 119
Billings, R. 131
Blackburn Olympic 23, 25
Blackburn Rovers 4, 23, 24–5, 55–6, 102, 132
Bohemia 82, 90, 91, 111
Bolton Wanderers 25, 29, 76

Brazil 1, 89, 111, 127, 131; Corinthian tours to 120–6; origins of soccer in 6–7, 118–19; standard of soccer in 123–4, 126
Brighton and Hove Albion 55
British Football Association 24
British Imperialism (P.J. Cain and A.G. Hopkins) 119
Bury 46–7, 85

Caldecott Corinthians 134
Canada 2, 16, 105, 108, 113, 136; Corinthian tours 110, 111–12; early development of soccer in 101–2
Cambridge University 4, 22, 24, 46, 51, 72, 82, 130
Cardiff Corinthians 43, 134
Casuals 10, 31, 33, 55, 57, 82, 111
Cavallini, R. 97, 130
Chamberlain, J. 7
Charterhouse School 54
Chelsea 30, 53, 131
Civil Service 82
civilising process and sport 3
Clapton 66, 83
Cobbold, W.N. 9, 49, 56
Cochrane, Sir Ernest 104, 108
College football (USA) 103–4, 112
Corbett, B.O. (Bertie) 6, 7, 9, 42, 44, 73–4, 87, 105, 106, 130
Corinthian FC 3–4, 41–2; and AFA-FA split 15, 47–52, 73, 86, 112–13, 126; amateurism and 3–4, 6, 85, 94; clubs named after 42–3; in decline 81, 86, 95–6, 111, 113, 126; declining quality of opposition 44–5, 49–51, 86, 90; in FA Cup 55–8; financial guarantees and expenses 28, 29, 34, 67, 74–5, 94, 106, 109, 112; fixtures in London of 30–3; impact of 130–8; merger with Casuals

57, 111; Nazi salute 97; origins of 3, 21–2; social exclusivity of 3, 11, 21, 33, 107, 136–7; style of play 4, 9, 27, 46–7, 70, 85, 94, 104, 130, 132–3 as a touring club 5–8, 22, 24–9, 33–4, 44–5, 49–50, 53–5, 86–97; in Austria 86–7, 94; in Bohemia 86–7, 90–1; in Belgium 92–3; in Brazil 120–6; in Canada 105–6, 109, 111–12; in Denmark 87, 92–3, 96; in France 87, 89–90, 92, 94–5; in Germany 86, 88, 96–7; in Hungary 86, 87; in the Netherlands 81, 88–9, 92–4; in South Africa 65–77; in Sweden 87, 88; in Switzerland 91, 96; in United States of America 103, 107–8, 112
Corinthian FC, Kent 131
Corinthian-Casuals 57–8, 131–2
Corinthian League 131
Corinthian Shield 131
Corinthians & Cricketers (E. Grayson) 10, 46, 130
Les Corinthiens de Paris 95
Les Corinthiens Françaises 91–2
County Ground, Leyton 31–3, 47
Cox, O. 7, 119
Craig, R.D. 73
Creek, F.N.S. (Norman) 12–13, 31, 44, 54, 56, 90, 130, 136
Crystal Palace, London 5, 20, 32, 36, 44, 46, 55
Currie, Sir D. 64
Cursham, H.A. 26

Daily Mail 42, 103
Day, S.H. 42
De Zwaluwen (Swallows) 89, 92, 93
Denmark 6, 84, 85, 87, 91, 92–3, 96, 111
Derby County 34, 103, 133
Deutscher Fussball Bund (DFB) 86, 94, 97
Dewhirst, F. 26
Dominion Football Association (Canada) 102
Dunn, A. T. B. (Arthur) 134–5

England 34; versus Scotland 1; versus Wales 5, 35
English Wanderers 83, 126
Essex County Cricket Club 32–3, 35
Everton 28, 45, 118

Fabian A.H. (Howard) 10, 130, 133
Federación Argentina de Football 126
Fédération Français de Football 95–6

F.I.F.A. (*Fédératión Internationale de Football Association*) 1, 82, 89, 90, 91, 110, 126
financial arrangements 28, 29–30, 36, 67, 74–5, 107, 109, 112
First World War, impact of 52, 85, 92, 127
Fluminense 7, 190
Football 8, 21
Football Association (FA) 2–3, 16, 21, 77, 83, 103, 110; crisis over professionalism 23–5, 134; split with AFA 47–52, 91, 112, 113, 126; relations with FIFA 89–90, 92, 126; relations with Argentina 117–18, 126–7; relations with South African FA 64, 75, 76, 77
Football Association Challenge Cup (FA Cup) 23, 24, 31, 46; Corinthians record in the 55–7
Football Field (Bolton) 28, 29
Football League 36, 44, 50, 56–7, 58, 72, 103
Fore River 107
Foster, G.N. 53, 133
France 16, 82, 83, 85, 89, 94–5, 111
Fry, C.B. 4, 5, 9, 28, 30, 34, 42, 56

Germany 80, 82, 83, 84, 85, 91, 96–7
Glasgow Rangers 6, 28, 102
globalization and soccer 1–2, 7–8, 13, 136–7
Gosling, R.C. 28, 134
Green, G. 10, 13–14, 47, 130, 132
Greenwood, D.H. 106

Haagse Voetbal Vereniging (HVV) 88, 93
Harvard University 101, 103
Highgate School 52, 54
History of the Corinthian Football Club (F.N.S. Creek) 12, 44, 54, 130
Hornby, A. N. (Monkey) 29–30, 36, 67, 75, 109
Hughes-Onslow, H. 48
Hungary 82, 86
Hunt, Rev. K.R.G. 54, 133

In a Class of their Own: History of English Amateur Football (T. Morris) 10, 14, 22, 49, 52–3
Ince, Sir G. 131
informal empire 6, 118, 119
Ipswich Town 50
Ireland 81, 85
Islington Corinthians 131

Jackson, N. L. (Pa) 1, 3, 4, 8, 9, 23, 24, 25, 47, 56–7, 58, 64, 65, 69, 89, 97, 130, 135–6; allegations re expenses and guarantees 28–30; biography of 20–1; as England selector 34, 28, 32; as founder of Corinthians 21–2 offside law on 133; as tour organiser 25–8; relations with Sudell 25, 32, 37; resigns as secretary of Corinthians 42, 44; scratch teams controversy 35–6; Sheriff of London's Charity Shield 36
Jameson Raid (1895) 66–7

Kennington Oval, London 1, 31, 33, 34
Kim Yong Sik 134
Kinnaird, Lord 48
Kruger, President Paul 67

Les Lions de Flandres 92
Lindley, T. 28, 49
literaturisation 9
Liverpool 47, 123
Llewellyn, C.B. (Buck) 67–8
London Football Association 21, 47–8
London Nomads 91
Loughborough Corinthians 43

Magyar Testgyakorlók Köre (MTK) 85, 86
Malvern College 54
McGill University 101
Meisl, H. 83, 84, 133, 137
Miller, C. 6–7, 118, 122, 123
Mills-Roberts, R. H. 26
Milnes, F. 103, 104
'missionaries of empire' 7, 15, 72, 74
Morgan-Owen, M. 49, 54, 105, 106, 125
Moscow Dynamo 131
Murray, C.M. 103

Nederlandsche Corinthians 93–4
Nederlansche Voetbalbond (NVB) 80, 88, 93, 95
Needham, E. 45–6
Netherlands 14, 16, 80, 82, 83, 84, 85, 88, 91, 92–4, 95; early tours by English sides 83
Newcastle United 29, 47, 49, 56
Northern Nomads 55, 123
Norwich City 56
Nottingham Forest 32, 118, 102, 103, 119
Notts County 35, 45, 94

Oakley, W.J. 9, 42, 49
offside law 133
Old Etonians 23
Olympic Games (1908) 84
Outcasts (Corinthians Outcasts) 90
Oxford University 4, 6, 51, 57, 72, 83

Parker, G. A. 16, 69; biography 65–6, 103, 107, 109, 113
Pastime 8, 26
Pegasus 131
penalty kicks 7, 12, 48, 73, 76, 122, 134
The People (London) 103, 105
Pickford, W. 35
Pilgrims 103, 107, 137; in United States of America 103–5, 108
Play Up Corinth: History of the Corinthian FC (R. Cavallini) 14, 97, 130
press coverage of soccer in Britain 8–9, 42; in Europe 85, 88
Preston North End 4, 5, 23, 24–5, 35, 44; close links with the Corinthians 25–6, 37
professionalism 22–5, 48, 134; in Europe 86, 93, 94, 95–7; in Scotland 26; in the United States of America 102, 104; style of play 4, 133
public schools matches with 52–4; 'rush to rugby' in 53–4

Queen's Club, London 5, 31, 32, 35, 46, 47
Queen's Park 6, 15, 21, 24, 26, 34, 35, 46, 49; decline of interest in fixture with 55, 57; financial arrangements with Corinthians 28

Reading 57
Red Star Olympique 92, 95
Repton School 53
Rhodes, C.J. 63, 65, 73
Richmond Town Wanderers 83
Rio de Janeiro 119, 120–1, 123–4
Rivalries 35; amateur-professional 4–5, 10, 23, 135; Corinthians-Queen's Park 34, 35, 45; England – Scotland 1, 3, 21–2, 34, 89; North – South 4–5, 23, 24, 46, 135
Roosevelt, President Theodore 103, 104
Rowlandson, T. 73, 74–5
Royal Engineers 6, 22
Rugby Football Union 49
Rugby Union football 2, 53, 72, 83, 107; in South Africa 64–5, 69, 72

São Paulo 118–19, 121–2, 124–5
Scotch Canadians tour 102
Scotland 3, 5, 21–2, 24, 26, 27, 34, 49, 50, 53, 54–5, 57, 89, 102
Secretan, A. 22, 23, 24
Sheffield Wednesday 35, 36, 47
Sheffield United 20, 36, 41, 42, 44–5, 103
Sheriff of London's Charity Shield 36, 41, 42, 45–7, 57
shoulder-charging 70–1, 121–2
Shrewsbury School 54
Slavia 87, 90
Sloley, R. 57
Smith, Dr. J. 24, 26
Smith, G.O. 4, 9, 10, 42, 45–6, 49, 56, 87, 130
Snell, I. 125, 126
Sochaux 95
La Societé d'Encouragement du Football Association 87
South Africa 2, 7–8, 15, 47, 62–3, 113, 118, 119, 136; amateurism 72; British ex-professionals in 69–70, 76; Corinthians tours to (1897) 65–9, (1903) 69–72, (1907) 72–7; financial arrangements criticized 67, 74–5; origins of soccer in 63–4; standard of soccer in 68–9, 77; rugby and cricket tours to 64, 67
South African Football Association 7, 63–4, 65–6, 69, 72, 73, 75 attitude to AFA-FA split 72, 75; Brazilian tour 118, 119; invites English team to tour 65; invites Corinthians 69, 72
South African War 62, 69; touring in the aftermath of 69–72
Southampton 6, 34, 82, 118
Southern League 36, 45, 50–1
Spain 86, 91
Sport and the British (R. Holt) 11–12
Sport Club Internacionale 7, 119
Sports Club, London 29–30
Sports Club Corinthians Paulista 123, 131
sporting behaviour 6, 90, 92, 103, 104, 122, 134

Sportsman 9, 30, 52, 87, 90, 110
Stagg, A.A. 107
Stanton, W.S. (Pa) 9
Stoke City 44–5
Sudell, W. 23, 25, 37
Sunderland 45, 102
Surrey County Cricket Club 31–2
Surrey Wanderers 83
Sweden 82, 84, 87, 91, 137
Switzerland 12–13, 90, 91, 96, 137

Third Lanark 35, 57
Thompson, Dr H. 132
The Times (London) 10, 14, 31
Timmis W.U. 42, 49, 72, 84, 120
Topham, R. 67, 68, 69
Tottenham Hotspur 46, 53, 76, 118
tours by various sports clubs and associations 5–8, 83–4, 118, 101, 102, 111, 127

Union des Sociétés Françaises de Sports et Athlétiques (USFSA) 87, 89, 90, 91
United States of America 2, 7–8, 16, 89, 136, 137; Corinthians on tour in 110, 112–13; early soccer development in 102–3, 107–8
United States Football Association 110
Uruguay 118, 124, 126

Wall, F. 48, 109
Walters, P.M. 49
Wanderers FC 6, 21, 33
Welfare, H. 123
West Bromwich Albion 31, 52, 56, 126
West Ham United 52, 56, 126
Woodward, V. 53, 104
Woosnam, M. 127
Wreford-Brown, C. 45, 49, 69, 71, 107

Young Boys (Berne) 96

Zurich Grasshoppers 12, 96